# PHYSICAL OCEANOGRAPHY OF COASTAL WATERS

## ELLIS HORWOOD SERIES IN MARINE SCIENCE

*Series Editor:* Dr. T. D. Allan, Institute of Oceanographic Sciences, Wormley, Surrey

**SATELLITE MICROWAVE REMOTE SENSING**
T. D. ALLAN, Institute of Oceanographic Sciences, Wormley, Surrey

**PHYSICAL OCEANOGRAPHY OF COASTAL WATERS**
K. F. BOWDEN, University of Liverpool

**REMOTE SENSING IN METEOROLOGY, OCEANOGRAPHY AND HYDROLOGY**
A. P. CRACKNELL, Carnegie Laboratory of Physics, University of Dundee

**SATELLITE OCEANOGRAPHY**
I. S. ROBINSON, University of Southampton

**SUBMARINE GEOMORPHOLOGY**
R. C. SEARLE and R. B. KIDD, Institute of Oceanographic Sciences, Surrey

**MARINE CORROSION OF OFFSHORE STRUCTURES**
J. R. LEWIS, University of Aberdeen and A. D. MERCER, National Physical Laboratory, Middlesex

# PHYSICAL OCEANOGRAPHY OF COASTAL WATERS

K. F. BOWDEN
Department of Oceanography
University of Liverpool

ELLIS HORWOOD LIMITED
Publishers · Chichester

Halsted Press: a division of
JOHN WILEY & SONS
New York · Brisbane · Chichester · Ontario

82543

First published in 1983 by
**ELLIS HORWOOD LIMITED**
Market Cross House, Cooper Street, Chichester, West Sussex, PO19 1EB, England

*The publisher's colophon is reproduced from James Gillison's drawing of the ancient Market Cross, Chichester.*


**Distributors:**

*Australia, New Zealand, South-east Asia:*
Jacaranda-Wiley Ltd., Jacaranda Press,
JOHN WILEY & SONS INC.,
G.P.O. Box 859, Brisbane, Queensland 4001, Australia

*Canada:*
JOHN WILEY & SONS CANADA LIMITED
22 Worcester Road, Rexdale, Ontario, Canada.

*Europe, Africa:*
JOHN WILEY & SONS LIMITED
Baffins Lane, Chichester, West Sussex, England.

*North and South America and the rest of the world:*
Halsted Press: a division of
JOHN WILEY & SONS
605 Third Avenue, New York, N.Y. 10016, U.S.A.


©1983 K. F. Bowden/Ellis Horwood Ltd.

**British Library Cataloguing in Publication Data**
Bowden, K. F.
Physical oceanography of coastal waters. –
(Ellis Horwood series in marine science)
1. Oceanography
I. Title
551.46      G11.2

**Library of Congress Card No.** 83-18444

ISBN 0–85312–686–0 (Ellis Horwood Limited)
ISBN 0–470–27505–7 (Halsted Press)


Typeset in Press Roman by Ellis Horwood Ltd.
Printed in Great Britain by Camelot Press Ltd., Southampton

# Table of Contents

# Author's Preface

Coastal waters, comprising those on the continental shelf and in the adjoining seas, have features which are sufficiently distinctive to merit some consideration on their own. General textbooks of physical oceanography tend to give most of their attention to the deep oceans, while there are several books on estuaries. The present book is intended to fill a gap by concentrating on conditions in the intervening coastal zone.

The treatment in the book is based on courses of lectures given in the University of Liverpool and elsewhere over the years. The idea of expanding these into a book arose first from a course which I gave while on sabbatical leave in the Oceanography Department, University of Washington at Seattle several years ago. The approach throughout is a combination of the observational and the theoretical, since it is in this way that scientific progress is made. A certain amount of mathematics must play its part but it is kept as elementary as possible, while still being sufficiently rigorous, and does not require a mathematical knowledge beyond that provided by a first year university course in the subject.

It is hoped that the book will find a place as a text for undergraduate and graduate students of oceanography and ocean engineering and that marine biologists, chemists and geologists may also find it useful in providing a physical background to their work. For those wishing to pursue the various topics further, numerous references are given to more detailed texts and review papers. References to original research papers are given where appropriate but are used more sparingly.

I am grateful to the many colleagues who have helped me in the preparation of this book and in particular to the following who have read and made valuable comments on various chapters: Dr. R. I. Tait, Dr. E. D. Barton and Dr. S. R. Ferguson of the Oceanography Department, University of Liverpool, Dr. N. S.

Heaps of the Institute of Oceanographic Sciences, Bidston and Professor J. H. Simpson, Department of Physical Oceanography, University College of North Wales. I am also very grateful to Mr. J. Murphy for his help in preparing the figures.

K. F. BOWDEN
August 1983

# 1

# Introduction

## 1.1 DISTINCTIVE FEATURES OF COASTAL WATERS

The field of oceanography extends from the deep oceans to estuaries, wherever sea water penetrates. Many of the physical phenomena and theories relating to them are common to the whole range of situations, but coastal waters differ sufficiently from either the deep oceans or estuaries to merit some attention on their own. The three types of region are, of course, interconnected and dependent on one another so that, while focusing on coastal waters, we cannot completely ignore the others. The tides which produce the rise and fall of water in coastal areas were generated in the deep ocean. Swell breaking on the beaches may have received its energy from storms thousands of miles away. The river water, which often gives coastal zones their relatively low salinity and high concentration of nutrients, has frequently been modified by its passage through estuaries.

Coastal waters also have a special role from the economic and environmental points of view. Harbour installations must be sited at the coast and it is through coastal waters, often with strong tidal or wind-driven currents, that ships must be navigated when approaching and leaving port. The recreational use of coastal zones, with their beaches, swimming, sailing and other activities, is a far from negligible factor in many areas. Most of the world's major fisheries are on the continental shelf and in adjacent seas, and physical conditions often play a significant part in their productivity. Although the deep ocean may become a major source of mineral resources in the future, it is continental shelf waters which are being exploited for solid minerals and for oil and gas supplies at the present time.

## 1.2 PHYSICAL CHARACTERISTICS AND THEIR CONSEQUENCES

For the purpose of this book the term 'coastal waters' will be taken to comprise waters on the continental shelf and in adjacent semi-enclosed seas but not extending into estuaries.

The first characteristic feature of coastal waters is their shallow depth, typically less than 200 m, compared with depths of the order of 4000 m in the deep ocean. The edge of the continental shelf is usually marked by an abrupt increase in the bottom slope from an average of 1 in 500 to about 1 in 20. The presence of the bottom at a relatively shallow depth places a greater constraint on water movements than that which operates in deeper water. Currents near the bottom are often quite large and bottom friction, which is usually negligible in the ocean, plays a significant part in their dynamics.

The presence of a coastline acts as a lateral constraint on water movements, tending to divert currents so that they flow nearly parallel to it. By obstructing the flow of water towards it, the coastline causes surface slopes to develop and these in turn react on and modify the water movements. The restricting influence of the coastline varies greatly from one area to another. At one extreme is the case of a gentle curving coast bordering an ocean, like the Pacific coast of the USA and parts of Central and South America. At the other extreme is a largely enclosed sea such as the Baltic Sea, with a very restricted communication with other sea areas.

The influx of fresh water run-off from the land, often after passing through estuaries, has the effect of reducing the salinity, and hence also the density, of coastal water. For a similar heat flux through the sea surface, the shallower water near the coast undergoes larger changes in temperature than the deeper water. As a result of these effects, coastal waters are usually areas of relatively large horizontal gradients of salinity, temperature and density, often associated with changes in currents.

The above characteristics of coastal waters lead to some important physical consequences. In the first place tides and tidal currents are considerably modified, compared with their properties in deep water. Their magnitude is usually increased, sometimes by a large factor when resonance occurs between a tidal period and the natural period of oscillation of a coastal body of water. In particular, tidal currents become faster on the continental shelf and bottom friction has a greater influence on them.

Surface waves are a ubiquitous feature of oceans and seas and in some respects their properties are similar everywhere. As waves travel into shallower water, however, the proximity of the bottom induces considerable changes in them and eventually causes them to break, dissipating most of their energy on the shore. The release of energy from the waves leads to the movement of large amounts of beach material in some areas and exerts considerable forces on natural and man-made structures.

Wind-driven currents are also strongly affected by the presence of the coastline and the bottom. In some areas this gives rise to storm surges, while in others new effects are produced, such as the occurrence of upwelling or the generation of coastal jets.

Because of the large horizontal density gradients, density-driven currents are often a more significant feature in coastal waters than in the ocean. These currents have some features similar to those of estuarine circulation, which are also density driven, but the Coriolis effects, arising from the rotation of the earth, are more pronounced in the less restricted coastal waters.

Conditions in coastal seas cannot, however, be considered in isolation from those in the adjacent ocean. In some cases major ocean currents flowing along the continental slope, often varying in strength or meandering in direction, have a strong influence on conditions on the shelf. This may be by causing water masses of different properties to encroach on to the shelf or by entraining water from it. They may also induce currents on the shelf by producing gradients of sea level at the shelf edge.

## 1.3 PRACTICAL SIGNIFICANCE OF COASTAL WATERS

The history of oceanography shows many links between research and practical application. The needs of navigators and explorers provided the main incentive to research in the 17th and 18th centuries and the results included an improved knowledge of ocean currents. In the mid-19th century a new impetus was provided by the need to find suitable routes for trans-oceanic telegraph cables. The study of tides, unlike other branches of oceanography, started in coastal waters and indeed at the coast itself. Most early knowledge of tides came from measurements of the rise and fall of water level at ports and jetties. The theory of tides in coastal waters became well developed and coordinated with observations. Knowledge of ocean tides remained largely speculative, theory having to be tested by comparison with observations around the coasts of continents and islands. Only in recent years have reliable measurements of tides in deep water become possible.

Navigation through coastal waters, especially when entering or leaving port, requires a sound knowledge of the depth of water and how it is affected by tides. The increased draught of vessels, particularly tankers, has called for more accurate tidal predictions and for adequate warning of when meteorological conditions will cause significant deviations from the predictions. The manoeuvering of ships in restricted seaways also requires information on tidal streams and other currents.

The provision of adequate port and harbour facilities involves the construction of breakwaters, jetties and sea walls. Where the tidal range is high and enclosed docks are needed, dock gates and locks have to be built. The construction and maintenance of these facilities calls for a knowledge of wave conditions in the area: their heights, periods and directions of approach. Waves not only exert considerable forces on coastal structures but also affect the movement of beach and sea bed material, causing erosion at one place and siltation at another. Waves are much less predictable than tides but methods of forecasting them are vital. The need for predicting landing conditions on beaches in World War II provided a great stimulus to the study of waves and led to improved methods of forecasting. Today the stringent requirements of drilling rigs and other offshore structures are supporting further research on waves and their effects.

The needs of the fishing industry have, for many years, provided a stimulus to the study of oceanography. The foundation of ICES, the International Council for the Exploration of the Sea, in 1902 by the fishing nations of north-west Europe, joined later by Canada, USA and USSR, is an example which was followed by similar organisations in other parts of the world. Fishermen share with the crews of other vessels the need for navigational information and warnings of severe wave conditions. In addition the distribution of temperature, salinity and chemical constituents is often a good indication of the biological productivity of an area. A special case of this occurs in upwelling regions, where an understanding of the physical processes and, if possible, the ability to forecast times and areas of intense upwelling, is of particular value. The forecasting of oceanographic conditions, for this and other purposes, involves differing problems on various time scales: short-term from days to weeks, seasonal, year to year and long-term trends.

For centuries the sea has been used as a receptacle for waste, either directly or through the estuaries flowing into it. The ability of sea water to degrade organic waste and to kill bacteria has enabled the seas to cope fairly well with waste in the past. The problem has been aggravated in recent years by the growth of urban populations in coastal areas and by the introduction of chemicals, including industrial waste from factories, radioactive materials and the run-off of pesticides and herbicides used in agriculture. Many of these, like the heavy metals, DDT and the chlorinated hydrocarbons, are more persistent than organic waste, and their influence extends further from the coast. The ability of coastal waters to disperse such wastes away from the coastal zone and eventually transport them to deep water depends on the regime of tides and currents and, in some cases, on thermal or haline stratification and the presence of fronts.

A striking example of the increased use of coastal waters is the exploration for oil and gas reserves and their exploitation. The need for being able to forecast extreme wave conditions and the forces associated with them has been highlighted by a number of disasters to drilling rigs. Less spectacular but no less important is the requirement for an adequate knowledge of tides, waves and currents in the day-to-day operation of drilling rigs and production platforms and the fleet of support vessels and helicopters needed to service them. These requirements have provided a stimulus to oceanographic research in the fields of waves, tides and wind-driven currents and surges.

With so many people living in coastal areas or visiting them for recreation and sport, their amenity value is not a consideration to be ignored. The preservation of the quality of life as well as the commercial value of tourism means that the environmental impact of commercial and industrial activities should be carefully assessed and, where necessary, controlled. Beaches and the waters adjoining them should not only be free from bacteria and toxic chemicals but should be seen to be clean and attractive for bathing and other activities. Action may need to be taken to retain beaches against the effects of erosion and long-shore transport. In other areas it may be necessary to prevent the encroachment of sand bars or the deposition of silt. The popularity of sailing as a sport has brought a need for more detailed knowledge of currents and waves and for reliable methods of forecasting the effects of wind. Estimation of the likely impact of harbour works, power stations or waste-disposal plants requires a knowledge of the oceanographic conditions, as does the planning of preventive or remedial measures to combat any harmful effects.

The progressive use of coastal waters in the ways outlined above calls for research to improve our knowledge of oceanographic conditions and for its application by engineers, navigators, fisheries scientists and others. This book does not attempt to deal with the engineering problems. Nor does it aim to provide a comprehensive review of oceanographic knowledge sufficient for immediate application to any problem. This must be sought in specialist mono-graphs or original papers. Its objective is to present the observations and ideas which are basic to an understanding of the subject with, an indication of the directions being taken by present-day research. It is hoped, that in this way it will be a useful guide to oceanographers preparing to undertake research in the field, as well as to engineers and other potential users.

# 2

# Tides and tidal currents

## 2.1 INTRODUCTION

### 2.1.1 Main features of tides

The periodic rise and fall of the sea surface, known as the tide, is a conspicuous feature of many coastal areas. The most commonly encountered type of tide is that in which two high waters and two low waters occur each day, the times of high water and low water becoming later by approximately 50 minutes from one day to the next. This type of tide is found around nearly all shores bordering on the Atlantic Ocean, for example, but different patterns occur in some other parts of the world. In fact the tides everywhere are made up of a number of constituents of different periods. The tidal pattern described above is dominated by the lunar semidiurnal constituent, denoted by $M_2$, having a period of 12 h 25 m, which is half of a lunar day. The moon crosses the meridian at a given place at a time which is, on average, 50 minutes later each day, so that a lunar day has a period of 24 h 50 m. It is also well known that the range of tide, defined as the difference in height between a high water and the following low water, varies periodically with the phases of the moon. Tides of maximum range, known as spring tides, occur within a day or two of a new or a full moon, and those of minimum range, neap tides, near the first and third quarters of the moon. This sequence arises from the solar semidiurnal constituent, denoted by $S_2$ and having a period of 12 h 00 m, alternately reinforcing and opposing the lunar semidiurnal constituent.

It is frequently found that the two high waters on a given day are of different heights, the morning high waters on successive days, for example, being higher than the intervening afternoon high water. This feature is known as a 'diurnal inequality', and may also occur in the low waters. It is due to the superposition of diurnal tidal constituents, with periods of approximately a day, on the semidiurnal constituents. Around the coasts of the Atlantic Ocean the diurnal inequality is usually small and appears only as a slight perturbation of the semidiurnal tides. Along the western coast of North America, however, the diurnal inequality is more pronounced and the differences between successive high waters or low waters are so marked that the distinguishing nomenclature of higher high water, lower high water, higher low water and lower low water (abbreviated to HHW, LHW, HLW and LLW) is in common use. The diurnal effect often varies with time, passing through two maxima and two minima in the course of a lunar month. In other areas, including the Gulf of Mexico and parts of south-east Asia, the diurnal tide is dominant with only one high water and one low water occurring each day.

Horizontal movements of water, the tidal currents, are necessarily associated with the vertical rise and fall of the sea surface. The current associated with a rising water level is termed the flood and that with a falling level the ebb current. In a gulf or estuary the relation between elevations and currents is straight-forward but the situation is less clear off an open coast or well away from land. The phase relationship between elevation and current, e.g. the time interval between maximum flood and high water, then varies from place to place and, in general, the current rotates in direction as well as changing in magnitude during a tidal cycle.

### 2.1.2 Observations of tides

The observation of tides involves the measurement of water level at a given place as a function of time. In the simplest case, visual observations are made of the water level against a graduated scale but usually a form of recorder is used. This is frequently actuated by a float, rising and falling with the water level in a well which is connected to the sea by an orifice of such a diameter that it reduces wave action while not impeding the tidal movement. In the type of tide gauge which is still most commonly used, a curve of the changing water level is drawn on a paper chart. In some cases the recording may be done remotely and records from several tide gauges in different positions may be recorded in a central location. Digital recording, which facilitates the preparation of the data for analysis, is now being used to an increasing extent. As distinct from tide gauges which measure water level directly, there are other instruments, usually of the pressure gauge type, which may be laid on the sea bed, either adjacent to the shore or in an open sea position. As a rule they record internally, often on magnetic tape, and only need to be serviced at intervals of a month or longer. In some circumstances remote recording by radio from a surface buoy to a shore station may be used. Further information on tidal measurements is given by Glen (1979) and Huntley (1980).

The techniques for measuring tidal currents, which usually serve to measure currents of other origins at the same time, are very varied and include drift methods, such as poles or drogues, as well as many types of current meter. It is now fairly common to deploy moored current meters, which can be left to record for a month or longer before they are recovered. Techniques of current measurement are reviewed in the books by Neumann (1968) and Pickard and Emery (1982). A detailed description of the instrumentation for measuring tides and currents is beyond the scope of this book.

### 2.1.3 Oceanic and coastal tides

The forces which generate the tides arise from the gravitational attraction of the moon and the sun but, in the case of tides in coastal seas, the influence of these forces is largely indirect. The coastal tides are driven by oceanic tides, which are themselves produced by the tide-generating forces. Seas such as the Mediterranean or Baltic, which have only a restricted access to the ocean, experience relatively small tides except for regions which have a natural period close to a tidal period. It is true, however, that tidal forces act on any body of water, including lakes. The tides in Lake Michigan, for example, have been measured and studied. In the main basin of the lake the highest spring range is about 8 cm but ranges up to 18 cm are observed in Green Bay, a subsidiary basin in which resonance occurs.

The method adopted in this chapter is to start by describing briefly the generation of the oceanic tides and their properties. The dynamical equations of tides are then given as a basis for understanding the modifications experienced by tidal waves as they travel on to the continental shelf and the response which they produce in coastal bodies of water. A combined observational and theoretical approach is used in the rest of the chapter to describe the varied features of tides and tidal currents in coastal waters.

## 2.2 OCEAN TIDES

### 2.2.1 Tide-generating forces

The tide-generating forces (abbreviated to T.G.F.) were shown by Newton to arise as a consequence of the law of gravitation. Because the gravitational attraction of the moon on a particle of matter at the surface of the earth varies with its position, there is a force acting on it which tends to move the particle, if it is free to move, relative to the solid earth. Given the position of the moon relative to the earth, it is possible to calculate the distribution of the T.G.F. over the surface of the earth. The distribution of the T.G.F. due to the sun may be calculated in a similar way.

The method of deriving the T.G.F. due to the moon is illustrated in Fig. 2.1. The system consisting of the earth and moon is considered, neglecting the movement of them both around the sun. Regarding them as rigid spheres, the earth and moon would move, as a result of their mutual gravitational attraction, in elliptical orbits with the common centre of gravity as a focus. In deriving the tide-generating force, the moon's attractive force at the centre of the earth is subtracted, since it is balanced by the centripetal acceleration. The vector difference between the moon's attractive force on a particle at point P and the force on a particle of the same mass at the centre of the earth may be calculated and resolved into a horizontal and a vertical component. The vertical component is equivalent to a slight increase or reduction in $g$, the acceleration due to gravity, of the order of $10^{-7} g$ but it cannot cause the particle to move.

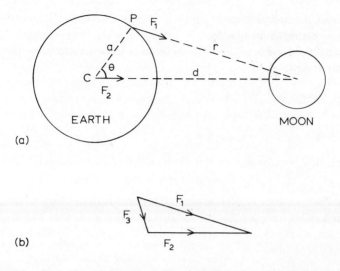

(a)

(b)

Fig. 2.1 – Derivation of the moon's tide-generating force. (a) The moon's attraction is represented by the vectors $F_1$ at P and $F_2$ at C. The magnitude of $F_1$ is
$GM/r^2$ and of $F_2$ is $GM/d^2$, where $G$ is the constant of gravitation. (b) In the
triangle of forces, $F_3$ is the vector difference of $F_1$ and $F_2$. In equation (2.1),
$F$ is the horizontal component of $F_3$.

The tide-generating force is the horizontal component of the differential force.
Thus the T.G.F. per unit mass at the point P, directed tangentially towards the
line joining the centre of the earth to the centre of the moon may be shown
to be given by,

$$F = \frac{3}{2} \frac{M}{E} \left(\frac{a}{d}\right)^3 g \sin 2\theta \ . \tag{2.1}$$

where     $M$   is the mass of the moon,
          $E$   is the mass of the earth,
          $a$   is the radius of the earth,
          $d$   is the distance between the centres of the earth and moon,
          $\theta$   is the angle between the line joining the centre of the earth
                to the centre of the moon and the radius vector from the centre
                of the earth to the point P.

The distribution of the tide-generating force around the earth, as given by
equation (2.1), is indicated in Fig. 2.3(a). The maximum force acting towards
the sublunar point, i.e. the point on the earth immediately below the moon,
occurs at $\theta = \pm 45°$. There is no horizontal force at the sublunar point itself
$(\theta = 0°)$. The maximum force acting towards a point diametrically opposite to
the sublunar point occurs at $\theta = \pm 135°$. In order to envisage the complete distribution of the tide-generating force one must imagine the diagram being

rotated about the line joining the centres of the earth and moon, since the force is axially symmetric about this line.

The maximum value of the ratio of the tide-generating force to the weight of a particle is given by

$$\frac{F_{max}}{g} = \frac{3}{2} \frac{M}{E} \left(\frac{a}{d}\right)^3 .$$

The appropriate numerical values are

$$M/E = 1/81.4, \quad a = 6.37 \times 10^3 \, km, \quad d = 3.84 \times 10^5 \, km .$$

Thus $F_{max}/g = 8.4 \times 10^{-8}$.

Since the distribution of tide-generating force is determined in relation to the position of the moon while the earth is rotating on its axis, the magnitude and direction of the T.G.F. at a given point on the earth's surface is changing continuously with time.

### 2.2.2 Equilibrium tide

The equilibrium tide is the response to the tide-generating forces of an ocean covering the whole earth, on the assumption that the water can respond instantly to the changing forces. Thus it represents the static response of the ocean to the distribution of the T.G.F. at any given time. In spite of these unrealistic assumptions, the equilibrium tide has proved to be a useful concept which exhibits a number of qualitative features of the actual tides. The elevation in the equilibrium tide, as will be seen shortly, is directly proportional to the potential of the tide-generating force and is a convenient way of representing this potential.

In the equilibrium tide the sea surface assumes a slope such that the tide-generating force is balanced by the horizontal pressure gradient. In a given vertical plane, as in Fig. 2.2, the slope $\alpha$ is given by

$$\tan \alpha = \frac{F_s}{g} = \frac{\partial \bar{\zeta}}{\partial s} , \tag{2.2}$$

where $\bar{\zeta}$ is the elevation in the equilibrium tide, $s$ is measured in a given horizontal direction and $F_s$ is the component of the T.G.F. in that direction. If $\Omega$ is the potential of the T.G.F., then

$$F_s = - \frac{\partial \Omega}{\partial s} ,$$

by the usual definition of potential. Thus, by integration,

$$g \bar{\zeta} = -\Omega . \tag{2.3}$$

The constant of integration has been taken as zero on the assumption that $\bar{\zeta}$ and $\Omega$ are measured from the same zero level. Then the distribution of $\bar{\zeta}$ is directly

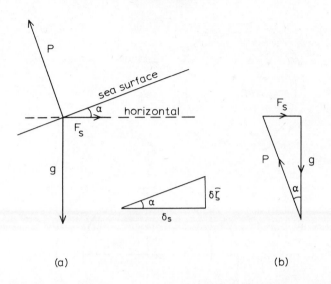

Fig. 2 .2 – Slope of the sea surface in the equilibrium tide. (a) $F_s$ is the tide-generating force, acting horizontally and $P$ is the resultant pressure force, normal to the sea surface. (b) The corresponding triangle of forces.

proportional to that of $\Omega$ but with a change of sign, so that the sea surface is raised where the potential of the T.G.F. is reduced.

From the distribution of tide-generating force, as given by equation (2.1) one may calculate the distribution of the equilibrium tide around the earth. In this way it is found that

$$\frac{\bar{\zeta}}{a} = \frac{1}{2} \frac{M}{E} \left(\frac{a}{d}\right)^3 (3 \cos^2\theta - 1) \tag{2.4}$$

This distribution is shown in Fig. 2.3(b).

The elevation has its maximum value $\bar{\zeta}_{\max}$ at $\theta = 0$ and $\pi$ and its minimum $\bar{\zeta}_{\min}$ occurs at $\theta = \pm \pi/2$. It is seen from (2.4) that $\bar{\zeta}_{\min} = -\frac{1}{2} \zeta_{\max}$ so that the maximum range is given by

$$\bar{\zeta}_{\max} - \bar{\zeta}_{\min} = \frac{3}{2} \frac{M}{E} \left(\frac{a}{d}\right)^3 a . \tag{2.5}$$

Since the diagram in Fig. 2.3(b) may be rotated about an axis joining the centre of the earth to the centre of the moon, the complete distribution of the equilibrium tide is represented by an ellipsoid of revolution with its major axis directed towards the moon. Maximum elevation occurs at the sublunar point, immediately below the moon and also at the corresponding point on the side of the earth away from the moon. As the earth rotates on its axis, the water level

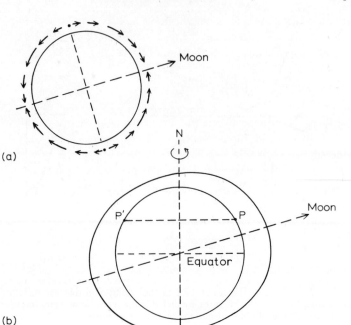

Fig. 2.3 -- (a) Distribution of tide-generating force around the earth. (b) The equilibrium tide due to the moon. A given point experiences two high waters, e.g. at P and P′, in a lunar day as the earth rotates on its axis.

will adjust itself so that the major axis of the ellipsoid continues to be directed towards the moon. In the course of a lunar day, a given point on the earth will experience a sequence of two high waters and two low waters, thus accounting for the lunar semidiurnal tides. In general the moon is not in the plane of the earth's equator but has a certain declination north or south of it. Taking this into account it is readily seen that the two high waters or the two low waters in a day are, in general, of unequal heights: the diurnal inequality. This inequality does not occur at the equator and it vanishes everywhere when the declination of the moon is zero, which happens twice in a lunar month.

Using the same numerical values as before for $M/E$, $a$ and $d$, it is found from equation (2.5) that the maximum range in the lunar equilibrium tide is given by

$$\bar{\zeta}_{max} - \bar{\zeta}_{min} = 53.5 \text{ cm} .$$

This value is of the same order as that observed at oceanic islands or measured by deep sea tide gauges but is an order of magnitude smaller than that measured at many coastal stations.

By considering the earth and the sun as a system and neglecting the moon, we may calculate the tide-generating force and the equilibrium tide due to the sun in a similar way. Denoting the mass of the sun by $S$ and its distance from the earth by $D$, the equation corresponding to (2.1) is

$$ F' = \frac{3}{2} \frac{S}{E} \left( \frac{a}{D} \right)^3 g \sin 2\theta' , \tag{2.6} $$

where $\theta'$ is the angle between the line joining the centre of the earth to the centre of the sun and the radius vector from the centre of the earth to the point considered.

The ratio of the maximum T.G.F. due to the sun to that due to the moon is thus

$$ \frac{F'_{max}}{F_{max}} = \frac{S}{M} \left( \frac{d}{D} \right)^3 $$

Since $S/E = 3.33 \times 10^5$ and $D = 1.496 \times 10^8$ km, whereas $M/E = 1/81.4$ and $d = 3.84 \times 10^5$ km, it follows that

$$ F'_{max}/F_{max} = 0.46 . $$

By writing down the equation corresponding to (2.4) for the sun's equilibrium tide it is seen that the ratio of the maximum ranges in the solar and lunar tides is given by the same factor. Thus the sun's greater distance from the earth more than compensates for its much greater mass and its equilibrium tide has a range less than half that due to the moon.

By considering the relative positions of earth, sun and moon at the various phases of the moon it is seen that the solar and lunar equilibrium ellipsoids reinforce one another at new and full moon and oppose one another at the first and third quarters. Thus the alternation of spring and neap tides, as well as the occurrence of solar and lunar semidiurnal tides and diurnal inequalities, may all be explained qualitatively in terms of the equilibrium tide.

### 2.2.3 Harmonic constituents of the tides

Using the notation of spherical trigonometry, the angle $\theta$, shown in Fig. 2.1 and appearing in equations (2.1) and (2.4) for the moon's tide-generating force and equilibrium tide respectively, may be expressed in terms of the latitude, longitude and time at a given point P and the declination and hour angle of the moon relative to a standard meridian. The angle $\theta'$ relating to the sun may be expressed in a similar way.

The positions of the moon and sun relative to the earth vary with the revolution of the moon in its orbit around the earth and with that of the earth in its orbit around the sun. The resultant tide-generating potential is thus a complicated function of time which may be resolved into the sum of a large number of harmonic constitutents. These constituents fall into three main classes or 'species':

(1) Semidiurnal constituents, with periods of approximately half a day. The main ones are $M_2$ with a period of half a lunar day, 12 h 25 m, and $S_2$ with a period of half a solar day, 12 h 00 m.

(2) Diurnal constituents, with periods approximately a day. Thus $K_1$ has a period of a sidereal day, 23 h 56 m.

(3) Long period constituents, with periods of two weeks and longer. The lunar fortnightly constituent Mf, for example, has a period of 13.66 days.

**Table 2.1** – Harmonic constituents of the tides.

| Species | Constituent | Symbol | Period |
|---------|-------------|--------|--------|
| | | | (hours) |
| Semidiurnal | Principal lunar | $M_2$ | 12.42 |
| | Principal solar | $S_2$ | 12.00 |
| | Larger lunar elliptic | $N_2$ | 12.66 |
| | Luni-solar | $K_2$ | 11.97 |
| Diurnal | Luni-solar | $K_1$ | 23.93 |
| | Principal lunar | $O_1$ | 26.87 |
| | Principal solar | $P_1$ | 24.07 |
| | | | (days) |
| Long period | Lunar fortnightly | Mf | 13.66 |
| | Lunar monthly | Mm | 27.55 |
| | Solar semiannual | Ssa | 182.70 |

Table 2.1 shows the more important harmonic constituents to which reference will be made from time to time in this chapter. In a full development of the tide-generating potential many more constituents have been distinguished. These constituents all appear in the elevation of the equilibrium tide although many are of very small amplitude. Of more practical importance is the fact that they may all be expected to occur in the actual tides. By a general dynamical principle due to Laplace, it may be deduced that for every harmonic constituent of the equilibrium tide there exists a harmonic constituent, of the same period, in the actual tides. This point will be considered in more detail later.

### 2.2.4 Dynamical response of the oceans
The response of the actual oceans to the tide-generating forces is a dynamical problem, since the variation of the forces with time and the inertia of the water

must be taken into account. The appropriate equations were formulated and
the first attempt to solve them was made by Laplace in 1775, nearly a century
after Newton had derived the tide generating forces and the form of the equilibrium tide. Following Laplace many eminent mathematicians, including Airy,
Kelvin, Sir George Darwin and, in the present century, Proudman and Doodson
made contributions towards solving the dynamical equations for ocean tides.
For many years the efforts were devoted to finding analytical solutions for
oceans of simple geometrical shapes, e.g. an ocean of uniform depth covering the
whole earth, a hemisphere, or an ocean bounded by certain meridians and
parallels of latitude. Oceans bounded by realistic coastlines and of variable
depth could only be treated by numerical methods and little progress could be
made before the advent of digital electronic computers. There has been much
activity in this field in recent years and a number of solutions have been given
for the world ocean, starting with Pekeris and Accad in 1969, as well as for

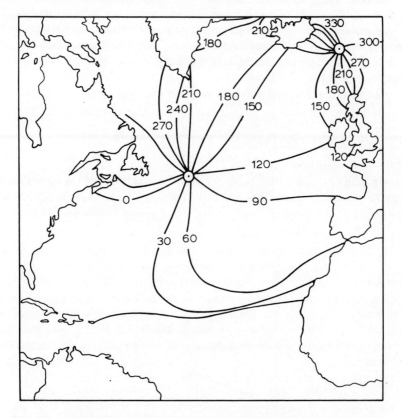

Fig. 2.4 – Cotidal lines for the $M_2$ tide in the North Atlantic. The numbers are
the phases in degrees (relative to the time of the moon's transit over Greenwich).
From Huntley (1980), by courtesy of Elsevier Scientific Publishing Co.

individual oceans or more limited oceanic areas. A review of this work was given by Hendershott (1977).

Observations of tides at positions around the continental coasts and at mid-ocean islands have been collected for many years and charts of cotidal lines, joining points at which high water occurs at the same time, were constructed. The way in which the cotidal lines were drawn across the open ocean was largely arbitrary but was usually guided by some general idea of how the oceans responded to the tidal forces. The charts produced by Harris in 1904, for example, were based on the idea that an ocean could be regarded as being built up of a continuous series of basins, each of which was of such dimensions that its natural period corresponded to that of the tidal period considered. This idea was a significant advance at the time and Harris's charts were the first to show amphidromic points from which cotidal lines radiated. The term 'amphidromic point' is used in tidal terminology for a nodal point, at which there is no vertical rise or fall of the tide. The range of tide increases with radial distance outwards from such a point so that lines of equal range, known as corange lines, encircle it. The whole pattern of the amphidromic point with its associated cotidal and corange lines is known as an 'amphidromic system'. Amphidromic systems are now known to be important features of the oceanic tides although Harris's ideas were oversimplified.

An example of a cotidal chart is shown in Fig. 2.4.

## 2.3 DYNAMICAL EQUATIONS

### 2.3.1 Basic equations

Over a limited region of the earth, for which the curvature of the earth's surface may be neglected, right-handed rectangular axes will be taken, as in Fig 2.5, with the origin in the mean sea surface, the $x$ and $y$ axes horizontal and the $z$ axis

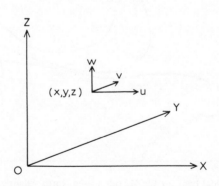

Fig. 2.5 – Rectangular axes for the equations of motion.

vertically upwards. The velocity components parallel to the $x$, $y$ and $z$ axes, at a point $x$, $y$, $z$, will be denoted by $u$, $v$ and $w$. The pressure is denoted by $p$, the density of the water by $\rho$ and $F_x$, $F_y$ denote the components of force per unit mass (other than the pressure force) in the $x$ and $y$ directions. It is assumed that the only significant force in the $z$ direction is that due to apparent gravity $g$, which includes the centrifugal force due to the rotation of the earth, and that vertical accelerations are negligible. Then the equations of motion in the $x$, $y$ and $z$ directions respectively are

$$\frac{Du}{Dt} - fv = -\frac{1}{\rho}\frac{\partial p}{\partial x} + F_x \, , \tag{2.7}$$

$$\frac{Dv}{Dt} + fu = -\frac{1}{\rho}\frac{\partial p}{\partial y} + F_y \, , \tag{2.8}$$

$$0 = -\frac{1}{\rho}\frac{\partial p}{\partial z} - g \, , \tag{2.9}$$

where $$\frac{D}{Dt} = \frac{\partial}{\partial t} + u\frac{\partial}{\partial x} + v\frac{\partial}{\partial y} + w\frac{\partial}{\partial z} \, ,$$

and $f = 2\omega \sin \phi$ where $\omega$ is the angular rate of rotation of the earth ($= 7.29 \times 10^{-5}$ radians per second) and $\phi$ is the latitude, positive to the north of the equator. $-fv$ and $fu$ are the Coriolis or geostrophic acceleration terms arising from the earth's rotation.

To these equations must be added the equation of continuity of volume

$$\frac{\partial u}{\partial x} + \frac{\partial v}{\partial y} + \frac{\partial w}{\partial z} = 0 \, . \tag{2.10}$$

A full derivation of these equations is given in standard textbooks of oceanography such as Pond and Pickard (1978) or Neumann and Pierson (1966).

Integrating (2.9) with respect to $z$, assuming $\rho$ to be independent of $z$

$$p = p_a + g\rho\,(\zeta - z)$$

where $p_a$ is the atmospheric pressure and $\zeta$ is the elevation of the sea surface above its undisturbed value, taken as the zero for the $x$, $y$ plane.

If $p_a$ is independent of $x$ and $y$ and if $\rho$ is independent of $x$ and $y$ as well as of $z$,

$$\frac{1}{\rho}\frac{\partial p}{\partial x} = g\frac{\partial \zeta}{\partial x} \quad \text{and} \quad \frac{1}{\rho}\frac{\partial p}{\partial y} = g\frac{\partial \zeta}{\partial y} \, . \tag{2.11}$$

In the case of tidal motions, the components of horizontal force, $F_x$ and $F_y$, will include the tide-generating force and also frictional stresses in the water, where they are significant. For the tide-generating forces

$$F_x = - \frac{\partial \Omega}{\partial x}, \qquad F_y = - \frac{\partial \Omega}{\partial y},$$

where $\Omega$ is the tide-generating potential.

Since        $\Omega = - g \bar{\zeta}$ ,

where $\bar{\zeta}$ is the elevation in the equilibrium tide,

$$F_x = g \frac{\partial \bar{\zeta}}{\partial x}, \qquad F_y = g \frac{\partial \bar{\zeta}}{\partial y}. \qquad (2.12)$$

The variation of $g$ and $\Omega$ with depth in the ocean is negligible so that in the absence of friction, the right-hand sides of equations (2.7) and (2.8) are independent of $z$ and hence the velocity components $u$ and $v$ are uniform with depth.

Frictional effects arise from the shearing stress of wind acting on the sea surface or the shearing stress at the bottom caused by the flow of water over the sea bed. These stresses are communicated to the rest of the water column by internal shearing stresses due to turbulence. The direct effect of molecular viscosity is usually negligibly small. In most cases only shearing stresses acting across horizontal planes need be considered. Then, as in Fig. 2.6, the stress per unit area across a surface perpendicular to the $z$ axis will have components $\tau_x$ and $\tau_y$ acting in the $x$ and $y$ directions respectively. The signs of $\tau_x$ and $\tau_y$ will be taken as positive if the water above the area considered acts on the water

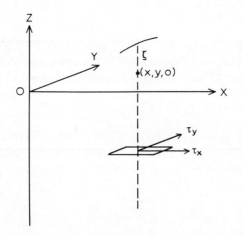

Fig. 2.6 – Components of shearing stress in the water.

below in the positive $x$ or $y$ direction. It may easily be shown that the additional force per unit mass acting on an element of water has components

$$\frac{1}{\rho}\frac{\partial \tau_x}{\partial z} \quad \text{and} \quad \frac{1}{\rho}\frac{\partial \tau_y}{\partial z} \; , \tag{2.13}$$

in the $x$ and $y$ directions respectively.

From equations (2.7), (2.8), (2.11), (2.12) and (2.13) the complete momentum equations in the $x$ and $y$ directions, valid at any point $x$, $y$, $z$ in the water are

$$\frac{Du}{Dt} - fv = -g\frac{\partial}{\partial x}(\zeta - \bar{\zeta}) + \frac{1}{\rho}\frac{\partial \tau_x}{\partial z} \; , \tag{2.14}$$

$$\frac{Dv}{Dt} + fu = -g\frac{\partial}{\partial y}(\zeta - \bar{\zeta}) + \frac{1}{\rho}\frac{\partial \tau_y}{\partial z} \; . \tag{2.15}$$

The hydrostatic equation (2.9) and continuity equation (2.10) are unchanged.

### 2.3.2 Depth-integrated equations

Let $h$ be the depth of water below the undisturbed level, $z = 0$. Then by integrating equations (2.14) and (2.15) from the bottom, $z = -h$, to the surface, $z = \zeta$, putting

$$\bar{u} = \frac{1}{h+\zeta}\int_{-h}^{\zeta} u \, dz \; , \quad \bar{v} = \frac{1}{h+\zeta}\int_{-h}^{\zeta} v \, dz \; ,$$

so that $\bar{u}$ and $\bar{v}$ are components of the depth-mean current, and making certain assumptions, the following equations may be derived:

$$\frac{\partial \bar{u}}{\partial t} + \bar{u}\frac{\partial \bar{u}}{\partial x} + \bar{v}\frac{\partial \bar{u}}{\partial y} - f\bar{v} = -g\frac{\partial}{\partial x}(\zeta - \bar{\zeta}) + \frac{\tau_{sx} - \tau_{bx}}{\rho\,(h+\zeta)} \; , \tag{2.16}$$

$$\frac{\partial \bar{v}}{\partial t} + \bar{u}\frac{\partial \bar{v}}{\partial x} + \bar{v}\frac{\partial \bar{v}}{\partial y} + f\bar{u} = -g\frac{\partial}{\partial y}(\zeta - \bar{\zeta}) + \frac{\tau_{sy} - \tau_{by}}{\rho\,(h+\zeta)} \; . \tag{2.17}$$

In these equations $\tau_{sx}$, $\tau_{sy}$ are the components of the stress on the surface and $\tau_{bx}$, $\tau_{by}$ are the components of the stress at the bottom. Integrating the continuity equation (2.10) in the same way gives

$$\frac{\partial}{\partial x}[(h+\zeta)\bar{u}] + \frac{\partial}{\partial y}[(h+\zeta)\bar{v}] + \frac{\partial \zeta}{\partial t} = 0 \; . \tag{2.18}$$

The wind stress acting on the surface is an important term in the study of wind effects and storm surges (Chapter 4), but in considering the tides alone we assume that $\tau_{sx} = \tau_{sy} = 0$. The resultant bottom stress $\tau_b$ may be related to the bottom current $U_b$ by a quadratic law, i.e. $\tau_b = k\rho U_b^2$ where $U_b$ is measured at a standard reference height, usually taken as 1 m, $\tau_b$ is assumed to be in the direction of $U_b$ and $k$ is a coefficient of friction. If $U_b$ has components $u_b, v_b$ in the $x$ and $y$ directions, then $\tau_b$ has components $\tau_{bx}, \tau_{by}$ given by

$$\tau_{bx} = k\rho U_b u_b \, , \qquad \tau_{by} = k\rho U_b v_b \, , \qquad (2.19)$$

where $\qquad U_b = (u_b{}^2 + v_b{}^2)^{1/2} \, .$

A typical value of the friction coefficient would be $k = 2 \times 10^{-3}$. For a bottom current $U_b$ of 0.5 m s$^{-1}$ (about 1 knot), this would give a bottom stress $\tau_b$ of approximately 0.5 N m$^{-2}$ (Newtons per square metre).

### 2.3.3 Linearised equations

Equations (2.16), (2.17) and (2.18), with $\tau_{sx} = \tau_{sy} = 0$ and $\tau_{bx}, \tau_{by}$ given by (2.19) are the complete equations for tidal motion. They are non-linear but can be linearised by making certain assumptions. If the acceleration terms are small, then terms like $\bar{u}\partial u/\partial x$ can be neglected. If the tidal elevation $\zeta$ is small compared with the depth of water $h$, then $(h + \zeta)$ can be replaced by $h$ in equation (2.18).

In the case of a harmonic constituent of velocity it is also possible to linearise the expressions for $\tau_{bx}$ and $\tau_{by}$. To illustrate this point, let the bottom velocity be in the $x$ direction so that $v_b = 0$. Then

$$\tau_{bx} = k\rho \, |u_b| \, u_b \, .$$

Let $\qquad u_b = C_b \cos \sigma t \, ,$

so that $C_b$ is the amplitude of the bottom current and $\sigma$ is its angular frequency. Then

$$\tau_{bx} = k\rho C_b{}^2 \, |\cos \sigma t| \cos \sigma t \, .$$

The expression $|\cos \sigma t| \cos \sigma t$ may be expanded as a Fourier series such that

$$|\cos \sigma t| \cos \sigma t = a_1 \cos \sigma t + a_2 \cos 2 \sigma t + \dots$$

where the Fourier coefficients $a_1, a_2, \dots$ are determined in the usual way. It is found that

$$a_1 = \frac{8}{3\pi} \, .$$

Thus $\qquad \tau_{bx} = \dfrac{8}{3\pi} k\rho C_b{}^2 \cos \sigma t + \text{terms in } \cos 2 \sigma t, \dots$

As far as the harmonic constituent of angular frequency $\sigma$ is concerned,

$$\tau_{bx} = \frac{8}{3\pi} k\rho C_b u_b = K'\rho u_b \, ,$$

where $K' = (8/3\pi)kC_b$, so that $\tau_{bx}$ is linearly proportional to $u_b$. The higher-order terms correspond to higher harmonics and these will be considered in a later section.

If the velocity profile has a standard form so that $u_b/\bar{u}$ may be regarded as constant, then $\tau_{bx}$ may be related to $\bar{u}$ instead of to $u_b$, with a suitably modified value of the factor $K'$.

In the more general case, when the bottom current has components $u_b$, $v_b$, a similar argument may be applied, although the details are more complicated (Heaps, 1978). Introducing the depth-mean current, with components $\bar{u}$, $\bar{v}$, it may be shown that

$$\tau_{bx} = K\rho\bar{u}, \qquad \tau_{by} = K\rho\bar{v}, \tag{2.20}$$

where $K = Ak\bar{C}$, $\bar{C}$ denoting the amplitude of the resultant depth-mean current and $A$ being a factor of order unity.

With these linearising assumptions and $\tau_{sx} = \tau_{sy} = 0$, equations (2.16), (2.17) and (2.18) become

$$\frac{\partial \bar{u}}{\partial t} - f\bar{v} = -g\frac{\partial}{\partial x}(\zeta - \bar{\zeta}) - \frac{K\bar{u}}{h}, \tag{2.21}$$

$$\frac{\partial \bar{v}}{\partial t} + f\bar{u} = -g\frac{\partial}{\partial y}(\zeta - \bar{\zeta}) - \frac{K\bar{v}}{h}, \tag{2.22}$$

$$\frac{\partial}{\partial x}(h\bar{u}) + \frac{\partial}{\partial y}(h\bar{v}) = -\frac{\partial \zeta}{\partial t}. \tag{2.23}$$

In these equations $K$ is a constant at a given position, having the dimensions of a velocity. It varies from one position to another since $\bar{C}$, the amplitude of the tidal current, and possibly also $k$, the friction coefficient, may vary. Over a restricted area, however, it may be adequate to treat $K$ as a constant, independent of position.

The linearised equations may be solved for a particular harmonic constituent in a given sea area, applying the appropriate boundary conditions. The solutions for several constituents may then be superposed to give the resultant tide due to these constituents.

### 2.3.4 Equations in polar coordinates
The equations given above are valid over an area of the earth's surface which is sufficiently small to be regarded as a plane. Over a larger area, on which the curvature of the lines of latitude and longitude is significant, a polar coordinate system must be used. Then equations (2.21), (2.22) and (2.23) are replaced by

$$\frac{\partial \bar{u}}{\partial t} - f\bar{v} = -\frac{g}{a\cos\phi}\frac{\partial}{\partial \chi}(\zeta - \bar{\zeta}) - \frac{K\bar{u}}{h}, \tag{2.24}$$

$$\frac{\partial \bar{v}}{\partial t} + f\bar{u} = -\frac{g}{a}\frac{\partial}{\partial \phi}(\zeta - \bar{\zeta}) - \frac{K\bar{v}}{h} , \qquad (2.25)$$

$$\frac{1}{a \cos \phi}\left\{\frac{\partial}{\partial \chi}(h\bar{u}) + \frac{\partial}{\partial \phi}(h\bar{v} \cos \phi)\right\} = -\frac{\partial \zeta}{\partial t} , \qquad (2.26)$$

where
- $\chi$ is the longitude measured positive eastwards from a standard meridian,
- $\phi$ is the latitude,
- $\bar{u}, \bar{v}$ are mean velocity components in the directions of $\chi$ and $\phi$ increasing,
- $a$ is the radius of the earth and $\zeta, \bar{\zeta}, h$ and $f$ have the same meanings as before.

Equations (2.24), (2.25), and (2.26), apart from the frictional terms, were first given by Laplace in 1775, and they form the basis of modern methods of modelling numerically the ocean tides.

### 2.3.5 Progressive waves

If the surface of the ocean is distorted in any way and the disturbing force is removed, the distortion will tend to travel to other parts of the ocean as a free wave. It has been useful in the study of ocean tides to regard them as being due to the superposition of waves of various types, generated by the tide-generating forces. Such waves are forced but their amplitude is increased if there is a tendency to resonance between the tidal forces and free waves of the same period. A useful insight into the tidal movements may be obtained, therefore, by considering free waves in the ocean.

The linearised equations for free waves travelling in an ocean of constant depth, without friction, are obtained from (2.21), (2.22) and (2.23) by setting $h = $ constant and $\bar{\zeta} = 0$ and omitting the frictional terms. Then

$$\frac{\partial u}{\partial t} - fv = -g\frac{\partial \zeta}{\partial x} , \qquad (2.27)$$

$$\frac{\partial v}{\partial t} + fu = -g\frac{\partial \zeta}{\partial y} , \qquad (2.28)$$

$$h\left(\frac{\partial u}{\partial x} + \frac{\partial v}{\partial y}\right) = -\frac{\partial \zeta}{\partial t} . \qquad (2.29)$$

In these equations $\bar{u}$ and $\bar{v}$ have been replaced by $u$ and $v$ since, in the absence of friction, the velocity is uniform with depth. The assumption made at the beginning of section 2.3.1, that vertical accelerations are negligible, restricts the above equations to so-called 'long waves' and they are not applicable to surface waves, for example.

A particular solution may be obtained for a progressive wave travelling in the $x$ direction if we assume that the water particles move in the $x$ direction only, so that $v = 0$. The above equations may then be written

$$\frac{\partial u}{\partial t} = -g\frac{\partial \zeta}{\partial x} , \tag{2.30}$$

$$fu = -g\frac{\partial \zeta}{\partial y} , \tag{2.31}$$

$$h\frac{\partial u}{\partial x} = -\frac{\partial \zeta}{\partial t} . \tag{2.32}$$

Eliminating $u$ from equations (2.30) and (2.32) by differentiating (2.30) with respect to $x$ and (2.32) with respect to $t$ leads to the equation

$$\frac{\partial^2 \zeta}{\partial t^2} = gh\frac{\partial^2 \zeta}{\partial x^2} . \tag{2.33}$$

Thus $\qquad\qquad \dfrac{\partial^2 \zeta}{\partial t^2} = c^2\dfrac{\partial^2 \zeta}{\partial x^2} , \tag{2.34}$

where $\qquad\qquad c^2 = gh . \tag{2.35}$

Equation (2.34) is the wave equation for oscillations of $\zeta$ travelling in the $x$ direction with a velocity of propagation $c$, given by (2.35). By eliminating $\zeta$ from (2.30) and (2.32) a similar equation is obtained for $u$, i.e.

$$\frac{\partial^2 u}{\partial t^2} = c^2\frac{\partial^2 u}{\partial x^2} . \tag{2.36}$$

A wave of general form travelling in the $x$-direction which satisfies (2.34) is

$$\zeta = Y(y)F(x - ct) \tag{2.37}$$

where $Y(y)$ is a function of $y$ only.
From (2.30) using (2.35),

$$u = \frac{c}{h} Y(y)F(x - ct) \tag{2.38}$$

From (2.31) it is found that

$$Y(y) = Ae^{-fy/c} , \tag{2.39}$$

where $A$ is a constant.

The factor $\exp(-fy/c)$ occurs in (2.37) and (2.38) for both $\zeta$ and $u$, showing that the amplitude of the wave decreases exponentially in the $y$ direction. The type of motion represented by equations (2.37), (2.38) and (2.39) is known as a Kelvin wave. As a special case we may take a wave of simple harmonic form of wavelength λ by setting

$$F(x - ct) = \cos \frac{2\pi}{\lambda}(x - ct)$$

The period is given by $T = \lambda/c$, so that by writing $\kappa = 2\pi/\lambda$ and $\sigma = 2\pi/T$ the solution may be written

$$\zeta = Ae^{-y/b} \cos(\kappa x - \sigma t) \qquad (2.40)$$

$$u = Ue^{-y/b} \cos(\kappa x - \sigma t) \qquad (2.41)$$

where $\quad U = \dfrac{c}{h}A \,, \qquad\qquad\qquad\qquad\qquad (2.42)$

$$b = \frac{c}{f}\,, \qquad\qquad\qquad\qquad\qquad (2.43)$$

and $\quad c = \sqrt{gh}\,. \qquad\qquad\qquad\qquad\qquad (2.44)$

These equations represent a Kelvin wave travelling in the $x$ direction. By referring to the coordinate system given in Fig. 2.6, it is seen that the amplitude increases exponentially in the negative $y$ direction if $f$ is positive. Thus the amplitude increases to the right of the direction of propagation in the northern hemisphere and to the left in the southern hemisphere, where $f$ is negative. A Kelvin wave in the northern hemisphere is illustrated in Fig. 2.7.

By putting in suitable numerical values we can get an idea of the dimensions and speed of travel of Kelvin waves in the ocean. For the ocean basins a typical value of depth is $h = 4000$ m. Taking $g = 9.80$ m s$^{-2}$, equation (2.44) gives $c = 198$ m s$^{-1}$. For a wave with the period of the M$_2$ tide, $T = 12$ h 25 m ($= 44,700$ s) and the relation $\lambda = ct$ gives the wavelength as $\lambda = 8850$ km. The rate of change of amplitude across the wave front depends on latitude. In latitude 30°N, for example, $f = 7.29 \times 10^{-5}$ s$^{-1}$ and hence, from (2.43), $b = 2720$ km. Thus the amplitude would increase by a factor $e$ ($= 2.78$) in a distance 2720 km measured to the right along the wavefront.

In the open ocean the amplitude of the tidal wave is unlikely to exceed about 0.5 m. Taking $A = 0.5$ m and the above values of $h$ and $c$, equation (2.42) gives $U = 2.5$ cm s$^{-1}$ which is typical of tidal currents in the open ocean.

Because a wave with an amplitude increasing indefinitely in a direction normal to the direction of propagation would be unrealistic, a Kelvin wave is likely to be found travelling parallel to a coast, with the coast on its right-hand side in the northern hemisphere. Its amplitude would then decrease to a small value in the centre of the ocean.

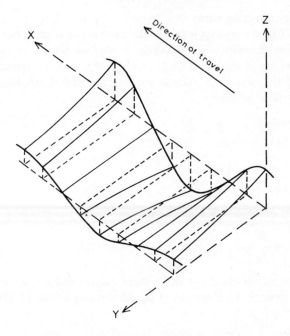

Fig. 2.7 – Schematic representation of a Kelvin wave, travelling with a coast
on its right-hand side, in the northern hemisphere.

Other wave-like solutions of equations (2.27), (2.28) and (2.29) are possible
if the restriction $v = 0$ is not imposed. One type is the Poincaré wave, in which
the amplitude varies sinusoidally, instead of exponentially, in the transverse
direction. The amplitude of the transverse component of velocity $v$, also varies
sinusoidally in the $y$ direction so that $v = 0$ at certain values of $y$. Such a wave
could travel parallel to a coast, provided that one of the lines along which
$v = 0$ lay along the coastline.

A solution to equations (2.27), (2.28) and (2.29), in which the waves have
horizontal crests, can be obtained by putting $\partial \zeta / \partial y = 0$ in (2.28) and $\partial v / \partial y = 0$
in (2.29). The $u$ and $v$ components of current are 90° out of phase so that the
resultant current vector traces out an ellipse in the course of a tidal period. The
velocity of propagation of such waves is greater than that of Kelvin waves and is
given by

$$c^2 = \frac{gh}{1 - f^2 / \sigma^2} .$$

Waves of this type were described by Sverdrup in 1926 and used in his explanation of tides on the North Siberian shelf (Defant, 1961, vol. II).

## 2.3.6 Frictional effect on waves

The effect of friction on long waves in the deep ocean is small but it becomes important when the waves are travelling in shallow water. In that case the frictional terms, as in equations (2.21) and (2.22), must be retained. For the special case of free waves travelling in water of constant depth, with $\bar{\zeta} = 0$ and $\bar{v} = 0$, the equations become

$$\frac{\partial \bar{u}}{\partial t} = - g \frac{\partial \zeta}{\partial x} - \frac{K\bar{u}}{h} , \tag{2.45}$$

$$h \frac{\partial \bar{u}}{\partial x} = - \frac{\partial \zeta}{\partial t} . \tag{2.46}$$

Since $\bar{v} = 0$, the coefficient $K$ is given by

$$K = \frac{8}{3\pi} k\bar{U} , \tag{2.47}$$

where $\bar{U}$ is the amplitude of the depth-mean current and $k$ is a friction coefficient defined to apply to $\bar{U}$ instead of $u_b$. Eliminating $\bar{u}$ from (2.45) and (2.46) gives

$$\frac{\partial^2 \zeta}{\partial t^2} = c_0^2 \frac{\partial^2 \zeta}{\partial x^2} - \frac{K}{h} \frac{\partial \zeta}{\partial t} , \tag{2.48}$$

where $c_0^2 = gh$.

This is the wave equation with a damping term proportional to the particle velocity $\partial \zeta / \partial t$. It has a progressive wave solution of the form

$$\zeta = A e^{-\mu x} \cos (\kappa x - \sigma t) \tag{2.49}$$

where $\kappa = 2\pi/\lambda$ and $\sigma = 2\pi/T$, as previously.

By differentiation and substitution in (2.48) it is found that

$$\sigma^2 = (\mu^2 - \kappa^2) c_0^2 ,$$

and
$$2\mu\kappa = \frac{K\sigma}{hc_0^2} .$$

The wave velocity $c = \sigma/\kappa$ is given by

$$c^2 = c_0^2 \left( 1 - \frac{\mu^2}{\kappa^2} \right) \tag{2.50}$$

and
$$\mu = \frac{1}{2} \frac{Kc}{hc_0^2} \cong \frac{1}{2} \frac{K}{hc_0} , \tag{2.51}$$

since usually $\mu \ll \kappa$.

Using equation (2.47) for $K$,

$$\mu = \frac{4}{3\pi} \frac{k\bar{U}}{hc_0} ,$$                    (2.52)

thus relating the damping coefficient $\mu$ to the friction coefficient $k$.

The corresponding solution for $\bar{u}$ is

$$\bar{u} = \bar{U}e^{-\mu x} \cos(\kappa x - \sigma t - \alpha)$$                    (2.53)

where    $$\bar{U} = \frac{\sigma A}{h(\kappa^2 + \mu^2)^{1/2}} .$$                    (2.54)

and    $$\tan \alpha = \frac{\mu}{\kappa} .$$                    (2.55)

Equations (2.49) and (2.53) represent the elevation and depth-mean current in a damped Kelvin wave travelling in the $x$-direction. Equation (2.53) shows that the current is no longer in phase with the elevation, as in a frictionless progressive wave, but reaches its maximum a time interval $\alpha/\sigma$ before the elevation reaches its peak.

## 2.4 TIDES ON THE CONTINENTAL SHELF

### 2.4.1 Effects of reduced depth

When the tidal movements which are generated in the open ocean travel as waves towards the continental slope and shelf, they undergo certain changes due to the decrease in depth. An estimate of the order of magnitude of these changes may be made by considering the rate of transport of energy. For a wave travelling in the $x$ direction, the rate of transmission of energy across an area $\delta y \delta z$ of a vertical plane perpendicular to the direction of propagation is given by

$$p'u\delta y\delta z$$

where $p'$ is the excess of pressure, above the hydrostatic pressure in the absence of wave motion, and $u$ is the particle velocity in the wave.

For a long wave, $p' = g\rho\zeta$ and is independent of $z$. Considering a progressive wave, as in equations (2.40) and (2.41) but neglecting the variation in the $y$ direction.

$$\zeta = A \cos(\kappa x - \sigma t)$$

$$u = U \cos(\kappa x - \sigma t)$$

where $A$ and $U$ now represent the amplitudes of the elevation and current respectively.

From equations (2.42) and (2.44)

$$U = \frac{c}{h} A = \left(\frac{g}{h}\right)^{1/2} A .$$

Thus the rate of transmission of energy across a vertical strip of unit width and extending from surface to bottom is given by

$$g\rho h A U \cos^2 (\kappa x - \sigma t)$$

Taking the average value over a tidal period, the mean rate of transmission of energy per unit width perpendicular to the direction of propagation is

$$E = \frac{1}{2} g\rho h A \bar{U} \tag{2.56}$$

which can also be written

$$E = \frac{1}{2} \rho g^{3/2} h^{1/2} A^2 \tag{2.57}$$

by using the above relation between $U$ and $A$.

If we consider a wave travelling from an ocean of depth $h_1$ on to a shelf region of depth $h_2$, the velocity of propagation will be reduced in the ratio

$$\frac{c_2}{c_1} = \left(\frac{h_2}{h_1}\right)^{1/2}$$

A rough estimate of the changes in amplitudes of the elevation and current can be made by assuming that the rate of energy transmission is conserved as the tidal wave moves on to the shelf. Then from (2.57),

$$\frac{A_2}{A_1} = \left(\frac{h_1}{h_2}\right)^{1/4}$$

and

$$\frac{U_2}{U_1} = \left(\frac{h_1}{h_2}\right)^{3/4}$$

If we take $h_1 = 4000$ m for the ocean and $h_2 = 100$ m as being typical for a continental shelf, then the above equations give

$$c_1 = 198 \text{ m s}^{-1} , \qquad c_2 = 31.3 \text{ m s}^{-1}$$
$$A_2 = 2.51 A_1 , \qquad U_2 = 15.9 U_1$$

If $A_1 = 0.5$ m and $U_1 = 2.5$ cm s$^{-1}$, as in the example taken previously, then $A_2 = 1.26$ m and $U_2 = 39.8$ cm s$^{-1}$. Thus the velocity is increased to a much greater extent than is the elevation.

This method does not provide more than an order of magnitude estimate of the changes because various assumptions made are not valid:

(1) Changes taking place on a sloping bottom cannot be inferred directly from equations derived assuming a constant depth.
(2) A portion of the energy will be reflected back from the sloping bed, so that less will be transmitted on to the shelf.
(3) Some energy will be dissipated by friction arising at the sea bed.

Considering a Kelvin wave on the continental shelf, it is seen from (2.43) that $b = c/f$, so that for the same latitude, $b_2/b_1 = c_2/c_1$. In latitude 30°N, as taken previously, $b_1 = 2720$ km so that, in a depth of 100 m, $b_2 = 430$ km, indicating that the amplitude of a Kelvin wave on the shelf decreases much more rapidly with distance from the coast than in deep water.

### 2.4.2  East coast shelf of USA

As an example of the changes in tide occurring on a continental shelf we may consider the treatment by Redfield (1958) of tides along the east coast of USA. It may be seen from the cotidal chart of the Atlantic Ocean in Fig. 2.4 that, along the east coast from Florida to the Gulf of Maine, high water occurs at approximately the same time: about 12 hours after a transit of the moon across the Greenwich meridian. This suggests that the $M_2$ tidal wave approaches the coast almost at right angles along this length. As pointed out by Redfield, the range of tide at the coast increases with width of the continental shelf, being lowest at Cape Hatteras and increasing both northwards to New England and southwards to Georgia, indicating that the variation at the coast is associated with changes while crossing the shelf.

Treating the tide on the shelf as a free co-oscillation, driven by the ocean tide and reflected at the coast, and using a method originally employed by Sterneck in 1915, Redfield calculated the changes in amplitude and phase of the tide as it crossed the shelf from the 1000 m contour to the coast. Working back from the values at coastal stations, he was thus able to estimate the range of tide and time of high water along the 1000 m contour.

The calculated variation across a section of the shelf off Atlantic City of the elevation at high water and the maximum tidal current normal to the coast is shown in Fig. 2.8. The charts of corange and cotidal lines are shown in Fig. 2.9 and Fig. 2.10 respectively. It is seen that the range and the time of high water are more uniform along the 1000 m contour than at the coast. Over the whole area considered, the variation in range is 2.7 ft (0.83 m) at the coast compared with 0.65 ft (0.20 m) at the 1000 m contour while the high water intervals vary from 11.90 hr to 12.59 hr at the coast but only from 11.75 hr to 12.18 hr at the 1000 m line. The high water interval is the interval of time between a transit of the moon at Greenwich and the occurrence of high water.

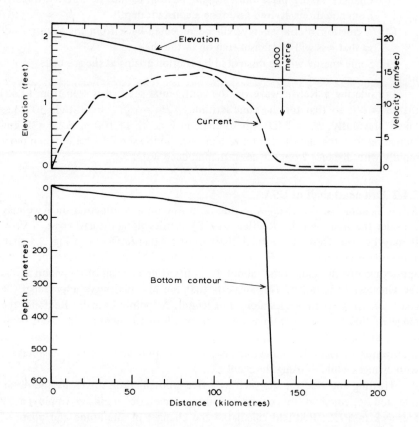

Fig. 2.8 – Profile of the USA continental shelf off Atlantic City (below) and the distribution of estimated elevation at high water and maximum velocities of onshore and offshore tidal currents across the shelf (above). From Redfield (1958), by courtesy of the *Journal of Marine Research*.

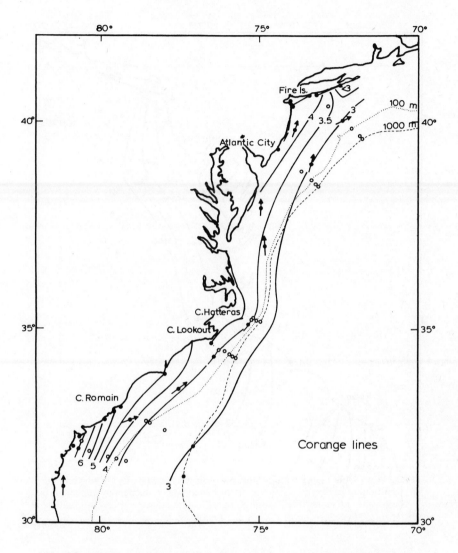

Fig. 2.9 – Estimated mean range of tide, in feet, on the continental shelf off the eastern coast of USA. Arrows show the direction of observed currents at high water. From Redfield (1958), by courtesy of the *Journal of Marine Research*.

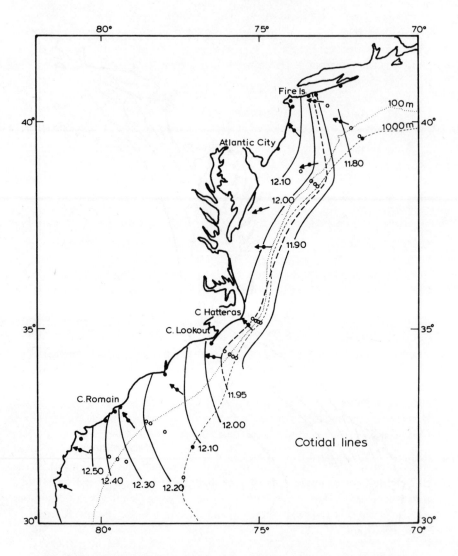

Fig. 2.10 – Estimated time of high water, in hours after the moon's transit at Greenwich, on the continental shelf of USA, assuming a damping factor $\mu\lambda$ of o.5. Arrows show the directions of currents 3 hours before high water. From Redfield (1958), by courtesy of the *Journal of Marine Research*.

In estimating the change in time of high water, Redfield allowed for damping of the tidal wave as it crossed the shelf by introducing a damping coefficient $\mu$ as in section 2.3.6. Thus the amplitude is attenuated by $\exp(-\mu\lambda)$ while the wave travels one wavelength. If $\zeta_{HO}$ is the elevation at HW at a coastal barrier and $\zeta_H$ is the elevation at HW at a position distant $x$ seaward from the barrier, it may be shown that

$$\zeta_H/\zeta_{HO} = \frac{1}{2}(\cosh 2\mu x + \cos 2\kappa x)^{1/2}$$

as in equation (2.73) of section 2.5.3, where $\kappa = 2\pi/\lambda$ and $\mu$ is defined as in section 2.3.6.

In order to obtain satisfactory agreement with observations, Redfield took the product $\mu\lambda$ as 0.5 for the continental slope off the east coast of USA. In a previous investigation (Redfield, 1950), he had found it necessary to take $\mu\lambda = 1.0$ to obtain agreement with observations in the Bay of Fundy and Long Island Sound and $\mu\lambda = 1.5$ to 2.0 for tides in the Straits of the Juan de Fuca and Georgia, on the west coast of North America.

In 1974 bottom pressure gauges were laid at several positions on the eastern USA continental shelf and the data from them showed Redfield's model of the $M_2$ tide to be essentially correct, except for an area to the east of Mountauk Point, at the tip of Long Island, where there was a discrepancy attributed to the influence of Long Island Sound.

In the past, theoretical models of the ocean tides have usually been matched to observations at coastal stations and mid-ocean islands. Studies such as that of Redfield show that it is unreliable to take observations at positions on a continental coast as boundary conditions for the oceanic tide, unless allowance is made for the modification as it crosses the continental shelf. As more data from open sea tide gauges become available it is possible to make direct comparisons between tides at coastal stations and at the shelf edge. Observations from instruments at the edge of the continental shelf to the southwest of the British Isles, for example, have shown that the amplitudes of the semidiurnal constituents there are about half of those at corresponding ·coastal stations such as Newlyn in Cornwall, England, and Brest in Brittany, France (Cartwright *et al.*, 1980).

### 2.4.3 Other areas
The case of the semidiurnal tide approaching the east coast of USA is particularly simple because the tidal wave approaches the continental shelf almost normally and the coast is relatively free from large bays and indentations. On the opposite side of the Atlantic Ocean the $M_2$ tide, as seen from Fig. 2.4, can be represented approximately as a Kelvin wave travelling northwards, parallel to the coast of western Europe, including the British Isles. An offshoot of the wave turns eastwards into the Celtic Sea, at latitude about 50°N, and

divides again into waves entering the English Channel and the Irish Sea. Meanwhile the main part of the wave continues northwards, along the shelf off the west of Ireland and Scotland, and then turns eastwards and southwards into the North Sea. The response of these shelf seas is too complex to be regarded simply as the reflection of a damped progressive wave and is considered again in section 2.6.

Another example of a tidal wave from deep water approaching a continental shelf almost at right angles is found on the North Siberian Shelf. This comprises the largest area of continental shelf in the world, extending from Cape Chelyuskin, Russia, about 106°E, to Point Barrow, Alaska, 157°W, and to a distance of 1300 km from the coast at its widest point. The tides of this region were described by Sverdrup in 1926 on the basis of observations of tidal elevations at coastal stations and of currents at a number of anchor stations on the 'Maud' expedition of 1924–25. The cotidal chart which he produced indicated that the tidal wave approached from the deep water of the Arctic Ocean with its wavefronts approximately parallel to the bottom contours of the shelf. The sea surface over the shelf is covered with ice for most of the year and friction at the ice surface as well as at the bottom causes a high rate of damping of the wave as it approaches the coast. On the shelf, away from the coast, the tidal currents rotate clockwise during a tidal period and the velocity or propagation of the tidal wave exceeds that given by $c = \sqrt{gh}$. In some cases the velocity approximated to that given at the end of section 2.3.6 for waves with horizontal crests. In other cases the velocity was between that for a Kelvin wave and that for a horizontally crested wave, suggesting that intermediate types of wave could exist (Defant, 1961, vol. II).

A general effect of the slope of the sea bed near a coast is that the wave energy approaching at an angle to the coast tends to become trapped in a coastal band. Since the velocity of propagation decreases as the depth decreases, an approaching wavefront is refracted towards the coast. The reflected wave moving away from the coast will also be refracted back towards it and a caustic line, parallel to the coast, may exist beyond which the energy cannot escape. Apart from Kelvin waves, other types of trapped waves can occur but their frequencies may not fall within the main semidiurnal and diurnal tidal bands.

## 2.5 TIDAL CO-OSCILLATION IN A GULF

### 2.5.1 Narrow rectangular gulf, without friction

The response of a partially enclosed body of water, such as a gulf, to the driving force exerted by the ocean tide at its entrance is influenced to a considerable extent by the natural modes of oscillation of the body of water and the extent to which there is a tendency to resonance with the tidal periods. A useful insight into the effects may be obtained by considering the idealised case of a rectangular gulf of length $l$ and constant depth $h$ communicating with a deep ocean at its open end. It is assumed that the gulf is sufficiently narrow for Coriolis effects to be neglected. Frictional effects are also neglected in the first instance. Axes may be taken as in Fig. 2.11, with the $x$ axis along the centre line of the gulf, with $x = 0$ at the closed end and $x = l$ at the open end. Then the equations of motion and continuity are the same as (2.30) and (2.32) in section 2.3.5, i.e.

$$\frac{\partial u}{\partial t} = -g\frac{\partial \zeta}{\partial x} \tag{2.30}$$

$$h\frac{\partial u}{\partial x} = -\frac{\partial \zeta}{\partial t} \tag{2.32}$$

where $\zeta$ is the surface elevation and $u$ is the velocity parallel to the centre line of the gulf.

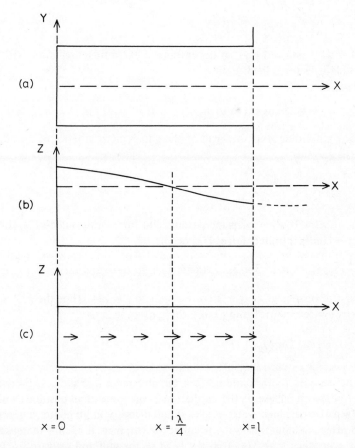

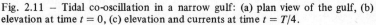

Fig. 2.11 – Tidal co-oscillation in a narrow gulf: (a) plan view of the gulf, (b) elevation at time $t = 0$, (c) elevation and currents at time $t = T/4$.

At the closed end there can be no velocity normal to the coast, so that at $x = 0$, $u = 0$ for all values of $t$. A solution is assumed in the form of a standing wave, such that

$$u = U \sin \kappa x \sin \sigma t \tag{2.58}$$

where $\kappa = 2\pi/\lambda$, $\sigma = 2\pi/T$, $\lambda$ is the wavelength and $T$ is the period. Then from (2.30) it is found that

$$\zeta = A \cos \kappa x \cos \sigma t \tag{2.59}$$

where $\qquad A = \dfrac{\sigma U}{g\kappa} \tag{2.60}$

From (2.32)

$$\sigma^2 = gh\kappa^2 \tag{2.61}$$

i.e. $\qquad \lambda^2 = ghT^2 \tag{2.62}$

It is now assumed that, at the entrance $x = l$, a tidal oscillation with a given amplitude $A_l$ is prescribed.

Then at $x = l$,

$$\zeta = A \cos \kappa l \cos \sigma t = A_l \cos \sigma t \tag{2.63}$$

Thus the amplitude $A$ at the head of the gulf is given in terms of the amplitude $A_l$ at the entrance by

$$A = \frac{A_l}{\cos \kappa l} \tag{2.64}$$

If $\cos \kappa l = 0$, then resonance occurs and for a finite value of $A_l$ the amplitude $A$ becomes infinitely large. This occurs at

$$\kappa l = \pi/2, \, 3\pi/2, \ldots (2n-1)\pi/2, \, n = 1, 2, \ldots$$

The first resonance at $\kappa l = \pi/2$ corresponds to $l = \lambda/4$. Thus the gulf acts as a quarter-wave resonator. From (2.62), this corresponds to

$$l = \frac{1}{4} T\sqrt{gh} \tag{2.65}$$

The cases of $l < \lambda/4$ and $l > \lambda/4$ are illustrated in Fig. 2.12, showing that when $l < \lambda/4$ the phase of the oscillation is the same at all positions within the gulf. In particular, high water occurs simultaneously at all points, a quarter of a period after maximum inward current at the entrance. If $l > \lambda/4$ there is a nodal line at a distance $x = \lambda/4$ from the head of the gulf and seaward of this line, where $x > \lambda/4$, the oscillation is in opposite phase to that near the head.

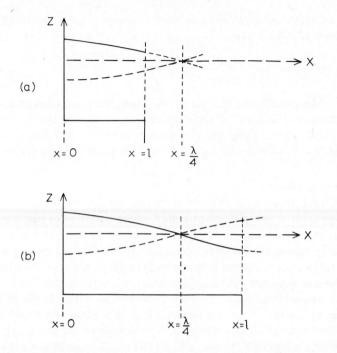

Fig. 2.12 – Tidal co-oscillation in a narrow gulf: (a) case of $l < \lambda/4$, (b) case of $l > \lambda/4$. In both cases the full line represents the elevation at time $t = 0$ and the broken line the elevation at time $t = T/2$.

In practice the amplitude at the head of the gulf will not become infinite at resonance because, as resonance is approached and the amplitude increases, the simplifying assumptions are no longer valid. Frictional forces will become significant and so may the non-linear terms in the equations of momentum and continuity. Nevertheless, useful deductions may frequently be made about the tidal response of a sea area by applying the simple theory of a frictionless co-oscillation in a rectangular gulf.

The Bay of Fundy, between Nova Scotia and New Brunswick in Canada, has the largest range of tide in the world, with spring tides reaching a range of 15.4 m (50.5 ft) at the head of the Bay. Its length is about 250 km and its average depth is 70 m. Putting $l = 250$ km and $h = 70$ m in equation (2.65) gives the period T at which the Bay would act as a resonator as T = 10.6 hr, which is approaching the $M_2$ tidal period of 12.4 hr. The validity of this estimate is doubtful, however, and the tides of the Bay of Fundy will be considered again later in this chapter.

When a gulf is not rectangular in cross-section an improved estimate of its response to an imposed oscillation at its mouth may be made by allowing for the varying width and depth along its length. Equation (2.30) remains unchanged but equation (2.32) is replaced by

$$\frac{\partial}{\partial x}(bhu) = -b\frac{\partial \zeta}{\partial t}$$

where $b$ is the breadth and $h$ is the depth: $b$ and $h$ are functions of $x$. Methods for the numerical solution of these equations to determine the distribution of elevation and current along the gulf were described by Proudman (1953). In particular, the resonant period may be determined from these equations.

### 2.5.2 Coriolis effects

Hitherto the gulf has been considered narrow enough for the Coriolis effects to be neglected. If the gulf is wider the Coriolis effects will cause a transverse oscillation to be superposed on the longitudinal motion. This is seen from Fig. 2.13 by noting that when the current at the entrance to the gulf is flowing inwards the surface will slope upwards to the right in the northern hemisphere. The transverse slope will vanish at high water, when the current is zero but will be in the opposite direction when the current flows outwards. There is thus a transverse oscillation of the sea surface which is a quarter of a period out of phase with the longitudinal oscillation. If the length of the gulf is greater than a quarter of a wavelength, so that a nodal line would occur at $x = \lambda/4$ when the Coriolis effect is neglected, allowing for this effect means that only the centre point of this line remains unchanged in level. Thus the nodal line is reduced to a nodal point, called an 'amphidromic point' in tidal terminology.

In Fig. 2.13(e) the amphidromic point is at C while the lines CA, CB, CA' and CB' radiating from it are cotidal lines for high water occurring at $t = 0$, $T/4$, $T/2$ and $3T/4$ respectively. The cotidal lines for increasing times of high water rotate in a counter-clockwise direction in this diagram, which is drawn for the northern hemisphere.

The appropriate equations of motion including the Coriolis effects are (2.27), (2.28) and (2.29) in section 2.3.5. In general it is not permissible to assume $v = 0$ in these equations, but it is possible to obtain an indication of the character of an amphidromic region by considering the standing oscillation produced in a channel, open at both ends, by the superposition of two Kelvin waves, travelling in opposite directions. Taking the $x$ axis along the centre line of the channel with the origin $x = 0$ at the point where the elevations due to the two waves are always equal and opposite, the resultant elevation may be written

$$\zeta = Ae^{y/b}\cos(\kappa x + \sigma t) - Ae^{-y/b}\cos(\kappa x - \sigma t) \qquad (2.66)$$

At high water, $\partial\zeta/\partial t = 0$, so that

$$e^{y/b}\sin(\kappa x + \sigma t) + e^{-y/b}\sin(\kappa x - \sigma t) = 0 \ .$$

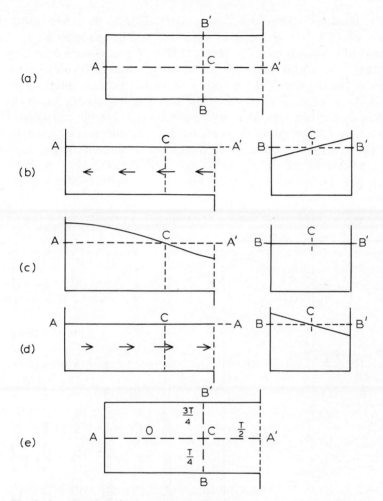

Fig. 2.13 – Coriolis effect on the co-oscillation in a gulf: (a) plan view. (b), (c) and (d) elevations along sections AA' and BB' at times $t = -T/4$, 0 and $T/4$ respectively; (e) resultant amphidromic system.

This may be regarded as the equation for the cotidal line for time $t$. After some manipulation it becomes

$$\tan \sigma t = -\frac{\tan \kappa x}{\tanh y/b} .$$  (2.67)

The cotidal lines for $t = 0$, $T/4$, $T/2$ and $3T/4$ are the coordinate axes, while near the origin, which is an amphidromic point, the radiating cotidal lines are given by

$$y = \kappa b x \cot \sigma t .$$  (2.68)

An analytical solution for the standing oscillation in a rectangular gulf produced by a Kelvin wave entering the mouth and being completely reflected at the closed end was given by Taylor (1920). The results are reproduced in Fig. 2.14, in which (a) shows the distribution of cotidal and corange lines and (b) shows the end-points of the current vectors at various positions. Near the mouth the solution corresponds to the superposition of two Kelvin waves, travelling in opposite directions, with currents parallel to the centre line. Near the head, in order to satisfy the condition that the current component normal to the boundary must vanish, the currents rotate in direction. This example is a first approximation to the $M_2$ tide in the North Sea, excluding the Southern Bight south of a line from Great Yarmouth on the English coast to the Hook of Holland.

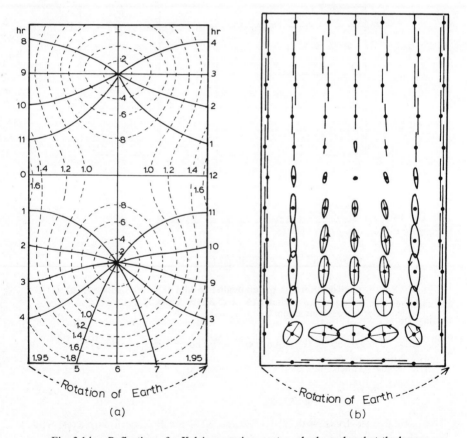

Fig. 2.14 – Reflection of a Kelvin wave in a rectangular bay; closed at the lower end, in the diagram. (a) Distribution of cotidal lines and corange lines (broken lines); (b) corresponding current diagrams. From Taylor (1920) by courtesy of the London Mathematical Society.

### 2.5.3 Frictional effects

To consider the basic features of the effects of friction on the co-oscillation in a gulf, we return to the case of a gulf which is sufficiently narrow for the Coriolis effects to be neglected. The standing oscillation given by equations (2.58) and (2.59) may be expressed as the superposition of two progressive waves of equal amplitude, travelling in opposite directions, one towards the head of the gulf and the other away from it, representing the case of total reflection. In the resultant oscillation, $u = 0$ at $x = 0$ for all values of $t$. Then

$$\zeta = \frac{1}{2} A \cos (\kappa x - \sigma t) + \frac{1}{2} A \cos (\kappa x + \sigma t) \qquad (2.69)$$

$$u = \frac{1}{2} U \cos (\kappa x - \sigma t) - \frac{1}{2} U \cos (\kappa x + \sigma t) \qquad (2.70)$$

where $U = cA/h$, as before. It is easily verified that these two equations are equivalent to (2.59) and (2.58) respectively.

When friction is included, each progressive wave of constant amplitude should be replaced by a damped progressive wave with a damping factor $\mu$, as in equations (2.49) and (2.53). Then again assuming total reflection, (2.69) is replaced by

$$\zeta = \frac{1}{2} A e^{-\mu x} \cos (\kappa x - \sigma t) + \frac{1}{2} A e^{\mu x} \cos (\kappa x + \sigma t) \qquad (2.71)$$

with a corresponding equation for $u$ replacing (2.70).

The time $t_H$ of high water at any position $x$ occurs when $\partial \zeta / \partial t = 0$. Hence it may be shown from (2.71) that

$$\sigma t_H = \text{arc tan} \, (-\tan \kappa x \tanh \mu x) \qquad (2.72)$$

In the absence of damping, high water occurred at $t = 0, T, \ldots$ for $0 < x < \lambda/4$ and changed discontinuously at $x = \lambda/4$ to $t = T/2, 3T/2, \ldots$ for $\lambda/4 < x < 3\lambda/4$. It may be shown from (2.72) that, in the damped case, the change in time of high water takes place gradually over a range of values of $x$ on either side of $x = \lambda/4$.

The height $\zeta_H$ of high water at any position $x$ may also be derived from (2.72), showing that

$$\zeta_H = A \left[ \frac{1}{2} (\cosh 2\mu x + \cos 2\kappa x) \right]^{1/2} \qquad (2.73)$$

In the undamped case it was found that resonance occurred if $\kappa l = \pi/2$ and that, for a prescribed amplitude $A_l$ at $x = l$, the amplitude $A$ at $x = 0$ would become infinitely large. Equating $\zeta_H$ at $x = l$ to $A_l$, it is seen from (2.73) that, at resonance,

$$A = A_l \left[ \frac{1}{2} (\cosh 2\mu l - 1) \right]^{-1/2} \tag{2.74}$$

Thus $A$ remains finite if $\mu$ is finite and the ratio $A/A_l$ decreases as $\mu$ increases in value. The derivation of equations (2.72) and (2.73) was given by Redfield in 1950 and is reproduced by Officer (1976).


### 2.5.4 Coriolis effects with friction

When Coriolis and frictional effects are both significant, it becomes more difficult to find an analytical solution to the equations but a qualitative indication of the combined result can be obtained as follows. In the case of two Kelvin waves of equal amplitude travelling in opposite directions along a channel, the amphidromic point due to their superposition lies on the centre line of the channel. If the waves are damped, however, at some distance from the head of the gulf the reflected wave will have a smaller amplitude. Looking towards the head of the gulf, assumed to be in the northern hemisphere, the amplitude at the right-hand side, due mainly to the incoming Kelvin wave, will be greater than at the left-hand side, where it is due mainly to the outgoing reflected wave. The amphidromic point will be displaced, therefore, from the centre of the channel towards the left-hand side. Examples of this effect are found in the North Sea, as mentioned later, and in many other areas.

An alternative approach was adopted by Hendershott and Speranza (1971), who assumed that the reflection of the incoming Kelvin wave at the head of the gulf is incomplete. This could be due to the dissipation of energy in an area of shallow water there, for example. The reflected wave then starts on its outward journey with a reduced amplitude. Neither the incident nor the reflected waves are damped by friction as they travel, in opposite directions, in the main part of the gulf. The problem is the same as that treated by Taylor, as described in section 2.5.2, except that at the head of the gulf, instead of the boundary condition $u = 0$, it is assumed that:

At $x = 0$, $u = \alpha\zeta$

where $\alpha$ is a parameter increasing with the rate of dissipation.

The effect on the amphidromic systems of increasing the value of $\alpha$ is shown in Fig. 2.15. In the case of complete reflection, Fig. 2.15(a), $\alpha = 0$ and the amphidromic points are on the centre-line. With $\alpha = 0.056$ s$^{-1}$ as in Fig. 2.15(b), the amphidromic points are displaced to the left of the centre line while with $\alpha = 0.28$ s$^{-1}$, Fig. 2.15(c) shows that there are no amphidromic points within the gulf, but the cotidal lines appear to radiate from a point beyond the landward boundary. This effect is well known from empirical charts of cotidal lines, where it is known as a 'degenerate amphidromic point'. Comparing these diagrams with Fig. 2.16 in section 2.6 of tides in waters around the British Isles, it is seen that displaced amphidromic points, as in Fig. 2.15(b) occur in the North Sea and degenerate amphidromic points in the English Channel and Irish Sea.

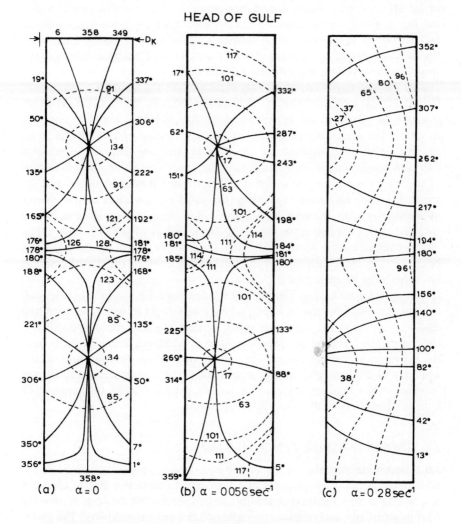

Fig. 2.15 – Complete and partial reflection of a Kelvin wave at the head of a rectangular bay: (a) complete reflection, $\alpha = 0$; (b) and (c) partial reflection with $\alpha = 0.056$ s$^{-1}$ and $\alpha = 0.28$ s$^{-1}$ respectively. From Hendershott and Speranza (1971), by courtesy of Pergamon Press.

### 2.5.5 Tides of the Bay of Fundy

Because of its large range of tide, the Bay of Fundy has been under consideration for a number of years as the possible site of a tidal power scheme. Various
analytical and numerical studies of the tides in the region have been carried out
with a view to estimating the changes which might occur following the construction of barriers across different sections. A simple calculation based on the
dimensions of the Bay, as in section 2.5.1, gives a natural period less than that
of the $M_2$ tide. It has been realised, however, that it is unsatisfactory to regard
the Bay of Fundy as co-oscillating directly with the tides of the Atlantic Ocean
because of the intervening, and relatively shallow, Gulf of Maine. Later work
has been devoted to treating the Bay of Fundy/Gulf of Maine combination as a
single system, co-oscillating with the Atlantic tides.

By comparing the response of the system to the $M_2$, $S_2$ and $N_2$ constituents,
Garrett (1972) estimated that its resonant period was 13.3 ± 0.4 h. The construction of barriers at the upper end of the Bay of Fundy would be expected
to reduce the period bringing it closer to the $M_2$ period of 12.42 h and so increasing slightly the amplitude of the $M_2$ tide. This was contrary to previous
estimates, made on the assumption that the conditions at the outer boundary
of the system would be unchanged, that the construction of barriers would decrease the tidal amplitude. Following the usual nomenclature in the physics
of resonant systems, the amplitude magnification at resonance may be expressed
by a factor $Q$, such that a fraction $2\pi/Q$ of the energy of the system would be
dissipated in one cycle. Garrett estimated the $Q$ of the system for the $M_2$ tide to
be 5.25 ± 1.5. More than 90% of the tidal energy entering the Bay of Fundy is
estimated to be dissipated there.

In a subsequent paper Garrett (1974) described a general method for calculating the tidal response of a gulf, taking into account its interaction with the
adjoining ocean. In the first stage of the process, the response of the gulf and
ocean separately to the tide generating force is calculated, assuming the boundary between them to be closed. The calculated level on the two sides of the
boundary is different and, in the second stage, the flux of water through the
boundary when it is opened is calculated. In the third stage, the response of
both gulf and ocean to this mass flux is calculated.

## 2.6 TIDES IN PARTIALLY ENCLOSED SEAS

### 2.6.1 General treatment

Some applications of the concept of a tidal co-oscillation in a gulf to the tides
in a sea have been mentioned already. In this section the methods of treating
tides in a partially enclosed sea are considered in a more general way. The observations available normally consist of records of the tidal elevations at a number
of positions, usually ports, around the coast and records of tidal currents at a
number of stations within the sea, from anchored ships, drifting buoys or

moored current meters. By analysing the records of tidal elevations at a given place, the amplitudes and phases of the various harmonic constituents there may be determined. From this information and data on the corresponding constituents in the tide generating potential, predictions may be prepared for the tides during a future period at the same place.

The observations of tidal currents at a particular station may be analysed in a similar way and the data used to make prediction of currents for a future period. This may be done for a position of special interest, such as the approach to a port, but such predictions of tidal streams are less commonly made than those of elevations. For navigational purposes charts are often prepared which show, by an array of arrows, the direction and speed of the tidal current over an area at a series of times relative to high water at a standard port.

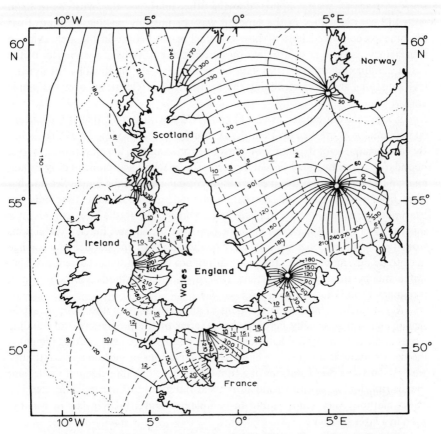

Fig. 2.16 – Cotidal and corange lines for the $M_2$ tide on the north-west European continental shelf. Solid lines: cotidal lines showing phase lag in degrees relative to a transit of the moon at Greenwich. Broken lines: corange lines with underlined numbers giving the range in feet. From Huntley (1980), by courtesy of Elsevier Scientific Publishing Co.

In order to obtain a representation of tides over the whole sea area, and hence be able to infer the tides at intermediate positions where observations have not been made, charts of cotidal and corange lines may be constructed. If a cotidal chart is drawn for a particular constituent, such as $M_2$, as in Fig. 2.16, the time of high water shown by a given line is usually expressed as the interval following a transit of the moon across a standard meridian. The corange lines on such a chart will show a range which is twice the amplitude of the $M_2$ constituent. On the other hand, for an area where the semidiurnal constituents are dominant, the chart may show the corange lines for average spring tides, in which case the range in question would be twice the sum of the $M_2$ and $S_2$ amplitudes.

A cotidal or corange chart may be drawn empirically using only the observations of tides at coastal points, drawing other lines over the sea so as to fit in with the coastal values in the simplest way, or possibly making qualitative use of some preconceived idea of how the tidal waves behave in the area. A more satisfactory method is to use data on currents at positions in the interior of the sea in conjunction with coastal data on elevations, relating them by the dynamical equations and so determining the distribution of elevations over the whole area.

It is seen from equations (2.21) and (2.22), with $\bar{\zeta} = 0$, that if the current components $\bar{u}$, $\bar{v}$ are known then $\partial \zeta/\partial x$ and $\partial \zeta/\partial y$ are also known at that point. By integrating along the line $x = $ constant, for example, the elevation from one boundary to another may be determined. This method was pioneered by Proudman and Doodson in 1924 in preparing a cotidal chart of the North Sea and has since been widely used. An alternative method, due to Defant, uses only the continuity equation (2.23), applied to current values at the four corners of a square, to calculate the elevation at the centre of the square. Further deductions from the equations of motion enable the directions of the cotidal and corange lines to be determined from the phase difference between the occurrence of high water and maximum flood current. Details of these methods will be found in Proudman (1953) and Defant (1961, vo. II).

A reasonably good understanding of the dynamics of the tides in a particular region may usually be obtained in terms of the progressive and standing waves and other analytical solutions already discussed. A further development is the use of numerical modelling in which the equations of motion and continuity are applied to a grid of stations in a finite difference or finite element model and the distribution of elevations and currents as functions of time are computed. These methods vary considerably in complexity and a brief review of them is given in a later section.

### 2.6.2 North-west European shelf
As an example of the response of partially enclosed sea areas to forcing by the

oceanic tide and its representation by cotidal charts, the $M_2$ tide in the shelf seas of north-west Europe will be described.

A chart of cotidal and corange lines for this area, including the North Sea, English Channel, Irish Sea and Celtic Sea is given in Fig. 2.16 taken from Huntley (1980). The construction of a cotidal chart for the North Sea by Proudman and Doodson in 1924 has been described already. Using the same method, Doodson and Corkan prepared corresponding charts for the English Channel and Irish Sea. These charts have been refined subsequently in the light of results from a series of numerical models but in general the modifications required have been small.

A simplified dynamical explanation of the features shown in Fig. 2.16 may be given as follows. The tide from the Atlantic Ocean approaches from the south as a north-going Kelvin wave, part of which turns north-eastward into the Celtic Sea, between south-west Ireland and Brittany. This wave generates co-oscillations in the English Channel to the east and in the Irish Sea and Bristol Channel to the north. The English Channel acts approximately as a half-wave resonator with maximum amplitudes, in opposite phase, at its two ends and a nodal line across the centre. Coriolis and frictional effects are important, however, so that the response may also be described as a damped progressive Kelvin wave travelling up the Channel, giving a large range of tide on the French side, particularly in the Gulf of St. Malo. A portion of the energy is reflected at the Straits of Dover and a weak Kelvin wave travels back down the Channel. The superposition of the two waves reduces the notional nodal line to a degenerate amphidromic point, somewhere inland from the English coast, from which the cotidal lines in the centre part of the Channel appear to radiate.

In the Irish Sea the tide moves as a progressive wave northward through St. George's Channel, between Southern Ireland and Wales, but the broad northern part of the Irish Sea acts approximately as a quarter-wave resonator. High water throughout most of the northern area occurs within 2 to 3 hours after maximum inflow from St. George's Channel. The situation is complicated to some extent by currents flowing southwards into the Irish Sea through the North Channel between north-east Ireland and south-west Scotland. Maximum inflow occurs, in fact, at the same time from north and south, but the volume of water entering from the north is much less. The Coriolis force is again in evidence, accounting for the greater range on the eastern side of the sea and the degenerate amphidromic point in south-east Ireland.

The approximate representation of the North Sea as a wide rectangular gulf has been mentioned already. The tide enters from the north as a progressive Kelvin wave, having been refracted around the north of Scotland. Much of the energy of this wave is dissipated in the Southern Bight of the North Sea but a portion is reflected as a damped Kelvin wave, travelling to the north. As a result of the superposition of the incoming and reflected Kelvin waves, three amphidromic regions are produced. The one in the Southern Bight is about midway between the coasts of East Anglia and the Netherlands, but the two northerly ones are displaced a considerable distance to the east of the centre line. This is an indication of the dissipation of energy in the southern part of the North Sea and in the reflected wave as it travels northward.

## 2.7  SUPERPOSITION OF TIDAL CONSTITUENTS

### 2.7.1  Harmonic constants and tidal predictions

The tide-generating force, and hence the elevation in the equilibrium tide at any place, may be resolved into a number of harmonic constituents, as explained in section 2.2. By a principle due to Laplace, the elevation in the actual tide at any place may be represented by the same harmonic constituents but with different amplitudes and phases. Thus the resultant elevation at a given place as a function of time may be written

$$\zeta = \sum_{n}^{N} H_n \cos(\sigma_n t + \alpha_n - \gamma_n) \tag{2.75}$$

where the suffix $n$ refers to the $n^{\text{th}}$ harmonic constituent, and $N$ is the total number of constituents considered; $H_n$ is the amplitude of the $n^{\text{th}}$ constituent, of angular speed $\sigma_n$; $\alpha_n$ is its phase at time $t = 0$ in the equilibrium tide; $\gamma_n$ is the phase lag of the constituent in the actual tide behind that of the same constituent in the equilibrium tide.

The values of $\sigma_n$ for the various constituents can be expressed in terms of certain angular speeds such as those of the rotation of the earth on its axis, the movement of the moon in its orbit around the earth and the movement of the earth in its orbit around the sun. The angular speed $\sigma_n$ of a constituent is related to its period $T_n$ by $\sigma_n = 2\pi/T_n$. The periods of some of the main constituents are given in Table 2.1. The values of $\alpha_n$ at a given zero of time, e.g. 00.00 h on 1 January of a particular year, are determined by astronomical data on the apparent positions of the moon and sun relative to the earth. The values of $H_n$ and $\gamma_n$ cannot be determined from first principles but have to be derived for the tide at a particular place by the analysis of observations. A typical set of data for this purpose would be the heights of water level every hour for a year, obtained by a recording tide gauge. Methods of analysis, which would be done with a digital computer, are described fully by Godin (1972) and Franco (1981).

Once the harmonic constants $H_n$ and $\gamma_n$ for the various constituents have been determined, they may be used to describe the characteristics of the tide at that particular place. They may also be used to predict the tides for a future period, by adding the contributions of all constituents for each time $t$, as in equation (2.75). This method of tidal analysis and prediction was devised by Lord Kelvin who also invented a machine to simulate the harmonic constituents and their summation. Tide-predicting machines operating on the same principle were used for many years for preparing tidal predictions but they have now been superseded by electronic computers.

## 2.7.2 Types of tides

Although as many as 60 or more constituents may have to be taken into account in order to make tidal predictions of sufficient accuracy, the general character of the tides can be expressed by the first few diurnal and semidiurnal constituents. The factor $F$, defined by

$$F = \frac{K_1 + O_1}{M_2 + S_2}$$

where $K_1$, $O_1$, $M_2$ and $S_2$ are the amplitudes of the corresponding constituents, may be used as an indicator of the type of tide as follows:

$$
\begin{aligned}
F : 0 \quad &\text{to } 0.25 \quad : \text{semidiurnal} \\
0.25 &\text{ to } 1.5 \quad : \text{mixed, mainly semidiurnal} \\
1.5 \quad &\text{to } 3.0 \quad : \text{mixed, mainly diurnal} \\
\text{greater than } 3.0 \quad &\quad : \text{diurnal}
\end{aligned}
$$

Figure 2.17 shows typical tidal curves for Hampton Roads, Va., Pensacola, Fla., and San Francisco, Cal., on the Atlantic, Pacific and Gulf of Mexico coasts of the USA. It is seen that they are of the semidiurnal, diurnal and mixed types, respectively, and their $F$ numbers are 0.19, 9.1 and 0.90.

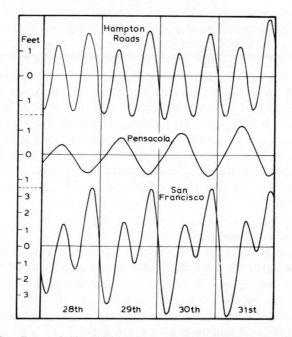

Fig. 2.17 — Types of tide. Tidal curves for Hampton Roads, Pensacola and San Francisco are representative of semidiurnal, diurnal and mixed tides respectively. From Marmer (1951), by courtesy of US Coast and Geodetic Survey.

For positions on an open oceanic coast, the type of tide reflects the response of the adjacent ocean to the tide-generating force. In the Atlantic Ocean the response is predominantly semidiurnal while the diurnal response is more significant, although not usually dominant, in the Pacific Ocean. The amphidromic sytems in a given ocean are quite different in form and distribution for the diurnal and semidiurnal constituents. In the neighbourhood of an amphidromic point for the semidiurnal tide the diurnal tide may be dominant, although over the region as a whole the diurnal response may be less than the semidiurnal. On the shores of the Pacific Ocean the tides are usually of the mixed type but mainly semidiurnal according to the $F$ factor defined above. The tides are mainly diurnal in the northern part of the ocean, along the west coast of Canada and Alaska, the Aleutian Islands and the Kamchatka Peninsula. This is also the case in the Philippines, New Guinea and some other Pacific islands. In the Indian Ocean the tides are mainly semidiurnal with the exception of places on the southern part of the west coast of Australia, where the semidiurnal constituents are very small.

In partially enclosed seas it is the response of the co-oscillating tide which determines the type of tide and wide variations in the ratio of the diurnal to the semidiurnal amplitudes occur from one area to another. A detailed account of the tides in many sea areas may be found in Defant (1961).

In regions where the semidiurnal tides predominate, the ratio of mean spring range to mean neap range is given by $(M_2 + S_2)/(M_2 - S_2)$, where $M_2$ and $S_2$ denote the amplitudes of the respective constituents. The ratio does not usually vary much in a given region, since the response for the $S_2$ tide is unlikely to differ greatly from that for the $M_2$ tide, unless a natural period lies very close to one or the other. In north-west European waters, for example, the $S_2/M_2$ ratio is about $1/3$, so that the spring range is about twice the neap range. In some other areas, however, the $S_2/M_2$ ratio approaches 1 and then the neap range becomes very small. An extreme example is found along the south coast of Australia from the south-west corner of the continent to Adelaide, where the $M_2$ and $S_2$ amplitudes are almost equal. At neap tides the semidiurnal oscillation vanishes and only a small diurnal oscillation occurs. This phenomenon is known as 'dodge tides'.

### 2.7.3 Shallow water constituents

If the response of the water in a particular area to simple harmonic forcing by the incoming tide is not linear, then higher harmonics occur in the equations for the elevations and currents. It was indicated in section 2.3.3 that this effect can be produced by bottom friction which is proportional to the square of the current speed. A similar effect is produced in shallow water if the elevation $\zeta$ is no longer small compared with the depth $h$ of the water.

We consider, as in section 2.3.6, free waves travelling in the $x$ direction in water of uniform undisturbed depth $h$, with $v = 0$. Friction is neglected this time but allowance is made for the $u\partial u/\partial x$ term in $Du/Dt$ and the depth of water is set as $(h + \zeta)$. Then equation (2.30) is replaced by

$$\frac{\partial u}{\partial t} + u \frac{\partial u}{\partial x} = - g \frac{\partial \zeta}{\partial x} \tag{2.76}$$

Equation (2.32) is replaced by

$$\frac{\partial}{\partial x} (h + \zeta) u = - \frac{\partial \zeta}{\partial t}$$

which may be written

$$(h + \zeta) \frac{\partial u}{\partial x} + u \frac{\partial \zeta}{\partial x} = - \frac{\partial \zeta}{\partial t}. \tag{2.77}$$

Comparing the above equations with (2.45) and (2.46), $u$ is used instead of $\bar{u}$ since, in the absence of friction, there is no variation of current with depth.

A solution to (2.76) and (2.77) is obtained by taking

$$\zeta = \zeta_1 + \zeta_2, \quad u = u_1 + u_2$$

where $\zeta_1, u_1$ represent the solution in the linearised case and $\zeta_2, u_2$ represent the second order solution due to the additonal terms. As shown previously, the first order solution for a progressive wave is given by

$$\zeta_1 = A \cos (\kappa x - \sigma t)$$

$$u_1 = \frac{c}{h} A \cos (\kappa x - \sigma t)$$

Substituting from these equations in (2.76) and (2.77), retaining terms of order $A^2$ but neglecting those of order $A^3$ or higher, a pair of equations is obtained for $\zeta_2$ and $u_2$. In this way it is found that

$$\zeta = \zeta_1 + \zeta_2 = A \cos (\kappa x - \sigma t) - \frac{3}{4} \frac{\kappa x A^2}{h} \sin 2 (\kappa x - \sigma t) \tag{2.78}$$

so that a higher harmonic term in $2(\kappa x - \sigma t)$ is present, with an amplitude which is proportional to $A/h$ and increases with distance $x$. The corresponding equation for $u$ contains a similar term. If terms of higher order in $A/h$ are retained, further harmonic terms in $3 (\kappa x - \sigma t)$, $4 (\kappa x - \sigma t) \ldots$ are found.

The superposition of the second term in (2.78) on the first gives a distortion of the simple harmonic form, which becomes greater the further the wave travels. By considering the elevation at a fixed point, i.e. for a given value of $x$, it is found that the distortion is such that the level $\zeta$ rises more rapidly to its peak than it falls. This feature is commonly found in tidal records in shallow water and it becomes very pronounced when the tidal wave travels up an estuary of decreasing depth. The current experiences a similar distortion with the flood current being shorter in duration and higher in speed than the ebb. The extreme case is that of a tidal bore, in which the flood current advances at a considerable speed up the estuary and the initial rise in water level takes place very rapidly.

As a result of non-linear effects a particular harmonic constituent, such as the semidiurnal constituent $M_2$, can give rise to a series of higher harmonics, e.g. $M_4$, $M_6$, $M_8$, . . . with frequencies which are multiples of the basic frequency. The constituent $S_2$ gives rise similarly to constituents $S_4$, $S_6$, . . . In addition it may be shown that terms arising from the interaction between constituents occur, so that $M_2$ and $S_2$ give rise to a quarter-diurnal constituent $MS_4$, which has a frequency equal to the sum of the individual frequencies of $M_2$ and $S_2$. A whole range of shallow-water constituents, such as $M_4$, $S_4$ and $MS_4$, are generated in this way. These constituents do not occur in the equilibrium tide but have frequencies which are multiples or sums of the frequencies of constituents in the equilibrium tide. Naturally they have to be taken into account in making tidal predictions of ports at which the range of tide is an appreciable fraction of the total depth of water.

The particular form of distortion described above depends on the second term in equation (2.78) being 90° out of phase with the first. In less simple cases different phase relationships may occur between the first and higher harmonic terms, leading to different forms of distortion. The phenomena of double high waters or double low waters may be explained in this way. In the English Channel, double high waters occur at Southampton while at Portland, about 100 km to the west, double low waters occur. Both these places are in the central part of the Channel, near a degenerate amphidromic point where the amplitude of the $M_2$ tide is relatively small.

## 2.8 TIDAL CURRENTS

### 2.8.1 Treatment of tidal current observations

A typical set of current observations at a particular station would consist of measurements of the speed and direction of the current as a function of time at a series of depths. If the measurements at a given depth are plotted as vectors, the end-points of the vectors will tend to trace out an ellipse in the course of a tidal period. The form of the eillipse may be distorted if the flood and ebb flows are unsymmetrical or a mean flow is superimposed on the tidal current. In a narrow channel, where the direction of flow is restricted by the boundaries, the ellipse may be so elongated that it is practically reduced to a straight line. In general, when the currents at various depths at a given station are plotted, the current vectors may vary with depth in direction as well as in magnitude and the ellipses may vary in eccentricity and even reverse in direction of rotation.

For analysis it is usual to resolve the measured velocities into two components, $u$ and $v$, in perpendicular directions which are normally taken towards east and north respectively. It is sometimes more convenient, however, to take the $u$ component parallel to a coast line or the axis of a channel and the $v$ component perpendicular to it. The $u$ and $v$ components may be presented as a plot against time or their values over a given interval of time may be analysed for the mean value and trend over the interval and the amplitude and phase of various harmonic constituents.

A given constituent of angular frequency $\sigma$ may be represented as

$$u = A_1 \cos \sigma t + B_1 \sin \sigma t$$
$$v = A_2 \cos \sigma t + B_2 \sin \sigma t$$

(2.79)

where $t$ is measured from a convenient time origin. If the resultant velocity is plotted on a vector diagram as a function of time, the end points of the vectors will trace out a perfect ellipse for a harmonic constituent. At this stage it is possible, if desired, to transform to axes parallel to the major and minor axes of the ellipse. Denoting the velocity components relative to these axes by $u'$ and $v'$, we can write

$$u' = a \cos (\sigma t - \epsilon)$$
$$v' = b \sin (\sigma t - \epsilon)$$

(2.80)

where $a$ and $b$ are the semi-major and semi-minor axes of the current ellipse and

$$\frac{u'^2}{a^2} + \frac{v'^2}{b^2} = 1 \ .$$

The values of $a, b$, the phase angle $\epsilon$ and the inclination $\alpha$ of the major axis to the original $x$ axis may all be calculated from the coefficients $A_1, B_1, A_2$ and $B_2$, as shown in the book by Godin (1972). The relation between the two methods of representation is indicated in Fig. 2.18(a).

An alternative method of representing a rotating tidal current, introduced by Thorade in 1928, is as the superposition of two circular components, rotating in opposite directions, as shown in Fig. 2.18(b). Considering the motion given by

$$u_1 = a_1 \cos \sigma t , \quad v_1 = a_1 \sin \sigma t$$

it is seen that the resultant current may be represented as a vector of constant length $a_1$ rotating to the left with increasing $t$. Similarly the motion

$$u_2 = a_2 \cos \sigma t , \quad v_2 = -a_2 \sin \sigma t$$

is represented by a vector of constant length $a_2$ rotating to the right. The resultant motion is given by

$$u = u_1 + u_2 = (a_1 + a_2) \cos \sigma t$$
$$v = v_1 + v_2 = (a_1 - a_2) \sin \sigma t$$

(2.81)

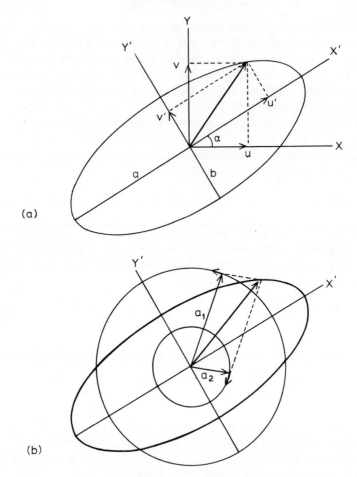

Fig. 2.18 – Tidal current ellipses: (a) transformation from axes $X$, $Y$ to axes $X'$, $Y'$ parallel to the major and minor axes of the ellipse; (b) representation of the current vector as the resultant of two rotating components.

Comparing equations (2.80) and (2.81), it is seen that (2.81) represents a tidal current ellipse for the special case, $\epsilon = 0$, so that the major axis is along the $x$ axis. The semi-major and semi-minor axes are given by

$$a = a_1 + a_2, \quad b = a_1 - a_2 .$$

The current vector in the ellipse will rotate to the left if $a_1 > a_2$ and to the right if $a_1 < a_2$. The case of $a_1 = a_2$ is that of a rectilinear current, oscillating in the $x$ direction only. The method of representation in a rotating coordinate system has some advantages in relating the currents to the surface gradients and the generating and frictional forces. Details are given in the book by Defant (1961).

### 2.8.2 Variability of tidal currents

Tidal currents are more variable than tidal elevations, in general, both in space and time. In order to satisfy continuity conditions, the speed of the current is increased in flowing around headlands, passing through a restriction in a channel or in passing from deeper to shallower water. Local variations in currents are, therefore, more pronounced than those of tidal elevations.

The currents measured at a given position are also more variable with time, in general, than the elevations recorded by a tide gauge. Surface waves may be a disturbing influence in both cases, although they are largely removed in a tide gauge by mechanical filtering and in many current meters by integrating the flow over a period of 5 or 10 minutes. Apart from wave effects the measured current frequently varies, in speed and direction, on time scales ranging from seconds to hours. The variations on scales from a few seconds up to several minutes may be attributed to the essentially turbulent character of the flow, involving irregular fluctuations with a horizontal and vertical structure. Variations on a longer time scale may be caused by eddies of topographic origin, shed by coastal features or irregularities of the sea bed. In addition variable currents induced by the wind may be present.

Apart from the variability actually present in the currents, various errors may arise in the measurements. If the current meter is suspended from an anchored ship or a moored buoy, the possible movement of the instrument relative to a fixed point on the sea bed is to be considered. The accuracy of a current meter itself is usually better for the measurement of speed than of direction. When the velocity is resolved into components, relatively large errors may occur in the smaller component due to fairly small errors in direction. As an overall result of the inherent variability of tidal currents and errors of measurement, the percentage error in the amplitudes and phases derived for the current constituents is usually an order of magnitude greater than for the elevations.

### 2.8.3 Variation of tidal current with depth

It is found from observations that the amplitude of a tidal current usually has its largest value near the surface and decreases with depth, at first slowly and then more rapidly as the bottom is approached. The phase often also changes with depth, usually in the sense that the phase is earlier near the bottom so that the current turns, e.g. changes from flood to ebb, at the bottom before it does at the surface. These general features and more quantitative deductions may be derived from the dynamical equations.

In discussing the general equations (2.14) and (2.15) of section 2.3.1, it was pointed out that the frictional stresses are the only terms which vary significantly with depth and in the absence of friction the current would be independent of depth. The equations were derived on the assumption that the density $\rho$ is constant. If the density varies with depth, baroclinic or internal tides may occur, which are characterised by vertical variations in the current. Apart from internal tides, which are not considered here, the variation of current with depth is due entirely to the frictional stresses arising from bottom friction.

The effect of bottom friction on the depth-mean current was considered in section 2.3.6, where it was shown that, in a progressive wave, friction caused the current to reach its maximum before the peak elevation occurred. It is a general result, applicable also to a standing wave, that friction causes a given phase of the current to occur earlier relative to the elevation. If it is assumed that frictional effects are likely to be greater near the bottom than near the surface, this result is consistent with observations of the tidal current turning earlier near the bottom than at the surface.

In order to calculate the vertical profile of velocity from the equations of motion, it is necessary to relate the shearing stress components $\tau_x$ and $\tau_y$ to the velocity components $u$ and $v$. This is done most simply by introducing the concept of a coefficient of eddy viscosity $N_z$, defined so that

$$\tau_x = \rho N_z \frac{\partial u}{\partial z}, \quad \tau_y = \rho N_z \frac{\partial v}{\partial z}. \tag{2.82}$$

If it is assumed that $N_z$ is independent of $z$, the frictional terms in (2.14) and (2.15) become

$$\frac{1}{\rho} \frac{\partial \tau_x}{\partial z} = N_z \frac{\partial^2 u}{\partial z^2}, \quad \frac{1}{\rho} \frac{\partial \tau_y}{\partial z} = N_z \frac{\partial^2 v}{\partial z^2}. \tag{2.83}$$

The boundary conditions to be satisfied are

$$\text{At } z = 0, \ \tau_{sx} = \tau_{sy} = 0 \text{ so that } \frac{\partial u}{\partial z} = \frac{\partial v}{\partial z} = 0$$

$$\text{At } z = -h, \ \tau_{bx} = \rho N_z \left( \frac{\partial u}{\partial z} \right)_b \text{ and } \tau_{by} = \rho N_z \left( \frac{\partial v}{\partial z} \right)_b \tag{2.84}$$

where the suffix $b$ indicates that the values are evaluated at $z = -h$. If the bottom friction is linearised, as in section 2.3.3,

$$\tau_{bx} = K' \rho u_b, \quad \tau_{by} = K' \rho v_b. \tag{2.85}$$

Instead of assuming that the conditions expressed by equations (2.84) or (2.85) apply at the sea bed itself, it is more realistic to apply them at the upper surface of a bottom boundary layer, of the order of one to several metres thick. There is a considerable amount of observational evidence to support the existence of a logarithmic bottom boundary layer, in which the velocity increases logarithmically with distance from the bottom. In the case of a rectilinear current $u$, so that $v = 0$ and $\tau_y = 0$,

$$u = \frac{u_*}{k_0} \log_e \frac{z'}{z_0} \tag{2.86}$$

where $z'$ is distance from the bottom, $u_* = (\tau_{bx}/\rho)^{1/2}$ is the friction velocity, $z_0$ is a roughness parameter and $k_0$ is von Kármán's constant, equal to 0.4 approximately. The logarithmic velocity profile is a well-known feature of boundary layer flow and is discussed in McLellan (1965) and Neumann and Pierson (1966).

The solution of the dynamical equations with eddy viscosity terms becomes quite complicated, even in fairly simple conditions. A general result is that the influence of bottom friction extends to a height $D$ above bottom of the order of

$$D = \pi \left( \frac{2N_z}{\sigma} \right)^{1/2} \tag{2.87}$$

Information on the magnitude of $N_z$ in various conditions is limited but there is some evidence that in currents of order 50 cm s$^{-1}$ values of $N_z$ of the order of 100 cm$^2$ s$^{-1}$ may be expected. Taking $N_z = 200$ cm$^2$ s$^{-1}$ and $\sigma = 1.4 \times 10^{-4}$ s$^{-1}$ for the $M_2$ constituent, it follows from (2.87) that $D = 53$ m. Thus in water appreciably shallower than 50 m frictional effects would probably extend throughout the whole depth. In water deeper than 100 m, on the other hand, friction may influence only the lower half of the water column, the velocity being practically constant in the upper half.

For a rectilinear tidal current in water which is shallow enough for friction to be effective throughout the depth, a velocity amplitude profile which appears to fit a number of observations is obtained by assuming the logarithmic law, given by equation (2.86), to apply for $0 < z' < \alpha h$, where $\alpha$ is a certain fraction of the total depth, and a parabolic profile to hold above it. Thus, for $\alpha h < z' < h$,

$$U = U_1 + U_2 \left[ \frac{z'}{h} - \frac{1}{2} \left( \frac{z'}{h} \right)^2 \right] \tag{2.88}$$

where $U_1$ and $U_2$ are constants which may be determined if the velocities at the top of the logarithmic layer, $z' = \alpha h$, and at the surface, $z' = h$, are specified. Observations in several areas suggest that $\alpha$ is approximately 0.14.

## 2.9 MODELLING TIDES

### 2.9.1 Hydraulic and analogue models

Physical models have been used for many years to study the tides in particular areas, particularly rivers and estuaries, in which engineering works have been proposed. For practical reasons, the vertical scale is exaggerated relative to the horizontal scale. In order to retain dynamical similarity between the actual and model flows, the Froude number given by $U/\sqrt{gh}$, where $U$ is a representative velocity and $h$ is the depth, is kept the same. This determines the tidal period in the model which is usually of the order of several minutes corresponding to the semidiurnal tide, so that a large number of tidal periods may be simulated in a reasonable length of time. Models of this type which have been of practical use include those of the Severn Estuary and the Wash in Great Britain, Puget Sound in USA and the Delta area in the Netherlands (McDowell, 1977.)

Hydraulic models are not usually able to include Coriolis effects but a notable exception is the model of the English Channel, constructed on a rotating table at the C.N.R.S. Laboratoire de Mécanique des Fluides in Grenoble, which has been used to study, in particular, the tides in the Gulf of St. Malo, where a pilot tidal power scheme has been installed.

Electrical analogue models, first used by Van Veen in the Netherlands, are an alternative and more versatile method of modelling tides and storm surges in shallow waters. The real sea area is simulated by an array of electrical circuits which represent the interactions specified in the hydrodynamic equations, including the Coriolis and frictional terms. A varying voltage, representing the tidal driving force, is applied to the model and the response can be measured at various sections of the model. (Ishiguro, 1972.)

### 2.9.2 Numerical modelling

The most common form of modelling in use today is that of solving the basic equations numerically on a digital computer. The sea area in question is represented by a network of points, at which the elevations or current components are to be calculated, and appropriate boundary conditions are applied. Until recently, most models have been of the two-dimensional or depth-integrated type, for which the basic equations are (2.16), (2.17) and (2.18) of section 2.3.2, if the rectangular coordinate system can be used.

A considerable simplification is possible if a linearised model can be used, using equations (2.21), (2.22) and (2.23) of section 2.3.3. For a single harmonic constituent, the time factor by which $\zeta$, $\bar{u}$ and $\bar{v}$ vary can be set as $e^{i\sigma t}$, where $i = \sqrt{-1}$. Since

$$e^{i\sigma t} = \cos \sigma t + i \sin \sigma t$$

the corresponding amplitudes of $\zeta$, $\bar{u}$ and $\bar{v}$ are taken as complex numbers. By substitution in (2.21), (2.22) and (2.23), the $e^{i\sigma t}$ term drops out and the resulting equations represent relations between the complex amplitudes, or alternatively the amplitudes and phases of the constituent. Given the necessary data on the elevations or currents at the boundary, the model then enables the corresponding values to be calculated at all the internal grid points. Usually the elevations are of primary interest but the velocity components can be included in the output if required. The friction coefficient $K$ is often regarded as a disposable parameter which can be adjusted to give the optimum agreement between the model output and observations.

In many sea areas the assumptions involved in formulating a linear model are not justified. The tidal elevation is not small relative to the depth of water and the non-linearity arising from the field acceleration and frictional terms may be appreciable. In this case a non-linear model, using the full equations (2.16),

(2.17) and (2.18), must be used. The computation is started by assigning initial values to the variables at zero time and then proceeding by steps in time as well as in position to calculate the succession of elevations and currents over the whole area. In a non-linear model, even if simple harmonic forcing terms are applied at an open boundary, a series of harmonics will be developed in the response of the sea to them. A non-linear model can be used to study the inter-action between several constituents or the combined effect of tidal and meteoro-logical forcing.

Most of the models used to date, whether linear or non-linear, have been of the depth-integrated type, yielding the surface elevations and depth mean currents. For many purposes this is sufficient but for others a knowledge of the distribution of current with depth is needed. In some cases the tidal models are used to investigate the effects of wind stress imposed on the surface, or of the density distribution arising from the influx of fresh water, and the variation of current with depth is then a feature of prime interest. For these purposes three-dimensional models have been developed. These are either of the multi-layer type in which the two-dimensional $x$, $y$ grid is extended into the $z$ dimension, or a type in which the dependence of the velocity components, $u$ and $v$, on depth is represented by analytical functions. One of the problems in formulating a three-dimensional model of either type is how to specify the shearing stresses in terms of the velocity components. An eddy viscosity model may be used, allowing the coefficient $N_z$ to vary with depth or a turbulence closure scheme may be incorporated, in which the stress is related to the turbulent kinetic energy, which is itself calculated in the course of the computation. A number of modelling techniques were described by Ramming and Kowalik (1980).

## 2.10 TIDAL ENERGY AND DISSIPATION

The rate of transmission of energy by a tidal wave across a vertical section is given, as in section 2.4.1, by $p'u$ per unit area, where $p'$ is the excess pressure and $u$ is the velocity normal to the section. Since $p' = g\rho\zeta$ for a long wave,

$$p'u = g\rho\zeta u \ .$$

Integrating vertically from $z = -h$ to $z = \zeta$ and assuming that $\zeta \ll h$, the rate of transmission of energy across a vertical strip of unit width is given by

$$E = g\rho h \overline{\zeta u}$$

For a given harmonic constituent let

$$\zeta = A \cos \sigma t$$

$$\overline{u} = U \cos (\sigma t - \delta)$$

where $\delta$ is the phase difference between the elevation and the current.

Then taking the mean rate of transmission of energy over a tidal period

$$\bar{E} = \frac{1}{2} g\rho hAU \cos\delta \qquad (2.89)$$

Equation (2.89) includes the case of energy being taken out of the sea by a reflected wave, since it is the resultant values of $\zeta$ and $\bar{u}$, as would be measured at the section, which are considered. Denoting by $\Sigma_w \bar{E}$ the value of $\bar{E}$ in (2.89) integrated across the width of the boundary section, $\Sigma_w \bar{E}$ represents the total transmission of energy due to the harmonic constituent which enters the sea. If the sea has no further opening, this is also the amount which is dissipated within the sea as in Fig. 2.19.

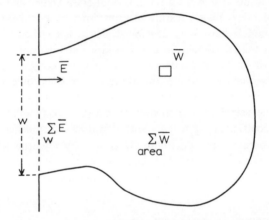

Fig. 2.19 – Tidal energy flux and dissipation in a closed sea. $\bar{E}$ is the rate of energy flux inwards, per unit width of section. $\bar{W}$ is the rate of frictional dissipation per unit area of bed.

An alternative calculation of the rate of dissipation may be made by considering the rate at which work is done by bottom friction. In the notation of section 2.3.2, let

$$\tau_b = k\rho \,|U_b|\,U_b$$

where $\tau_b$ is the bottom stress per unit area, $U_b$ is the bottom current and $k$ is the friction coefficient, having a magnitude of the order of $2 \times 10^{-3}$. The rate of doing work by the bottom stress is

$$W = \tau_b U_b = k\rho \,|U_b|\,U_b^2 \,.$$

If $U_b = C_b \cos \sigma t$, then the average rate of doing work over a tidal period, using the results of section 2.3.3 is

$$\bar{W} = \frac{4}{3\pi} k\rho C_b^3 \tag{2.90}$$

If $\Sigma_a \bar{W}$ denotes the integral of $\bar{W}$ taken over the whole bottom area of the sea, $\Sigma_a \bar{W}$ represents the total rate of dissipation of tidal energy by bottom friction. On the hypothesis that the net energy entering the sea is all dissipated within it by bottom friction, we should have

$$\Sigma_w \bar{E} = \Sigma_a \bar{W} .$$

The energy flux method of equation (2.89) was first used by Taylor in 1919 and was applied by Jeffreys in 1920 to calculate the loss of tidal energy in all the shallow seas of the world. Revised estimates were made by other authors and in particular by Miller (1966), who estimated that the world-wide dissipation of energy in the $M_2$ tide amounted to $1.7 \times 10^{19}$ erg s$^{-1}$, equivalent to $1.7 \times 10^6$ megawatts. This corresponds to the total energy in the world's tides being dissipated in about 2 days. Table 2.2 shows the rate of dissipation in a number of sea areas, expressed in units of $10^4$ megawatts and also as percentages of the total. The values given are based on Miller's data, except for the Bering Sea for which estimates, including that from a numerical model, are much lower than those given earlier, and for the north-west European shelf seas, for which recent values from a numerical model, not very different from earlier estimates, have been taken.

**Table 2.2** – Flux of $M_2$ tidal energy into coastal seas.

| Region | $10^4$ MW | Percentage of total |
|---|---|---|
| N.W. European Shelf Seas | 19 | 12 |
| Hudson Strait | 12 | 8 |
| Patagonian Shelf of S. America | 13 | 9 |
| Other Atlantic shelf regions | 9 | 6 |
| Bering Sea | 3 | 2 |
| Sea of Okhotsk | 21 | 13 |
| Other Pacific shelf regions | 29 | 19 |
| Northern Australian Shelf | 18 | 12 |
| Indian Ocean shelf regions | 23 | 15 |
| Arctic and Antarctic regions | 7 | 4 |
| Total | 154 | 100 |

The rate of doing work on the tides by the moon's gravitational force may also be calculated. It is relatively small over the shelf seas and large over the oceans. It appears, therefore, that the energy of the tides is generated mainly in the oceans but most of it is dissipated in the shallow seas. Some energy is dissipated, no doubt, by friction at the bed of the oceans and some is converted into energy of internal tides, principally on the steep continental slopes at the ocean margins.

# 3

# Surface waves

---

## 3.1 INTRODUCTION

### 3.1.1 Characteristics of surface waves

The occurrence of waves on the surface of the sea and their association with winds blowing over it are features which are familiar to everyone. The practical importance of surface waves in all aspects of sea travel, offshore engineering activities and the maintenance of coastal defences is well recognised. Although wind stress is obviously the primary cause of surface waves, the actual generation process has only recently received a satisfactory physical explanation. Fortunately the dynamical properties of waves, once generated, and the changes which occur as they propagate from deep into shallower water have been given a sound theoretical basis which is largely independent of a knowledge of the generation processes.

The main characteristics of surface waves may be summarised as follows:

(1) They are of relatively short period, mostly within the range 1 to 30 seconds.
(2) In deep water, their influence is restricted to a comparatively shallow layer, unlike tidal waves which extend throughout the whole depth.
(3) The water movements associated with them are of similar magnitude in the vertical and horizontal directions. This is in contrast to tides or wind-driven currents in which the vertical movement is small compared with the horizontal flow.
(4) The vertical accelerations in surface waves are significant and approach the order of magnitude of the acceleration due to gravity. This is again in contrast to ocean currents or tides in which vertical accelerations may be neglected.
(5) The accelerations, both vertical and horizontal, are large compared with the components of geostrophic acceleration, which can normally be neglected in the dynamics of surface waves.

The classical theory of surface waves, with a history going back more than a hundred and fifty years, deals with trains of waves of uniform amplitude, wavelength and period, travelling in a fixed direction. A casual observation of actual sea waves, however, shows that the sea surface is very irregular, with waves of different heights and periods, changing in character as they move. In order to bring some degree of order out of chaos, it is necessary to treat an actual wave field statistically. The simplest approach is to define average values of features such as height, period and wavelength. A second method is to recognise a distribution of values of each property around its mean value. A further advance is to determine a wave spectrum, representing the actual sea surface as a superposition of a large number of wave trains of different periods and amplitudes, travelling in general in different directions.

### 3.1.2  Observations of waves

Some basic definitions are illustrated in Fig. 3.1. The crest of a wave is defined as the highest point of that wave above the mean water level. The trough is defined as the lowest point below the same level. The height $H$ of a wave is the vertical distance between a trough and the following crest. In the case of a sinusoidal wave the crest and the trough are displaced symmetrically from the mean level and the height is twice the amplitude, but this is not true of a general wave form. The wavelength $\lambda$ is the horizontal distance between two crests and the period $T$ is the time interval between the passage of two successive crests past a fixed point. The velocity of propagation of a given crest (or trough) is denoted by $c$. The velocity $c$ is related to the wavelength and period by the equation $c = \lambda/T$, which is valid for all types of waves.

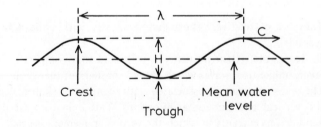

Fig. 3.1 – Definition of terms relating to waves.

Visual observations of the heights of waves reaching the shore may be made by noting the rise and fall of the sea surface against a vertical scale. The period may be determined by measuring the time interval between the arrival of successive crests at a fixed point. To estimate the wavelength directly it is necessary to be able to see a whole wave as it travels along a fixed structure, such as a jetty or sea wall.

Measurements of waves in the form of a record of the height of the water surface against time may be made in various ways. The changing water level may be measured by a float or indirectly by the change in electrical capacitance or resistance as the water level moves along a wire or set of contacts. Other types of wave gauge operate by measuring the change of pressure at a fixed point as the waves pass above it. Such a gauge may be attached to a fixed structure above the bottom or may be laid on the sea bed. The amplitude of the pressure oscillation, due to a wave of given surface amplitude, decreases with distance below the surface in a way described in section 3.2.2, and allowance for this must be made in converting the pressure oscillation to surface movement.

The vertical component of acceleration of a floating object, such as a buoy, may be measured by a suitable accelerometer and then a double integration, carried out electronically, will give the vertical displacement. The ship-borne wave recorder, described by Tucker (1956), uses a combination of accelerometer, measuring the vertical movement of a point on the ship's hull, and a pressure gauge, measuring the movement of water relative to that point. Various types of wave recorder were described by Draper (1961, 1967).

Measurements by the above types of instrument yield a record of sea surface height as a function of time, from which various mean values, statistical properties and energy spectra may be derived. They do not give any information on the direction of travel of the waves, however. For this purpose an array of recorders may be used, using the principle of wave interference, as in a directional radio aerial array, to determine the direction. Alternatively one may employ an instrument measuring the components of slope of the sea surface, such as the pitch and roll buoy, or one measuring the two components of wave particle velocity, from which the direction of travel may be determined (Cartwright and Smith, 1964).

In addition to instruments mounted in fixed positions, or on buoys or on board ship, there are several methods of measuring waves by remote sensing. Stereoscopic photographs from aircraft have been used to determine the directional wave spectrum. Radar reflections from surface waves, normally regarded as disturbing clutter, may be used to measure wave properties, employing suitable transmission and reception techniques, from shore-based stations or from aircraft. Remote sensing from satellites has also been applied to the measurement of wave properties over large areas of sea (Gower, 1981). An example is shown in Fig. 3.21. Meteorologists have found such measurements a useful method of estimating wind velocities.

### 3.1.3 Waves in oceanic and coastal areas

The waves which determine sea conditions in coastal waters and eventually break upon the shore may have been generated either in the open ocean, and travelled coastwards as swell, or in the coastal area itself by local winds. The initial wave generation process is largely similar in both cases but the shallower water depth begins to affect the waves when it is less than about half a wavelength. The longer waves are thus affected first when a spectrum of waves travels into shallower water. Waves are also modified in the presence of currents such as tidal currents, which are often stronger in coastal waters. The refraction of waves, due to the reduction in their velocity of propagation in shallower water, has an important influence on their properties near the shore.

The scheme of this chapter is to consider first the classical theory of waves of a single period, as this is basic to the treatment of more realistic distributions of waves. The statistical approach, including the definition of significant waves, energy spectra and directional spectra and the estimation of extreme conditions, will be considered next. The generation of waves, the propagation of waves as swell and the changes which occur as they enter shallow water will then be treated. The final sections will deal with breaking waves and such effects as wave set-up, rip currents and longshore drift.

## 3.2 DYNAMICS OF SURFACE WAVES

### 3.2.1 Basic equations

Right-handed rectangular coordinate axes will be taken, as in section 2.3.1, with the $x$ and $y$ axes horizontal and the $z$ axis vertically upwards. The corresponding velocity components will be denoted by $u$, $v$ and $w$, as before. In view of the characteristics of surface waves, noted in section 3.1.1, the vertical acceleration term must be included but the Coriolis terms may be neglected. Then the equations of motion in the $x$, $y$ and $z$ directions respectively may be written:

$$\frac{Du}{Dt} = -\frac{1}{\rho}\frac{\partial p}{\partial x} + F_x \tag{3.1}$$

$$\frac{Dv}{Dt} = -\frac{1}{\rho}\frac{\partial p}{\partial y} + F_y \tag{3.2}$$

$$\frac{Dw}{Dt} = -\frac{1}{\rho}\frac{\partial p}{\partial z} - g + F_z \tag{3.3}$$

together with the equation of continuity of volume:

$$\frac{\partial u}{\partial x} + \frac{\partial v}{\partial y} + \frac{\partial w}{\partial z} = 0 \ . \tag{3.4}$$

In the above equations

$$\frac{D}{Dt} = \frac{\partial}{\partial t} + u\frac{\partial}{\partial x} + v\frac{\partial}{\partial y} + w\frac{\partial}{\partial z}$$

and $F_x$, $F_y$ and $F_z$ denote the components of any force, other than pressure or gravity, acting in the body of the water.

The above equations will be simplified at this stage by confining our attention to waves with horizontal crests, travelling in the $x$-direction so that

$$v = 0 , \quad \frac{\partial}{\partial y} = 0 .$$

We will also consider the waves to be of relatively small amplitude, so that the higher-order acceleration terms may be neglected and thus

$$\frac{Du}{Dt} = \frac{\partial u}{\partial t} , \quad \frac{Dw}{Dt} = \frac{\partial w}{\partial t} .$$

Frictional terms, arising from molecular or eddy viscosity, will be assumed negligible, so that

$$F_x = F_y = F_z = 0 .$$

The density $\rho$ is taken as uniform.

With these simplifications, equations (3.1), (3.3) and (3.4) respectively become

$$\frac{\partial u}{\partial t} = - \frac{1}{\rho} \frac{\partial p}{\partial x} \tag{3.5}$$

$$\frac{\partial w}{\partial t} = - \frac{1}{\rho} \frac{\partial p}{\partial z} - g \tag{3.6}$$

$$\frac{\partial u}{\partial x} + \frac{\partial w}{\partial z} = 0 . \tag{3.7}$$

The above equations apply at any point within the water.

At the free surface, defined by $z = \zeta_0$, where $\zeta_0$ is the elevation of the surface above its undisturbed level, two boundary conditions are to be applied. The first expresses the fact that the surface is formed by the moving water particles, i.e.

$$\text{At } z = \zeta_0 , \quad w = \frac{\partial \zeta_0}{\partial t} . \tag{3.8}$$

The second expresses the condition that, if surface tension is neglected, the pressure at the sea surface is equal to the atmospheric pressure $p_a$. Thus

$$\text{At } z = \zeta_0 , \quad p = p_a . \tag{3.9}$$

The modifications required to the theory in the case of capillary waves, when surface tension cannot be neglected, are considered later.

A further assumption made in the classical theory is that the waves are irrotational, i.e. that they have no vorticity and the curl of the velocity vector is zero. For waves in which the motion is confined to the $x$-$z$ plane, as assumed above, the condition for irrotationality is

$$\frac{\partial u}{\partial z} = \frac{\partial w}{\partial x} \ .$$

In this case a velocity potential $\phi$ may be defined such that

$$u = \frac{\partial \phi}{\partial x} \quad w = \frac{\partial \phi}{\partial z} \ .$$

Irrotational flow may be generated by the action of pressure forces only, but if tangential stresses are significant the flow is no longer strictly irrotational. It is not clear from first principles that surface waves should be irrotational, since it is possible that the tangential component of wind stress on the surface might be significant, as might the effects of molecular or eddy viscosity. In fact observations show that, in most respects, surface waves approximate closely to the irrotational theory.

The solution of the basic equations may be expressed in terms of the velocity potential $\phi$ and this method is followed in most mathematical treatments, such as those of Lamb (1945) or Phillips (1977). In the present work, however, the solution will be derived in a simple way directly from the basic equations.

By differentiating equation (3.5) with respect to $x$, (3.6) with respect to $z$ and (3.7) with respect to $t$, it is found that

$$\frac{\partial^2 p}{\partial x^2} + \frac{\partial^2 p}{\partial z^2} = 0 \ . \tag{3.10}$$

### 3.2.2 Progressive waves of small amplitude

A solution of the above equations is sought for a simple harmonic wave travelling in the $x$ direction. The following form may be assumed

$$p = p_a - g\rho z + Z(z) \cos (\kappa x - \sigma t) \tag{3.11}$$

The first two terms on the right-hand side of (3.11) give the pressure at depth $z$ under undisturbed (hydrostatic) conditions. The third term represents a pressure wave of wavelength $\lambda = 2\pi/\kappa$ and period $T = 2\pi/\sigma$ with an amplitude $Z(z)$ which is a function of $z$ only. By substituting from equation (3.11) in (3.10), it is found that $Z(z)$ must satisfy the differential equation

$$\frac{d^2 Z}{dz^2} - \kappa^2 Z = 0 \ .$$

This has the solution

$$Z(z) = A e^{\kappa z} + B e^{-\kappa z} \tag{3.12}$$

where $A$ and $B$ are constants of integration.

(a) *In deep water*
In deep water it is known from observations that the effect of surface waves becomes negligible at great depth, i.e.

$$\text{As } z \to -\infty, \quad Z(z) \to 0 . \tag{3.13}$$

Thus in (3.12), $B = 0$ and from (3.11) the solution for $p$ is:

$$p = p_a - g\rho z + Ae^{\kappa z} \cos(\kappa x - \sigma t) \tag{3.14}$$

Applying the surface boundary conditions (3.8) and (3.9), it may be shown that $\kappa$ and $\sigma$ have to satisfy the equation

$$\sigma^2 = g\kappa . \tag{3.15}$$

This gives the velocity of propagation $c$, since

$$c = \frac{\lambda}{T} = \frac{\sigma}{\kappa} .$$

Thus from (3.15)

$$c^2 = \frac{g}{\kappa} = \frac{g\lambda}{2\pi} . \tag{3.16}$$

By writing $a = A/g\rho$ and using equations (3.5), (3.6), (3.8) and (3.14), it is found that

$$\zeta_0 = a \cos(\kappa x - \sigma t) \tag{3.17}$$

$$u = \sigma a e^{\kappa z} \cos(\kappa x - \sigma t) \tag{3.18}$$

$$w = \sigma a e^{\kappa z} \sin(\kappa x - \sigma t) \tag{3.19}$$

$$p = p_a - g\rho z + g\rho a e^{\kappa z} \cos(\kappa x - \sigma t) \tag{3.20}$$

In these equations $a$ is the amplitude of the vertical displacement of the sea surface while $u$ and $w$ are the horizontal and vertical components respectively of the particle velocity at a depth $z$.

The components $\xi$, $\zeta$ of the displacement of a water particle from its undisturbed position, as in Fig. 3.2, may be found, noting that

$$u = \frac{\partial \xi}{\partial t}, \quad w = \frac{\partial \zeta}{\partial t} .$$

Hence

$$\xi = - a e^{\kappa z} \sin(\kappa x - \sigma t) \tag{3.21}$$

$$\zeta = a e^{\kappa z} \cos(\kappa x - \sigma t) \tag{3.22}$$

Equations (3.21) and (3.22) show that the water particles move in circular

orbits of radius $a e^{\kappa z}$. Thus the displacements, the particle velocities and the
oscillatory part of the pressure all decrease exponentially with increasing depth,
with the attenuation factor $e^{\kappa z} = \exp(2\pi z/\lambda)$. At a depth equal to half a wavelength, this factor is $\exp(-\pi)$ which is 0.043, showing that the wave motion is
reduced to about 1/23 of its surface amplitude at a depth of half a wavelength
below the surface. In Fig. 3.2 the angle $\theta$ in radians represents $\sigma t - \kappa x$.

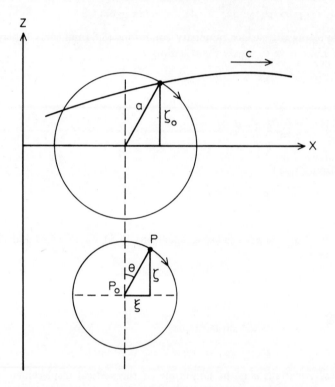

Fig. 3.2 – Displacement of water particles in wave motion.

From equation (3.16) for the velocity of propagation and the relation
$c = \lambda/T$, it is seen that the velocity and the wavelength may each be expressed in
terms of the period $T$. Thus

$$c = \frac{gT}{2\pi}, \quad \lambda = \frac{gT^2}{2\pi}. \tag{3.23}$$

Taking $g = 9.80$ m s$^{-2}$, these equations become

$$c = 1.56\,T, \quad \lambda = 1.56\,T^2$$

where $c$ is in m s$^{-1}$ and $\lambda$ in $m$ if $T$ is in $s$.

As a numerical example:

If   $T = 5\,\text{s}, \quad c = 7.8\,\text{m s}^{-1}, \quad \lambda = 39\,\text{m},$

if   $T = 10\,\text{s}, \quad c = 15.6\,\text{m s}^{-1}, \quad \lambda = 156\,\text{m}.$

A period of 5 s would be typical of waves generated locally in a coastal area while a period of 10 s would be more representative of waves in the open ocean.

(b) *In water of finite depth*
If the depth of water is not large compared with the wavelength, condition (3.13) must be replaced by the condition that, at the bottom, the vertical velocity of a water particle is zero. Thus

$$\text{At } z = -h, \quad w = 0 \tag{3.24}$$

where $h$ is the depth of water.

Both terms on the right-hand side of equation (3.12) are retained when $Z(z)$ is inserted in (3.11) and $w$ is found using (3.6). Condition (3.24) is applied, as well as the surface boundary conditions (3.8) and (3.9), leading to the following equations for $\zeta_0, c, p, u, w, \xi$ and $\zeta$:

$$\zeta_0 = a \cos (\kappa x - \sigma t) \tag{3.25}$$

$$c^2 = \frac{g}{\kappa} \tanh \kappa h \tag{3.26}$$

$$p = p_a - g\rho z + g\rho a \, \frac{\cosh \kappa \, (h + z)}{\cosh \kappa h} \cos (\kappa x - \sigma t) \tag{3.27}$$

$$u = \sigma a \, \frac{\cosh \kappa \, (h + z)}{\sinh \kappa h} \cos (\kappa x - \sigma t) \tag{3.28}$$

$$w = \sigma a \, \frac{\sinh \kappa \, (h + z)}{\sinh \kappa h} \sin (\kappa x - \sigma t) \tag{3.29}$$

$$\xi = -a \, \frac{\cosh \kappa \, (h + z)}{\sinh \kappa h} \sin (\kappa x - \sigma t) \tag{3.30}$$

$$\zeta = a \, \frac{\sinh \kappa \, (h + z)}{\sinh \kappa h} \cos (\kappa x - \sigma t) \tag{3.31}$$

Equation (3.26) for the velocity of propagation $c$ may be written

$$c^2 = \frac{g\lambda}{2\pi} \tanh \frac{2\pi h}{\lambda} \tag{3.32}$$

showing that the velocity now depends on the depth of water as well as the wavelength. The velocity in deep water, given by (3.16), may be recovered by letting $h \gg \lambda$, so that tanh $(2\pi h/\lambda) \to 1$ and $c^2 \approx g\lambda/2\pi$. At the other extreme, if the depth is small compared with the wavelength, i.e. $h \ll \lambda$, then tanh $(2\pi h/\lambda) \to 2\pi h/\lambda$ and

$$c^2 = gh \tag{3.33}$$

which is the equation for the velocity of long waves, including tidal waves, given in (2.35) of Chapter 2.

Broadly speaking, if the ratio $\lambda/h$ is less than 2, the equation for waves in deep water (3.16) may be used, while if $\lambda/h$ is greater than 20, one may use the equation for long waves (3.33) but if $\lambda/h$ is between 2 and 20, the complete equation (3.32) must be used. The wave velocity as a function of depth, together with the deep water and shallow water approximations, are shown in Fig. 3.3.

The orbits of the water particles, instead of being circular as in deep water, are seen from (3.30) and (3.31) to be elliptical, in general, with the major axis horizontal. As the bottom is approached the ellipses become flatter and at the bottom the water particles move to and fro horizontally in a straight line.

If the pressure is written as

$$p = p_a - g\rho z + P \cos (\kappa x - \sigma t)$$

so that $P$ is the amplitude of the oscillatory part, it is seen from (3.27) that

$$P = g\rho a \frac{\cosh \kappa (h + z)}{\cosh \kappa h} \tag{3.34}$$

giving the rate of attenuation of the pressure oscillation with depth. For a pressure gauge laid on the bottom we have:

$$\text{At } z = -h, \quad P = \frac{g\rho a}{\cosh \kappa h}. \tag{3.35}$$

This equation enables the surface amplitude $a$ of a wave of wavelength $\lambda (= 2\pi/\kappa)$ to be calculated from the pressure amplitude recorded by a gauge on the bottom.

### 3.2.3 Waves of greater amplitude

The waves may be regarded as of small amplitude if the amplitude $a$ is small compared with the wavelength $\lambda$. If this is not the case, the higher order acceleration terms may not be neglected. Then in equations (3.5) and (3.6),

$$\frac{\partial u}{\partial t} \text{ must be replaced by } \frac{\partial u}{\partial t} + u \frac{\partial u}{\partial x} + w \frac{\partial u}{\partial z}$$

$$\frac{\partial w}{\partial t} \text{ must be replaced by } \frac{\partial w}{\partial t} + u \frac{\partial w}{\partial x} + w \frac{\partial w}{\partial z}.$$

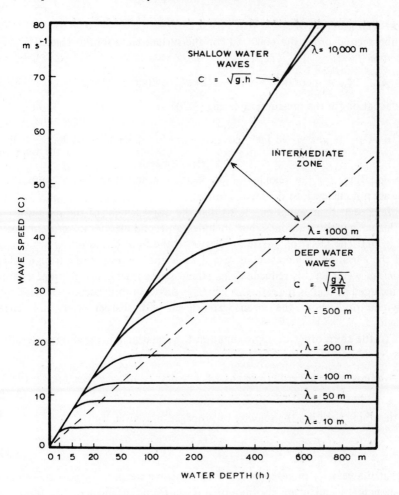

Fig. 3.3 — Wave speed as a function of water depth for various wavelengths λ. From Pond and Pickard (1978) by permission of Pergamon Press.

The surface boundary condition (3.8) becomes

$$w = \frac{\partial \zeta_0}{\partial t} + u \frac{\partial \zeta_0}{\partial x} \; .$$

The modified equations may be solved by a perturbation technique. It is no longer possible to find a solution in terms of a single simple harmonic constituent but higher harmonic terms must be included.

(a) *In deep water*

To the second order the equation for the surface elevation, instead of (3.17), becomes

$$\zeta_0 = a \cos(\kappa k - \sigma t) + 1/2\, \kappa a^2 \cos 2(\kappa x - \sigma t) \qquad (3.36)$$

The equation for the pressure, replacing (3.20), is

$$p = p_a - g\rho z + g\rho\, [a e^{\kappa z} \cos(\kappa x - \sigma t) + 1/2\, \kappa a^2 e^{2\kappa z} \cos 2(\kappa x - \sigma t)] \qquad (3.37)$$

The equations for the velocity of propagation $c$ and the velocity components $u$, $w$ are not changed, to the second order.

It is seen from equation (3.36) that the displacement of the sea surface is no longer purely sinusoidal but includes a second harmonic term in cos 2 $(\kappa x - \sigma t)$. The phase of this term relative to the term in $\cos(\kappa x - \sigma t)$ is such that the elevation of a crest is increased while the depression of a trough below the mean water level is reduced. This effect is accentuated if higher order terms are included so that as the ratio $a/\lambda$ increases the wave form becomes increasingly unsymmetrical about the mean water level, with sharper crests and flatter troughs.

To the third order of approximation the equation for the surface elevation $\zeta_0$ is

$$\zeta_0 = a\{\cos(\kappa x - \sigma t) + 1/2\, \kappa a \cos 2(\kappa x - \sigma t) + 3/8\, \kappa^2 a^2 \cos 3(\kappa x - \sigma t)\} \qquad (3.38)$$

To this approximation the velocity of propagation is given by

$$c^2 = \frac{g}{\kappa}(1 + \kappa^2 a^2) \qquad (3.39)$$

so that the velocity increases as the waves become steeper. The particle velocity components $u$ and $w$ are also modified when third- and higher-order terms are taken into account.

(b) *In water of finite depth*

If the wave height is relatively large compared with the wavelength, as well as the depth being small compared with the wavelength, the solutions to the wave equation become quite complicated. They will not be considered here but some special cases will be described later in dealing with waves entering shallow water.

### 3.2.4 Mass transport velocity

It was mentioned above that, to the second order approximation the particle velocity components $u$ and $w$, as functions of depth, were the same as in the first order solution. It may be shown, however, that the orbits of the individual water particles are no longer closed circles but that a given particle has a net movement in the direction of propagation at the end of a complete period. The mean velocity, known as the 'mass transport velocity', is given by

$$\bar{u} = \kappa \sigma a^2 e^{2\kappa z} . \tag{3.40}$$

The orbital velocity, with components $u$, $w$, given by (3.18) and (3.19), has an amplitude $\sigma a e^{\kappa z}$. At the surface the ratio of the mass transport velocity to the orbital velocity is given by

$$\frac{\bar{u}}{\sigma a} = \kappa a = \frac{2\pi a}{\lambda} .$$

The steepness of a wave, given approximately by $2a/\lambda$, seldom exceeds 0.1, and in that case $\bar{u}/\sigma a = 0.1\pi = 0.314$. This is an extreme example and indicates that the mass transport velocity is usually an order of magnitude smaller than the orbital velocity at the surface. Because of the $\exp(2\kappa z)$ term in (3.40), the mass transport velocity decreases rapidly with depth.

The mass transport is described as 'Lagrangian', since it is a consequence of considering the movement of an individual water particle rather than the velocity components observed at a fixed point in the fluid: the 'Eulerian' approach. As derived by the theory given above, originating with the work of Stokes in 1840, the unclosed orbits and the mass transport are consequences of assuming the wave motion to be irrotational.

Earlier than Stokes's work, Gerstner in 1802 described a wave motion in which the particle orbits were exact circles with radii decreasing exponentially with depth. The water surface had the form of a trochoid, i.e. the curve traced out by a point on a radius of a circle which was rolling on the underside of a plane surface. For very small waves the trochoid approximates to a sinusoidal surface but as the wave height increases the crests become increasingly sharper and the troughs flatter, resembling to some extent the higher approximations to a Stokes wave. The Gerstner wave is not irrotational but has a certain vorticity, which can be calculated.

The observed features of surface waves, including the occurrence of mass transport phenomena, indicate that they approximate more closely to irrotational waves than to Gerstner waves. One is justified, therefore, in using irrotational wave theory to describe real waves to a reasonable degree of approximation, although on some occasions the vorticity of the waves may need to be considered. A discussion of this point is given in the book by Kinsman (1965).

### 3.2.5 Energy of wave motion
A surface wave possesses both potential energy, arising from the displacement of water particles vertically from their undisturbed level, and kinetic energy due to the orbital velocity of the particles. The potential energy of a column of

water at height $\zeta_0$ and cross-sectional area $\delta x$ as in Fig. 3.4, considering unit width of wave front in the $y$ direction, is given by

$$\delta \text{ (P.E.)} = \frac{1}{2} g \rho \zeta_0^2 \, \delta x \ .$$

The average potential energy per unit horizontal area is found by integrating over a wavelength. For a simple harmonic wave, in which $\zeta_0$ is given by equation (3.17),

$$\text{mean P.E.} = \frac{1}{\lambda} \int_0^\lambda \frac{1}{2} g \rho a^2 \cos^2 (\kappa x - \sigma t) \, \mathrm{d}x = \frac{1}{4} g \rho a^2 \ . \tag{3.41}$$

The kinetic energy of a small volume of water $\delta x \, \delta z$, of unit width in the $y$ direction, is

$$\delta (\text{K.E.}) = \frac{1}{2} \rho (u^2 + w^2) \, \delta x \, \delta z \ .$$

For waves of small amplitude in deep water, from (3.18) and (3.19),

$$u^2 + w^2 = \sigma^2 a^2 e^{2\kappa z} \ .$$

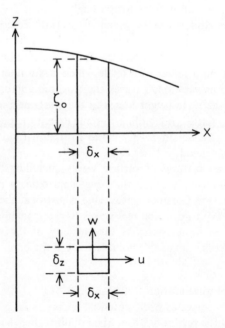

Fig. 3.4 — Potential energy and kinetic energy of wave motion.

Integrating over the whole depth and over a wavelength, the average kinetic energy per unit horizontal area is given by

$$\text{mean K.E.} = \frac{1}{\lambda} \int_0^\lambda \int_0^{-\infty} \frac{1}{2} \rho \sigma^2 a^2 e^{2\kappa z} \, dx \, dz$$

$$= \frac{1}{4} \frac{\rho \sigma^2 a^2}{\kappa} . \tag{3.42}$$

But, from (3.15), $\sigma^2 = g\kappa$ and so

$$\text{mean K.E.} = \text{mean P.E.} = \frac{1}{4} g\rho a^2 .$$

The total energy per unit area of sea surface is given by

$$E = \frac{1}{2} g\rho a^2 . \tag{3.43}$$

Thus the energy $E$ is independent of wavelength and depends only on the amplitude $a$ of the waves.

In water of finite depth it may be shown, from equations (3.28) and (3.29), that

$$E = \frac{1}{2} \frac{\rho \sigma^2 a^2}{\kappa} \coth \kappa h \tag{3.44}$$

### 3.2.6 Group velocity
If two or more wave trains of different wavelengths and periods, travelling in the same direction, are superposed, they will interfere in such a way that a pattern of groups of waves will be formed. The speed of advance of the groups is not necessarily the same as the velocity $c$ of a particular wave. An equation may be derived from the kinematics of wave motion in general, giving the group velocity $V$ by

$$V = \frac{d\sigma}{d\kappa} . \tag{3.45}$$

In the case of surface waves in deep water, from (3.15)

$$\sigma^2 = g\kappa .$$

Hence by differentiation and substitution in (3.45)

$$V = \frac{1}{2} \left( \frac{g}{\kappa} \right)^{1/2} = \frac{c}{2} . \tag{3.46}$$

The group velocity is half the wave velocity. This result is readily confirmed by observation of wave groups at sea. If attention is focused on a particular wave crest in a group, it will be seen to travel forwards through the group, losing its height and appearing to move out of the group. At the same time, new waves will appear in the rear of the group and move forwards into it, increasing in height to a maximum as they pass through the centre of the group.

In water of finite depth, it follows from equations (3.26) and (3.45) that

$$V = \frac{c}{2} \left[ 1 + \frac{2\kappa h}{\sinh 2\kappa h} \right] \tag{3.47}$$

In deep water, the second term in the bracket approaches zero and equation (3.47) reduces to (3.46). In very shallow water, the second term approaches 1 and (3.47) becomes

$$V = c$$

This result could have been obtained directly from (3.45), noting that in very shallow water $c^2 = gh$ so that the waves are non-dispersive.

A second interpretation of group velocity is that it is the velocity with which the energy of the wave motion is propagated. Referring to Fig. 3.5, the rate of doing work by water to the left of the vertical plane on water to the right of it at any instant is given by

$$dW = \int_{-\infty}^{\zeta_0} pu \, dz \, .$$

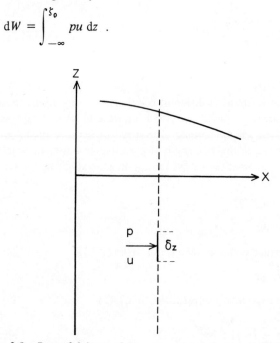

Fig. 3.5 – Rate of doing work by wave pressure across a vertical plane.

Over a complete period, the mean rate of doing work is

$$W = \frac{1}{T} \int_0^T \int_{-\infty}^{\zeta_0} pu \, dz \, dt \; .$$

For waves of small amplitude in deep water, the pressure $p$ and horizontal velocity $u$ may be substituted from (3.20) and (3.18), giving

$$W = \frac{1}{4} \frac{g\rho a^2 \lambda}{T} = \frac{1}{2} cE \qquad (3.48)$$

using (3.43).

In unit time a wave group advances a distance $V$ and the wave energy in this distance is $VE$. The rate at which energy crosses a vertical plane is equal to the rate of doing work across it so that, from (3.48), $V = 1/2 \, c$. In general the rate of transmission of energy is given by

$$W = VE \; .$$

### 3.2.7 Capillary waves

For waves of very short wavelength, surface tension has a significant effect on their properties. At a curved interface between air and water, surface tension results in an excess pressure $p_s$ acting towards the centre of curvature and given by

$$p_s = S \left( \frac{1}{r_1} + \frac{1}{r_2} \right)$$

where $S$ is the surface tension and $r_1$ and $r_2$ are the principal radii of curvature of the interface. The pressure boundary condition at the surface, given by equation (3.9) when surface tension is neglected, should be replaced by

$$\text{At } z = \zeta_0 \, , \quad p = p_a + p_s \; .$$

For two-dimensional wave motion in the $x$–$z$ plane, as considered previously, $p_s$ may be expressed in terms of the first and second derivatives of $\zeta_0$ with respect to $x$. In the case of waves in deep water the velocity of propagation $c$, given previously by equation (3.16), is found to be given by

$$c^2 = \frac{g}{\kappa} + \frac{\kappa S}{\rho} \; . \qquad (3.49)$$

The velocity of propagation $c$ as a function of wavelength $\lambda$, corresponding to equation (3.49) is shown in Fig. 3.6. The curves marked $c_1$ and $c_2$ correspond to the first and second terms on the right-hand side of (3.49) separately. For very short waves, the second term predominates and the velocity increases with

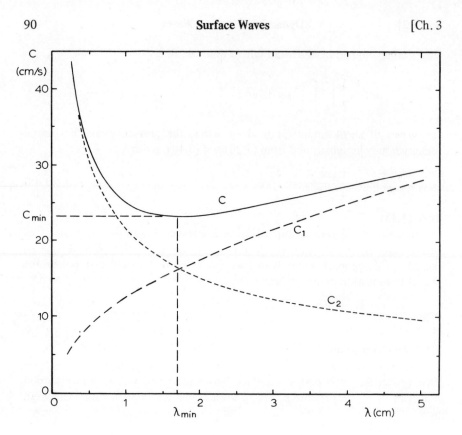

Fig. 3.6 — Velocity of propagation of capillary waves.

decreasing wavelength. In fact the velocity has a minimum for the value of $\kappa$ given by

$$\kappa^2 = \frac{g\rho}{S}$$

Taking $S = 74$ dyne cm$^{-1}$, this value of $\kappa$ is 3.64 cm$^{-1}$, corresponding to a wavelength $\lambda = 1.7$ cm and a minimum velocity $c_{min} = 23$ cm s$^{-1}$.

The group velocity may be shown to have a minimum value $V_{min} = 18$ cm s$^{-1}$ for waves of $\lambda = 4.4$ cm. For shorter waves the group velocity increases with decreasing wavelength and for very short waves it is related to the velocity of propagation by $V = 1.5c$.

The main interest of capillary waves in the sea is that they occur on the slopes of much longer waves and may thus affect the small-scale surface roughness and influence the process of wave generation and growth. Capillary waves occur most prominently on the crests of longer waves, particularly if their steepness is approaching the breaking point.

### 3.2.8 Dissipation of waves by viscosity

The rate of dissipation of the energy of surface waves due to molecular viscosity may be shown to be given by

$$\frac{dE}{dt} = - 2\mu\kappa^3 c^2 a^2 \qquad (3.50)$$

where $\mu$ is the coefficient of viscosity, $a$ is the amplitude, $\kappa$ is the wave number and $c$ is the velocity of propagation (Lamb, 1945). In the absence of any generating forces, the amplitude would decay according to the equation

$$a = a_0 \exp\left(-2\nu\kappa^2 t\right)$$

where $a_0$ is the amplitude at time $t = 0$ and $\nu$ is the kinematic viscosity, given by $\nu = \mu/\rho$. The time $\tau$ at which the amplitude would be reduced to $e^{-1}$ of its initial value is

$$\tau = \lambda^2/8\pi^2 \nu \ .$$

Taking $\nu = 0.0014$ cm$^2$ s$^{-1}$, valid for sea water at 10°C, this gives $\tau = 0.905\,\lambda^2$ in seconds if $\lambda$ is in centimetres. Thus capillary waves are very rapidly attenuated by viscosity but longer waves are little affected. The influence of viscosity on the longer waves is confined to thin boundary layers near the surface and, in shallow water, near the bottom.

In considering processes which may cause the dissipation of sea waves, molecular viscosity may usually be neglected in comparison with other processes, such as wave breaking or bottom friction.

## 3.3 STATISTICAL TREATMENT OF WAVES

### 3.3.1 Mean properties: significant waves

A record of waves passing a fixed point would normally have an irregular appearance, as represented in Fig. 3.7. Groups of high waves alternate with intervals

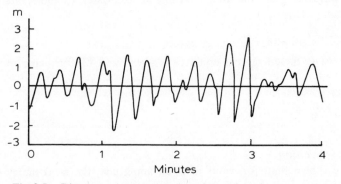

Fig. 3.7 – Diagrammatic representation of a portion of a wave record.

of lower waves and it is apparent that wave trains of a number of different periods have been superposed. The simplest way of describing such a record would be by defining a mean wave height and a mean period of all the waves on the record. Such definitions are of limited usefulness, however, since they give undue weight to the many low waves which occur between the groups of higher waves. At the other extreme, one might take the highest wave on the record and the corresponding period. For some purposes the extreme wave is a useful concept, but the highest wave on a given record is subject to a considerable sampling error. An alternative method, useful for many purposes, is to consider the highest one third of all the waves as being the 'significant waves' and to take the average height and period of these waves as the 'significant wave height' and 'significant wave period' respectively. This procedure gives more weight to the higher waves, which are of greater importance in relation to their effect on ships or coastal structures but retains a certain amount of averaging and avoids extreme values. Empirical methods of wave forecasting, referred to later in section 3.4.4, have been developed for the significant waves.

### 3.3.2 Wave spectrum

The next stage in representing a wave field is to formulate the wave spectrum, which takes into account the superposition of many wave trains of different wavelength and periods. Considering only waves travelling in the $x$ direction, the resultant elevation of the sea surface may be written

$$\zeta_0(x, t) = \sum_{n=1}^{\infty} a_n \cos(\kappa_n x - \sigma_n t + \epsilon_n) \tag{3.51}$$

where $a_n$ is the amplitude of the $n$th component which has a wavenumber $\kappa_n$ and angular frequency $\sigma_n$. $\epsilon_n$ is a phase lag which varies randomly within the range 0 to $2\pi$ radians from one component to another and the summation is carried out over all the components present.

For waves of small amplitude travelling in deep water, $\kappa_n$ and $\sigma_n$ are related by equation (3.15), i.e.

$$\sigma_n^2 = g\kappa_n . \tag{3.52}$$

For such waves the energy per unit area is given by (3.43) for each component, i.e.

$$E_n = \frac{1}{2} g\rho a_n^2 . \tag{3.53}$$

### (a) Energy spectrum

It may be shown that, for waves of small amplitude, the total energy of any number of superposed wave trains is given by the sum of their individual energies.

This enables an energy spectrum to be defined. Let $E(\sigma)\,d\sigma$ be defined as the energy per unit area of all wave trains with angular frequencies between $\sigma$ and $\sigma + d\sigma$. Then

$$E(\sigma)\,d\sigma \doteq \frac{1}{2}g\rho \sum_{\sigma}^{\sigma+d\sigma} a_n^2 \tag{3.54}$$

where the summation of $a_n^2$ is carried out for all components with angular frequency between $\sigma$ and $\sigma + d\sigma$. $E(\sigma)$ is the spectral density, which may be plotted as a function of $\sigma$, as in Fig. 3.8. $E(\sigma)\,d\sigma$ is represented by the area between the ordinates of $E(\sigma)$ at $\sigma$ and $\sigma + d\sigma$. The total energy of the wave field is obtained by summation over the whole spectrum. Thus

$$E = \int_0^\infty E(\sigma)\,d\sigma \ . \tag{3.55}$$

From (3.53) equation (3.55) is equivalent to

$$E = \frac{1}{2}g\rho \sum_{n=1}^\infty a_n^2$$

showing that the total energy per unit area of all the wave trains present is proportional to the sum of the squares of their amplitudes.

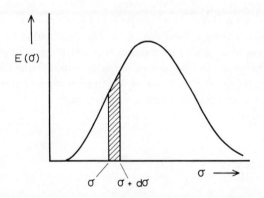

Fig. 3.8 – Energy spectrum of waves: $E(\sigma)$ as a function of angular frequency $\sigma$.

The energy spectrum has been defined above with the angular frequency $\sigma$ as the independent variable. It is possible to define the spectrum, if desired, in terms of the frequency $f$, period $T$, wavenumber $\kappa$ or wavelength $\lambda$, since all these quantities are related to $\sigma$. The form of the spectral curve will be different in each case but the total area under the curve always represents the total wave energy $E$.

If a record of sea surface elevation against time has been obtained for a certain length of time, say 12 minutes, then the energy spectrum of the record may be obtained by the methods of spectral analysis. In the early days of the study of wave spectra, the analysis was carried out by a mechanical wave analyser. It is now usual to digitise the record at suitable time intervals, or to record digitally in the first place, and to carry out the spectral analysis numerically, using a computer. The methods of analysis will not be described here but are given in books such as Kinsman (1965) or Bendat and Piersol (1971).

If the wave record has been obtained by a pressure gauge at the bottom, then a filter function must be applied to the spectral values as determined from the record in order to correct for the attenuation of the pressure oscillation with depth. For a pressure gauge on the bottom at a depth $h$, the attenuation factor is given by equation (3.35) as sech $\kappa h$, where the wavenumber $\kappa$ is related to the frequency $\sigma$ by

$$\sigma^2 = g\kappa \tanh \kappa h .  \tag{3.56}$$

### (b) *Directional spectrum*

The energy spectrum represents the distribution of energy among the waves of different frequencies but it takes no account of the direction of travel of the waves. A more complete description of the wave field specifies the direction of propagation of the various trains of waves as well as their frequency. Referring to Fig. 3.9, let $E(\sigma, \theta) \, d\sigma \, d\theta$ be the energy per unit area of waves with angular frequencies between $\sigma$ and $\sigma + d\sigma$ travelling in directions between $\theta$ and $\theta + d\theta$, where $\theta$ is measured from a fixed direction. The distribution of $E(\sigma, \theta)$ may be represented by contours drawn on a diagram in which $\sigma$ is denoted by the radial distance from the origin and $\theta$ is drawn in the appropriate direction. In Fig. 3.9, $d\sigma \, d\theta$ is represented by the shaded area for given $\sigma$ and $\theta$ and $E(\sigma, \theta)$ would be the value of the spectral density assigned to this area.

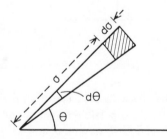

Fig. 3.9 – Definition of a directional wave spectrum: $E(\sigma, \theta)$ as a function of angular frequency $\sigma$ and direction of propagation $\theta$.

By integrating the value of $E(\sigma, \theta)$ over all values of $\theta$ for a given $\sigma$, the spectral density $E(\sigma)$ for the energy spectrum, as described above, is obtained. Thus

$$E(\sigma) = \int_0^{2\pi} E(\sigma, \theta)\, d\theta \ . \tag{3.57}$$

An example of a directional spectrum, obtained with a wave recording buoy in the North Atlantic, is shown in Fig. 3.10. The maximum spectral density is seen to occur for waves with a frequency of about 0.07 cycle per second travelling in an approximately south-east direction.

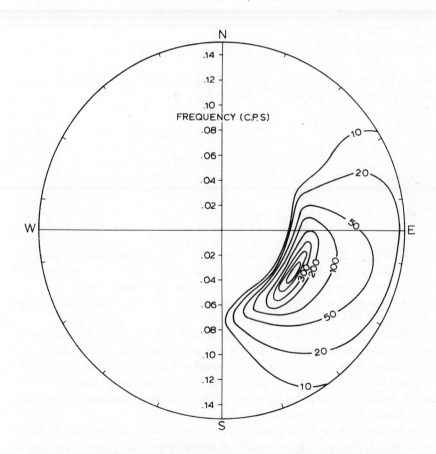

Fig. 3.10 – Example of a directional wave spectrum: data obtained by the first N.I.O. buoy. From D. E. Cartwright in *Ocean Wave Spectra,* by the National Academy of Science, © 1963. Reprinted by permission of Prentice-Hall, Inc., Englewood Cliffs, New Jersey.

### 3.3.3 Statistics of wave distributions

From a record of surface elevation $\zeta_0$ as a function of time, as in Fig. 3.7, a number of mean and statistical properties of the sea surface may be determined. The most fundamental is the root mean square displacement of the sea surface, denoted by $\zeta_{rms}$ and defined by

$$\zeta_{rms}^2 \equiv \overline{\zeta_0^2} = \frac{1}{T_L} \int_0^{T_L} \zeta_0^2 \, dt \tag{3.58}$$

where $\zeta_0$ is the elevation of the surface above its mean level, during a short time interval between $t$ and $t + dt$, and $T_L$ is the total length of the record.

For a train of simple harmonic waves of amplitude $a$, the mean square elevation is given by

$$\overline{\zeta_0^2} = \frac{1}{2} a^2 \ .$$

For a superposition of a number of simple harmonic wave trains of random phase, as assumed in equation (3.51), it follows that

$$\overline{\zeta_0^2} = \frac{1}{2} \sum_{n=1}^{\infty} a_n^2 \ . \tag{3.59}$$

In terms of the wave energy per unit area $E$ of the superposed wave trains,

$$E = \frac{1}{2} g\rho \sum_{n=1}^{\infty} a_n^2 = g\rho \zeta_{rms}^2 \ . \tag{3.60}$$

While $\zeta_{rms}$ is a precisely defined measure of the average displacement of the sea surface during the length of the record, the properties of the crests and troughs and of the wave heights are usually of more practical interest.

As a prelude to discussing these properties, the terms 'crest', 'trough' and 'wave height' will be examined more closely.

When waves of a wide range of periods and wavelengths are present, the sea surface may take on a form similar to that represented in Fig. 3.11. Defining a crest as a maximum of the curve of elevation against time, it is seen that, in addition to the main crests such as A, B and E, other crests such as C and D occur, some of which, like D, may be below the mean water level. If troughs are defined similarly as minima of the curve of elevation as at a, b, c, etc., some of them, like c in the diagram, may be above the mean level. These effects occur when the crests and troughs of shorter waves are superposed on the gentler slopes of much longer waves. It is a matter of some uncertainty whether all the smaller crests should be included when counting the number of waves on the record, in order to determine the properties of the significant waves, for

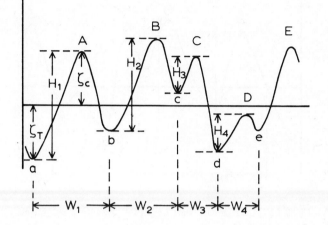

Fig. 3.11 – Definition of crest height and wave height for 'crest-to-trough' waves.

example. In fact the number of crests and troughs, defined as maxima and minima respectively, becomes greater if the resolution of the wave recording instrument is increased. From the point of view of the effects of waves on floating or fixed structures, the very short waves are unimportant and it is better to disregard them when determining the wave characteristics.

In the 'crest-to-trough' definition of a wave, the wave height $H$ is defined as the height of a crest above the preceding trough. In Fig. 3.11, $H_1, H_2, H_3$, and $H_4$ are the heights of the waves $W_1, W_2, W_3$ and $W_4$, having crests A, B, C, and D respectively. The elevation of a given crest above the mean level may be denoted by $\zeta_c$, as shown in the figure for crest A, and the depression of a given trough by $\zeta_T$, with $\zeta_T$ taken as positive for convenience. For the wave represented by crest A, it is seen that $H_1 = \zeta_c + \zeta_T$. One way of discriminating against the smaller waves would be to disregard those crests which are below the mean level. In that case, crest D in Fig. 3.11 would be disregarded.

An alternative definition is that of the 'zero up-cross' wave, illustrated in Fig. 3.12, in which the same surface elevation curve as in Fig. 3.11 is taken. A zero up-crossing occurs when the surface passes through the mean level in an upward direction. A zero up-cross wave is the portion of the record between two successive zero up-crossings. Thus $W_1$ and $W_2$ represent two zero up-cross waves. The height of the wave is the vertical distance between the highest and lowest points of the wave. The heights of waves $W_1$ and $W_2$ are therefore $H_1$ and $H_2$, as shown in Fig. 3.12. Crests C and D and troughs c and e are disregarded by this definition. The concept of the zero up-cross wave is an objective way of focusing attention on the larger waves and it has been found to be amenable to statistical treatment. The basic theory was described in papers by Longuet-Higgins (1952) and Cartwright (1958) and its practical application by Draper (1963).

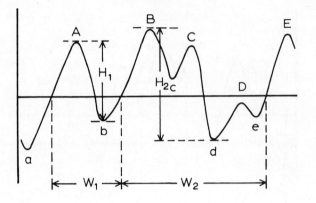

Fig. 3.12 – Definition of wave height for "zero up-cross" waves.

Let $N$ be the total number of zero up-cross waves in the record of duration $T_L$, then the root mean square wave height $H_{rms}$ is defined by

$$H^2_{rms} = \frac{1}{N} \sum_{n=1}^{N} H_n^2 \qquad (3.61)$$

where $H_n$ is the height of the $n$th wave.

In order to determine the significant wave height, the heights $H_n$ are arranged in decreasing order of magnitude from $H_1$ to $H_N$. Then the significant waves are those from $H_1$ to $H_{N/3}$, taking $N/3$ to the nearest integer, and the significant wave height $H_s$ is given by

$$H_s = \frac{3}{N}(H_1 + H_2 + \ldots + H_{N/3}) \qquad (3.62)$$

The average wave period may be defined in terms of either the zero up-cross waves or the number of crests. The mean zero up-crossing period is given by

$$T_z = \frac{T_L}{N}$$

where $T_L$ is the duration of the record and $N$ is the number of zero up-crossings. The mean crest period $T_c$ is defined similarly by

$$T_c = \frac{T_L}{N_c}$$

where $N_c$ is the number of crests, i.e. maxima, on the record.

The statistical properties of the distribution of crests and zero up-cross waves are related to the energy spectrum in a way which was described by

Cartwright (1962), based on original papers by Longuet-Higgins and by Cartwright. It is possible to derive an equation for the probability distribution of the crest heights $\zeta_c$ and hence obtain the expected value of the significant wave height or of the height of the highest wave on the record. On the assumption that the heights of the zero up-cross waves follow a Rayleigh distribution, for which there is good experimental evidence, it may be shown that the significant wave height is given by

$$H_s \cong \sqrt{2}\, H_{rms} \tag{3.63}$$

where $H_{rms}$ is the root mean square height of all the zero up-cross waves as in equation (3.61).

By making the additional assumption that the spectrum has a narrow band-width, i.e. that most of the energy is concentrated in frequencies near the spectral peak, it may be shown that

$$H_{rms} = 2\sqrt{2}\, \zeta_{rms} \tag{3.64}$$

where $\zeta_{rms}$ is the root mean square displacement of the sea surface as in equation (3.58). Hence from (3.63) and (3.64),

$$H_s \cong 4\zeta_{rms} \; . \tag{3.65}$$

### 3.3.4 Estimating maximum wave heights

A further statistic obtainable from the distribution discussed above is the most probable height $H_{max}$ of the largest wave on a record of $N$ waves. With the above assumption it may be shown that, to a first approximation

$$H_{max} = (\ln N)^{1/2}\, H_{rms} \tag{3.66}$$

Table 3.1 gives the values of $H_{max}/H_{rms}$ for certain values of $N$, taken from Longuet-Higgins (1952) using a closer approximation than equation (3.66).

**Table 3.1** – Most probable wave height $(H_{max})$ on a record of $N$ waves.

| $N$ | $H_{max}/H_{rms}$ | $N$ | $H_{max}/H_{rms}$ |
|---|---|---|---|
| 10 | 1.58 | 2,000 | 2.77 |
| 50 | 2.01 | 5,000 | 2.93 |
| 100 | 2.17 | 10,000 | 3.04 |
| 200 | 2.32 | 20,000 | 3.15 |
| 500 | 2.51 | 50,000 | 3.30 |
| 1,000 | 2.64 | 100,000 | 3.40 |

Using this method it is seen that on a 10-minute record, containing about 100 waves, one would expect the highest wave measured to be 2.17 times the root mean square or, using equation (3.63), about 1.54 times the significant wave height. One may extrapolate from the record to estimate the most probable height occurring during a given period, assuming the wave spectrum, of which the 10-minute record was a sample, to remain unchanged. Thus over a 3-hour period, containing about 1800 waves, the most probable value of $H_{max}$ would be about 2.75 $H_{rms}$ while over a period of 16 hours, containing about 10,000 waves, it would be about 3 $H_{rms}$. Clearly, the longer the period the less likely it is that the wave conditions will remain statistically unchanged.

The same distribution may be used to estimate the highest wave to be expected in a storm of a given duration, having predicted the significant wave height by one of the methods mentioned later in section 3.4.4.

Forecasting the maximum design wave height in relation to structures is a problem on a longer time scale. Oil platforms and other offshore structures are often designed to withstand the '50-year return values of wave height', which is the height exceeded on average once every 50 years. Methods of estimating this value usually depend on having wave records for the area concerned extending over at least a year and fitting a suitable statistical distribution in order to extrapolate to longer periods. The problem was discussed by Draper (1963) and reviewed recently by Carter and Challenor (1981).

## 3.4 GENERATION OF WAVES

### 3.4.1 Physical processes of generation
There are three aspects of the problem of the generation of surface waves by wind:

(1) Why does the surface of a body of water become wavy when a wind blows across it?
(2) How is energy transferred from the wind to the waves, so that they grow and develop the characteristic features of a rough sea?
(3) How may the occurrence of waves, their heights, periods and spectrum, be forecast for practical purposes?

The first is a stability problem which has been treated by a number of mathematicians over many years. The general view at present appears to be that, if the fetch is more than a few metres, winds of very low velocity, appreciably less than 1 m s$^{-1}$, are sufficient to cause waves of certain wavelengths to grow and propagate. We will not attempt to consider this problem further here but go on to the second aspect.

The first theory of wave generation with a realistic physical basis was proposed by Jeffreys in 1924. It did not consider the formation of waves from an initially flat surface but assumed that wave-like perturbations of small amplitude were present and considered how they could grow by extracting energy from a steady wind blowing over them. The streamlines in the air flow, parallel to the mean surface at some distance above it, would tend to follow the wave contours closer to them as in Fig. 3.13. It was assumed that separation of the flow would take place at some point on the leeward side of a wave, analogous to the boundary layer separation on a stalling aerofoil, with the production of eddy motion and a decrease in pressure, in accordance with Bernoulli's theorem. The flow was assumed to re-attach itself to the windward slope of the wave in front. There would thus be a lower pressure on the downstream side of a wave than on the windward side. The theory showed that the pressure difference was in the right phase relationship to the movement of the wave surface for the wind to do work on the waves and so increase their energy. The rate of dissipation of wave energy by viscosity was considered and the condition for the waves to grow was that the rate of energy transfer from the wind should exceed the rate of viscous dissipation.

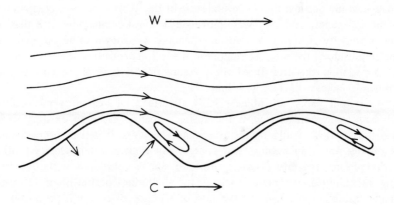

W ⟶

C ⟶

Fig 3.13 – Schematic representation of air flow over a wave surface.

The Jeffreys theory included a parameter called the 'sheltering coefficient', analogous to the drag coefficient $C_D$ for the stress of the wind on the sea surface, which had to be determined empirically. For the waves to grow at a rate consistent with observations, it seemed that the coefficient would have to be an order of magnitude greater than experimental evidence indicated. Another objection was that it was doubtful if separation of the air flow would occur on a wave of relatively low steepness, as assumed in the initial stages of the process. It now appears that separation occurs only with breaking waves, but that modification of the streamlines and a reduction of pressure on the downwind face can occur with unbroken waves. Although Jeffrey's theory was not quantitatively successful in its original form, the basic concept, of an existing wave form perturbing the air flow in such a way that it reacts on the waves and transfers energy to them, appears to be valid and is used in more recent theories.

The initial generation of waves from a plane surface, by the action of turbulent fluctuations of air pressure present in the wind, was first considered by Eckart in 1953. His theory led to a method of relating the height of the waves generated to the amplitude of the pressure fluctuations due to the 'gustiness' of the wind. The theory was not quantitatively satisfactory, however, as the pressure fluctuations likely to be present were an order of magnitude smaller than would be needed to generate waves of the observed amplitude. The state of theoretical and experimental knowledge on wave generation up to 1956 was well described by Ursell (1956).

Two papers were published in 1957 which form the basis of present-day theory of the generation of waves. The first, by Phillips (1957), described a resonance mechanism which postulated the presence of a random distribution of pressure fluctuations, changing slowly as it was being advected by the wind. Waves would be produced on the surface of the water by normal pressures and resonance would occur if the horizontal scale of the fluctuations was comparable with the wavelength and they were moving at a speed comparable with that of the wave velocity. The rate of transfer of energy was shown to be proportional to the amplitude of the pressure fluctuations but independent of the wave height. For a constant mean strength of the pressure fluctuations, the energy of the waves would increase linearly with time.

The second paper, by Miles (1957), described an instability mechanism which had some similarity with the Jeffreys theory. Over an existing wave profile the air flow would be disturbed and the pressure perturbations would react on the waves, increasing their energy. For a given wind velocity profile near the surface, the rate of energy transfer can be calculated, without introducing an empirical parameter such as the sheltering coefficient of Jeffreys. With the instability mechanism, the rate of increase of energy is proportional to the wave amplitude. As it is a feedback process, for a constant mean wind speed, the energy of the waves increases exponentially with time.

The two processes were combined in a mechanism described by Miles (1960). When a wind starts to blow over a calm sea, the resonance mechanism would come into action first, producing an initial rate of growth of wave energy linearly with time. As the waves become larger, the instability mechanism becomes more effective and the wave energy increases exponentially. The transition time, at which the instability process becomes dominant, can be calculated and shown to be dependent only on the parameter $(W \cos \alpha)/c$ where $W$ is the wind speed, $c$ the wave velocity and $\alpha$ the angle between the wind direction and the direction of travel of the waves.

### 3.4.2 Development of a wave spectrum

The simplified description given above should be taken as applying to each component of the waves, of a given angular frequency $\sigma$ or wavenumber $\kappa$, separately, as the rate of energy growth will be dependent on frequency and a spectrum of waves will be developed. The exponential rate of growth cannot continue indefinitely and eventually a stage will be reached, for each component, at which the gain of energy is balanced by losses due to molecular and eddy viscosity and wave breaking. Except for very short waves, breaking is probably the dominant process and in that case it was shown by Phillips, on dimensional grounds, that the spectral density would be given by

$$E'(\sigma) = \beta g^2 \sigma^{-5} \qquad (3.67)$$

where $E'(\sigma) = E(\sigma)/g\rho$ and $\beta$ is a constant. Thus, in the equilibrium range, where the rate of gain of energy from the wind is balanced by the loss due to breaking, the spectral density should be inversely proportional to the fifth power of the frequency.

The growth of a wave spectrum with time, for a wind starting at time $t = 0$ and continuing to blow at a constant speed, is illustrated diagrammatically in Fig. 3.14. At time $t_1$ the waves of higher frequency are already in the equilibrium state and $E(\sigma)$ follows the $\sigma^{-5}$ curve at the high frequency end of the spectrum. At a later time $t_2$, the waves of lower frequency have continued to

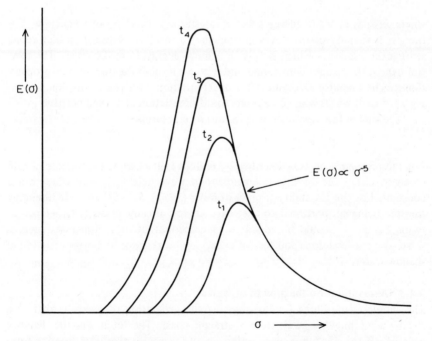

Fig. 3.14 – Growth of a wave spectrum: the form of the spectrum is shown at successive times $t_1, t_2, t_3$ and $t_4$.

increase in energy, while those previously in the $\sigma^{-5}$ range are unchanged, as they were already in equilibrium at time $t_1$. With increasing times $t_3$, $t_4$, ... the waves of lower frequency continue to gain energy, the peak of the spectrum moves towards a lower frequency and the $\sigma^{-5}$ range extend to lower frequencies as more wave components reach equilibrium.

The earlier theoretical work treated the growth of each component of the wave spectrum as taking place independently of those of other wavenumbers and frequencies. More recently much attention has been given to interactions between waves of different frequencies and wavenumbers, by which waves of a particular frequency may gain or lose energy by exchanges with waves of other frequencies. When such processes occur, the energy which a particular component wave train gains from the wind may be shared with waves of certain other frequencies. Observations have confirmed that wave–wave interactions do take place, sometimes resulting in a transfer of energy to both higher and lower frequencies and in other cases predominantly in one direction.

The growth of waves may be represented by the radiative transfer equation which, for the simplest case of waves propagating in one direction, may be written

$$\frac{DE}{Dt} \equiv \frac{\partial E}{\partial t} + V \frac{\partial E}{\partial x} = S \tag{3.68}$$

where $E(\sigma; x, t)$ is the energy spectral density as a function of frequency, $V$ is the group velocity of the waves of frequency $\sigma$ and $S$ is a source function, representing the processes which supply or remove energy from the waves. The spectral density $E$ changes with time $t$ and with position in the direction of propagation $x$. The operator $D/Dt$ indicates differentiation with respect to time following a group of waves while $\partial/\partial t$ refers to differentiation at a fixed position.

The source function may be split into several terms

$$S = S_1 + S_2 + S_3 + \ldots .$$

For the resonance process described by Phillips (1957), in which the rate of gain of energy from the wind is independent of wave height, $S_1 = \alpha$, where $\alpha$ is a constant. For the instability process of Miles (1957), $S_2 = \beta E$, the rate of energy transfer being proportional to the wave energy already present. Other source terms $S_3$, $S_4$, ... could be added to take account of other processes such as wave–wave interactions and loss of energy by breaking or by bottom friction in shallow water.

### 3.4.3 Observations on the growth of waves

The simplest conditions for investigating the generation of waves is that of a steady wind blowing away from a straight coast. The fetch, i.e. the distance over which the wind has been acting on the waves, is then the distance from the coast and the duration of the wind is irrelevant. Wave spectra were measured under these conditions by Burling (1959) at short fetches on a reservoir and his results were used in assessing theories of wave generation. A number of similar investigations have since been made with waves on the surface of lakes or the sea, coupled with measurements of the air flow over them. The most extensive investigation to date was the Joint North Sea Wave Project, known as JONSWAP, carried out in 1968 and 1969 west of the island of Sylt, West Germany. In the main experiment, a variety of instruments for recording the waves and the air flow above them were deployed at 13 stations along a line extending for 160 km westward from Sylt during the month of July 1969. The depth of water increased gradually from about 10 m near the coast to 50 m beyond 130 km from the coast. A full account of the experiment was published by Hasselmann *et al.* (1973).

Considering firstly the total energy of the wave motion, one may expect the energy to be proportional to the work done by the wind on the water. As a first approximation, this may be taken as the shearing stress of the wind multiplied by the fetch. Taking the stress as $\rho_a W_*^2$, where $W_*$ is the friction velocity of the wind and $\rho_a$ the density of the air (as discussed further in Chapter 4, section 4.3), and the distance $X$ from the coast as the fetch, we have

$$E \propto W_*^2 X .$$

(3.69)

Since $E = g\rho \zeta_{rms}^2$, where $\zeta_{rms}$ is the root mean square elevation of the sea surface, this can be written

$$\zeta_{rms} = \alpha W_* \left(\frac{X}{g}\right)^{1/2}$$

(3.70)

where $\alpha$ is a dimensionless constant. The JONSWAP data, like the smaller scale data of Burling, were shown by Phillips (1977) to follow this relationship with the constant $\alpha$ being about $1.26 \times 10^{-2}$.

A number of experiments have confirmed the existence of an equilibrium range in the spectrum, at frequencies higher than the spectral peak, in which the spectral density is proportional to $\sigma^{-5}$, as in equation (3.67). The value of the constant $\beta$ in (3.67), from a number of investigators, was found to be $1.23 \times 10^{-2}$ with an uncertainty of about 10% (Phillips, 1977).

In the JONSWAP data, as in other investigations, the shape of the spectrum at different fetches was found to be approximately similar, scaled by a factor which was a function of $\sigma/\sigma_0$, where $\sigma_0$ is the angular frequency of the spectral peak. This may be represented by the equation

$$E'(\sigma) = g^2 \sigma^{-5} f\left(\frac{\sigma}{\sigma_0}\right)$$

(3.71)

where the function $f \to \beta$ when $\sigma/\sigma_0 \gg 1$ and decreases rapidly to zero when $\sigma/\sigma_0$ is just less than unity. The value of $\sigma_0$ decreases with increasing fetch $X$.

By considering a number of investigations in which the development of the spectrum was limited by fetch, Phillips (1977) found that

$$\frac{\sigma_0 W_*}{g} \cong 2.2 \left(\frac{gX}{W_*^2}\right)^{-\frac{1}{4}} . \tag{3.72}$$

If $\lambda_0$ is the wavelength corresponding to the spectral peak, then for waves in deep water $\lambda_0 = 2\pi g/\sigma_0^2$ and the above equation gives

$$\lambda_0 \cong 1.3 \, W_* \left(\frac{X}{g}\right)^{1/2} . \tag{3.73}$$

Combining equation (3.73) with (3.70) for $\zeta_{rms}$, with $\alpha = 1.26 \times 10^{-2}$, it is seen that

$$\lambda_0 \cong 100 \, \zeta_{rms}$$

This result, which was pointed out by Charnock (1981), is a useful indication of where the peak in the spectrum may be expected.

The main objective of JONSWAP was to investigate the role of various energy transfer processes in the development of the wave spectrum. Non-linear interactions between waves of different frequencies were found to play a significant part. The various terms in the energy balance are shown schematically in Fig. 3.15. The spectrum as a function of frequency $f (f = \sigma/2\pi)$ is shown by the curve $E(f)$ while the curves $S_{in}$, $S_{nl}$ and $S_{ds}$ indicate the rates of energy transfer, as functions of $f$, by input from the wind, non-linear interactions and dissipation respectively. The energy input from the wind is seen to be distributed fairly broadly over a wide range of frequencies. The main effect of the inter-

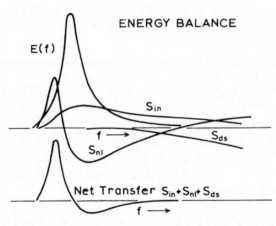

Fig. 3.15 – Schematic energy balance in the wave spectrum, based on JONSWAP data. $E(f)$ is the spectral density as a function of frequency $f$. $S_{in}$ is the rate of energy input from the atmosphere, $S_{nl}$ the non-linear wave–wave transfer rate and $S_{ds}$ the rate of dissipation. From Hasselmann *et al.* (1973), by courtesy of the Deutsches Hydrographisches Institut.

actions is to transfer energy from the peak of the spectrum towards lower frequencies. Dissipation becomes significant at the higher frequencies.

### 3.4.4 Wave predictions

The third aspect of the problem of wave generation, mentioned at the beginning of section 3.4.1, is the forecasting of waves for practical purposes. The development of methods of prediction has been largely empirical and has taken place almost independently of the theoretical and experimental studies just described. In World War II the forecasting of wave conditions on beaches was of vital importance in planning landing operations. A method of predicting the height and period of the significant waves for a given wind speed and duration or fetch was devised in the USA by Sverdrup and Munk, based on the minimum of physical ideas, since the knowledge of wave generating processes was very meagre at that time. In subsequent years the method was improved, largely by taking the increased number of observations into account, particularly by Bretschneider, and in its revised form it is sometimes known as the SMB (Sverdrup–Munk–Bretschneider) method.

At the same time, methods of forecasting the wave spectrum, from which the significant wave height and period could be derived, were being developed. One of the most widely used is that developed in the USA by Pierson, Neumann and James (1955), known as the PNJ method. Rather similar methods were developed in Great Britain by Darbyshire. The idea of a 'fully developed sea' was introduced, as applying to conditions in the open ocean, well away from land, when the wind had been blowing with a steady speed and direction long enough for all wave components to have reached a state of equilibrium. Under these conditions the spectrum, and also the significant wave height and period, may be expected to be a function of the wind speed only.

Using a large amount of data, available at the time, Pierson and Moskowitz (1964) derived the following equation for the spectrum in a fully developed sea:

$$E'(\sigma) = \alpha g^2 \sigma^{-5} \exp\left[-\beta\left(\frac{\sigma_0}{\sigma}\right)^4\right] \tag{3.74}$$

where $\sigma_0 = g/W$, $W$ is the mean wind speed at 19.5 m and $\alpha$ and $\beta$ are constants. From the data, the constants were evaluated as $\alpha = 8.1 \times 10^{-3}$, $\beta = 0.74$. It is seen that, at large values of the angular frequency $\sigma$, equation (3.74) gives $E'(\sigma) \propto \sigma^{-5}$, as in Phillips's theory of the equilibrium range. From the spectrum, the following expressions for the significant wave height $H_s$ and mean zero upcross period $T_z$ in a fully developed sea may be obtained (Neumann and Pierson, 1966, p. 351):

$$H_s = 2.12 \times 10^{-2} W^2$$

$$T_z = 0.52\ W$$

where $H_s$ in metres, $T_z$ in seconds and $W$ in metres per second.

When the state of the sea is limited by fetch (or wind duration if the fetch is unlimited), one would expect the spectrum, and also the significant wave height and period to be functions of fetch as well as of wind speed. The two variables may be combined by introducing the concept of 'dimensionless fetch', defined by $F = g\,X/W^2$. The prediction equations may then be expressed in dimensionless form, giving the dimensionless wave height $gH_s/W^2$ and dimensionless wave velocity $c/W$ each as a function of $F$. For the significant waves, $c$ is related to the period $T_s$ by the equation $c = g\,T_s/2\pi$, valid for deep water waves.

The following empirical equations were derived by Wilson in 1966 (cited by LeBlond and Mysack, 1978):

$$\frac{c}{W_{10}} = 1.37\,[1 - (1 + 0.008\,F^{1/3})^{-5}] \tag{3.75}$$

$$\frac{gH_s}{W_{10}^2} = 0.30\,[1 - (1 + 0.004\,F^{1/2})^{-2}] \tag{3.76}$$

It is interesting to compare the above empirical results, derived from observations in a number of areas, with those from the JONSWAP experiment. Equations (3.75) and (3.76) lead assymptotically to constant values of dimensionless velocity and wave height for very large values of $F$, but for small values of $F$ they agree well with the JONSWAP data, according to which

$$H_s \propto F^{1/2} \quad \text{and} \quad T_m \propto F^{1/3}$$

where $T_m$ is the period corresponding to the peak frequency $\sigma_m$.

Most wave prediction schemes have been developed for waves generated in deep water. Such waves may leave the generating area and travel as swell into shallower water. A forecast of their properties in coastal waters must include an allowance for changes as they move into shallow water, as discussed in section 3.6. Waves in coastal waters also include those generated on the continental shelf. From studies of waves recorded on weather ships in the North Atlantic and on light vessels around the coasts of Britain, Darbyshire (1963) deduced that there were significant differences in the properties of waves generated in deep water and those generated in water of depth less than about 200 m, for the same speed and fetch. He produced, therefore, separate prediction schemes for the two cases. Revised prediction formulae based on the JONSWAP results were derived by Carter (1982). Fig. 3.16 is taken from Carter's paper and shows predicted values of the significant wave height and zero up-crossing period in coastal waters as functions of wind speed and fetch or duration.

For graphical methods of forecasting waves generated in deep water, reference should be made to Darbyshire (1963), Pierson, Neumann and James (1955) or Bretschneider (1970). All these methods relate to waves generated by steady

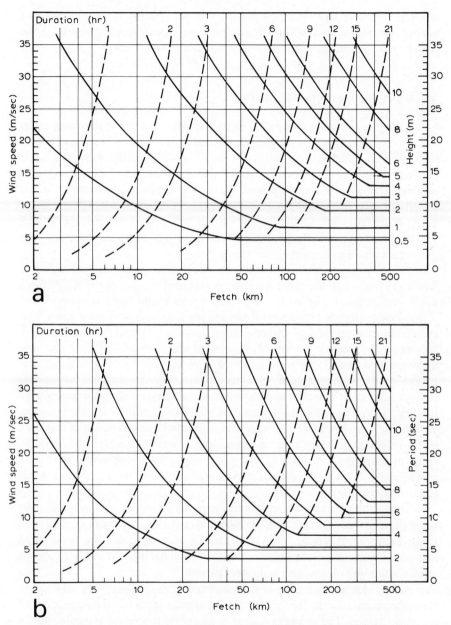

Fig. 3.16 – Graphs for the prediction of (a) significant wave height and (b) zero up-crossing wave period in coastal waters, based on JONSWAP results, from Carter (1982). In (a), enter with wind speed at left-hand side, move across until the limiting fetch or duration (broken lines) is reached, then move down the curve (full line) to the height scale. Similarly in (b), but moving down to the period scale.

winds in relatively large and slow-moving weather systems. Special methods are needed for waves generated in hurricanes and rapidly moving storms. Some references to this problem are given by Bretschneider (1973).


## 3.5 WAVE PROPAGATION: SWELL

In a storm area waves of many different wavelengths, travelling at varying angles to the wind direction are present. Once generated, waves of each component wavelength will continue to travel at their own velocity. The waves will travel beyond the storm area into previously undisturbed water, the energy being propagated at the appropriate group velocity. For waves in deep water the group velocity of waves of period $T$ is $V = c/2 = gT/4\pi$. Taking $g = 9.8 \text{ m s}^{-2}$, $V = 0.78T$ giving $V$ in metres per second when $T$ is in seconds. The waves of longer period, and thus of longer wavelength, will travel faster and arrive at a distant coast before shorter waves from the same storm area.

Pioneer work on the propagation of swell was carried out by Barber and Ursell (1948), using the spectra of waves recorded on the coast of Cornwall, south-west England, and originating from storms in the North Atlantic. Waves at the long period end of the spectrum arrived first, followed some hours later by the shorter period but higher energy waves at the peak of the generated spectrum. The form of the recorded spectrum thus changed with time, the peak appearing first at the longest period, then moving gradually towards the shorter periods while its height grew to a maximum and then declined. By drawing straight lines corresponding to the waves of various periods on a propagation diagram, as in Fig. 3.17, the distance of the storm centre from the recording station could be determined. Taking into account also the direction of approach of the waves, their origin could be identified on weather maps. In this way the speed of propagation of wave energy was confirmed as being by the theoretical group velocity and the height of the swell waves could be related to wind speeds in the corresponding storm area.

Some striking examples of the propagation of swell over long distances were given by Munk et al. (1963). Swell recorded on the coast of California could be traced to storms in the Southern Ocean and, in one case, even to an area near Madagascar in the Indian Ocean, the swell having travelled along a great circle route south of Australia and New Zealand.

Several changes take place in the properties of the waves as they travel away from the storm area. In the first place, the angular spread of their directions of travel is reduced. The spread is related to the angle subtended at a point by the dimensions of the generating area and this angle is reduced as the distance to the point increases. The energy density of the waves is decreased by geometrical spreading as they move further from the source. For waves from a point source the energy per unit length of wave front would be inversely proportional to the

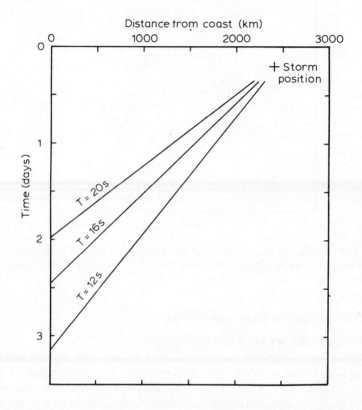

Fig. 3.17 – Propagation of swell waves of different periods. The distance of the storm from the coast and its approximate time of occurrence may be estimated from the successive times of arrival at the coast of swell waves of decreasing periods.

distance travelled, independently of the wavelength. Dissipative processes, of which wave breaking is probably the most important, although air resistance and turbulent friction may play some part, affect the waves of shorter wavelength more severely than the longer ones. The form of the spectrum therefore changes, as illustrated in Fig. 3.18, with the peak moving towards lower frequencies. As a consequence of these changes, the swell from a distant storm is characterised by waves of long period, relatively low steepness and long crests. Procedures for making quantitative estimates of the effects of these changes on the swell were included in the forecasting methods of Pierson, Neumann and James (1955).

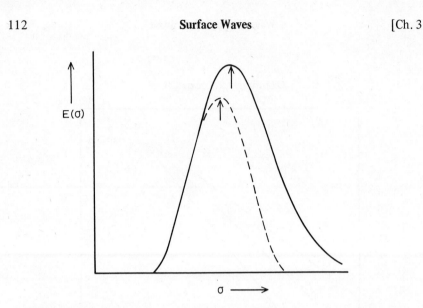

Fig. 3.18 – Change in spectrum of swell with increasing distance from the generating area. Full line: spectrum in generating area; broken line: spectrum at some distance away.

## 3.6 WAVES ENTERING SHALLOW WATER

### 3.6.1 Changes in velocity and wavelength

The classical theory described in section 3.2 may be used to predict the changes which occur as a train of waves enters shallow water. The term 'shallow' in this context is taken to mean water of depth less than half a wavelength. The velocity of propagation $c$ is reduced, in accordance with equation (3.32), but the period $T$ remains constant, since the number of waves passing a given point per unit time is conserved. The wavelength is reduced by the same factor as the velocity of propagation, as the equation $\lambda = cT$ continues to apply. The group velocity $V$ is also reduced, as given by equation (3.47), but not as rapidly with decreasing depth as the phase velocity $c$.

The relations between the angular frequency $\sigma$, wavenumber $\kappa$, phase velocity $c$ and group velocity $V$ in water of depth $h$ and the values $\sigma_0$, $\kappa_0$ and $c_0$ in deep water are given in the following equations.

In deep water, $h \gg \lambda/2$,

$$\sigma_0{}^2 = g\kappa_0, \quad c_0 = \left(\frac{g}{\kappa_0}\right)^{1/2} \tag{3.77}$$

In water of depth $h$,

$$\sigma = \sigma_0$$

$$\sigma^2 = g\kappa \tanh \kappa h \tag{3.78}$$

and thus

$$\kappa \tanh \kappa h = \kappa_0 \tag{3.79}$$

$$c = \frac{\kappa_0}{\kappa} c_0 \tag{3.80}$$

$$V = \frac{c}{2} \left( 1 + \frac{2\kappa h}{\sinh 2\kappa h} \right) \tag{3.81}$$

For waves of a given period $T$, corresponding to $\sigma_0 = 2\pi/T$, the wavenumber $\kappa$ is found from equation (3.79). The phase velocity $c$ and group velocity $V$ are then found from equations (3.80) and (3.81).

Fig. 3.19 shows the values of $c/c_0$ or $\lambda/\lambda_0$ and of $V/V_0$ as functions of $h/\lambda_0$.

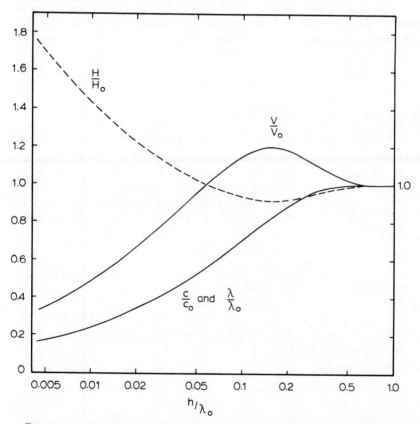

Fig. 3.19 – Wave changes in shallow water. The ordinates show relative changes in velocity $c/c_0$, wavelength $\lambda/\lambda_0$, group velocity $V/V_0$ and height $H/H_0$ as functions of $h/\lambda_0$, where $h$ is depth of water and $\lambda_0$ is the wavelength in deep water. $H/H_0$ is for the case of waves approaching perpendicular to the coast.

### 3.6.2 Refraction

If the wave fronts cross the depth contours at an angle, as a wave train moves
into shallower water, the wave fronts will be refracted. If the angle of incidence
$\theta$ is defined as the angle between the normal to the wave front and the normal to
the bottom contours, then the change in the angle $\theta$ with changing wave velocity
$c$ is given by

$$\frac{\sin \theta_1}{\sin \theta_2} = \frac{c_1}{c_2}$$

where $c_1$ and $c_2$ are the velocities at the points where $\theta$ has the values $\theta_1$ and $\theta_2$.
This is Snell's law, familiar in geometrical optics, and the procedures used to
trace light rays in a medium of variable refractive index may also be used for
surface waves.

The simplest case of plane waves approaching a straight coast over a uniformly sloping bottom is shown in Fig. 3.20. Waves approaching the shore at
right angles, for which $\theta = 0$, are slowed down but not refracted. Waves ap-

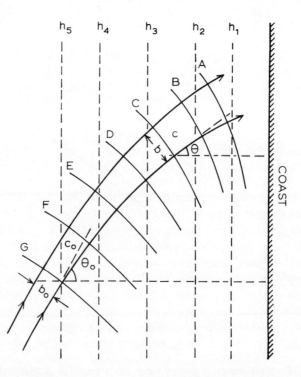

Fig. 3.20 – Refraction of waves approaching a straight coast. The bottom contours $h_i, h_2 \ldots$ are assumed to run parallel to the coastline. A, B, C . . . are wave
crests and the arrows show the direction of a ray, orthogonal to the crests.

proaching at an oblique angle, however, are refracted in such a way that the angle $\theta$ is decreased, corresponding to the wave fronts becoming more nearly parallel to the shore. If $\theta_0$ is the angle of incidence in deep water, where the velocity is $c_0$, then the value of $\theta$ at a·position where the velocity is $c$ is given by

$$\sin \theta = \frac{c}{c_0} \sin \theta_0 \qquad (3.82)$$

If two rays, defined as orthogonals to the wave front, a distance $b$, apart are considered, as in Fig. 3.20, then it is seen that the distance, measured along a wave front, is increased as the rays are refracted towards the coast. It can be shown that

$$b = b_0 \frac{\cos\theta}{\cos\theta_0} \qquad (3.83)$$

where $b$ is the perpendicular distance between the rays where the angle is $\theta$ and $b_0$, $\theta_0$ are the corresponding values in deep water. This result is relevant in considering the energy density of the waves.

Starting with a set of parallel rays in deep water, approaching at a given angle, the subsequent path of each ray may be traced for any distribution of bottom contours. In the simple case considered above, the rays remain nearly parallel although their direction is changed. If the bottom contours run approximately parallel to a curving coastline, then it is easily shown that the refracted rays will converge towards a headland and diverge when approaching a bay between two headlands. Since a convergence of the rays corresponds also to a convergence of the energy of a wave front, higher waves would be expected in the vicinity of a headland than in a bay. A number of examples are given in the book by Kinsman (1965) and procedures for constructing wave refraction diagrams are described by Pierson *et al.* (1955), Wiegel (1964), Wood and Fleming (1981) and in other textbooks of coastal engineering.

It should be noted that the change in wave velocity and hence the refraction pattern in a given area is a function of the wave period. The longer period waves, which have a longer deep water wavelength, are affected by the decreasing water depth at a greater distance from the coast and undergo greater refraction. For coastal engineering purposes it is necessary to prepare a series of wave refraction diagrams, for different wave periods and different directions of approach.

Figure 3.21 shows a satellite image of a swell approaching Sumburgh Head ($59° 52'$ N, $1° 17'$ W), at the southern tip of the main island of the Shetland Islands north of Scotland. This image was obtained by synthetic aperture radar (SAR) from SEASAT. It is a good example of how sea waves may be recorded from space and it shows clearly how the waves, approaching from a westerly direction, are refracted around the headland by shoaling water.

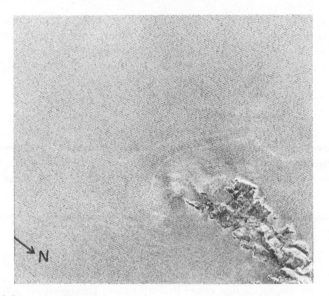

Fig. 3.21 – Satellite image of waves approaching Sumburgh Head, Shetland Islands, and being refracted around the headland. Obtained from SEASAT by SAR (synthetic aperture radar) on 15 September 1978. Reproduced by courtesy of Dr. T. D. Allan, Institute of Oceanographic Sciences

### 3.6.3 Changes in wave height

The rate of transmission of energy in the direction of propagation of the waves, per unit width of wave front, was shown in section 3.2.6 to be given by

$$W = EV \tag{3.84}$$

where $E$ is the energy per unit area of sea surface and $V$ is the group velocity. To estimate the change in $E$, and hence in the wave height, as waves travel into shallow water, we will assume that the energy of the waves between two given rays continues to be confined laterally by these rays and that dissipative processes can be neglected. If $b$ is the distance between the rays, as in Fig. 3.20, this means that $Wb$ remains constant. Then from equations (3.83) and (3.84)

$$EV \cos \theta = E_0 V_0 \cos \theta_0 . \tag{3.85}$$

For waves of a given period, approaching at a given angle $\theta_0$, the values of $V$ and $\theta$ as functions of $h$ may be determined from equations (3.80), (3.81) and (3.82). Since $E = 1/8 \, g\rho H^2$ for small amplitude waves of height $H$,

$$\frac{H}{H_0} = \left( \frac{E}{E_0} \right)^{1/2} = \left( \frac{V_0 \cos \theta_0}{V \cos \theta} \right)^{1/2} \tag{3.86}$$

The height of the waves is initially reduced as they enter water of depth less than $\lambda/2$ but it then increases rapidly to several times the deep water height. As the wavelength is decreasing at the same time, the waves become steeper and eventually reach the breaking point. The changes in wave height, as well as in wavelength and velocity, are illustrated in Fig. 3.19.

### 3.6.4 Waves on currents

If waves travelling initially in water with no mean motion enter a current, certain changes take place in the velocity, wavelength and height of the waves. We will consider first the simplest case of waves propagating in the $x$ direction encountering a current $U$ in the same direction. On the assumption that the number of wave crests is conserved, it may be shown that

$$\kappa(U + c) = \kappa_0 c_0 \tag{3.87}$$

where $\kappa_0$, $c_0$ refer to the wave number and velocity of propagation in the absence of the current and $\kappa$, $c$ to their values when the waves are superposed on the current.

Assuming, for simplicity, that the waves are effectively in deep water,

$$c^2 = g/\kappa , \quad c_0^2 = g/\kappa_0 \tag{3.88}$$

Hence from (3.87),

$$\frac{c^2}{c_0^2} = \frac{\kappa_0}{\kappa} = \frac{U + c}{c_0} .$$

This may be written as a quadratic equation in $c/c_0$ with the solution

$$\frac{c}{c_0} = \frac{1}{2}\left[1 + \left(1 + \frac{4U}{c_0}\right)^{1/2}\right] \tag{3.89}$$

When the current is flowing in the same direction as the waves are travelling, i.e. $U > 0$, the velocity $c$ and the wavelength $\lambda$ are increased compared with their values in still water. If the waves encounter an adverse current, i.e. $U < 0$, then $c$ and $\lambda$ are reduced. If the opposing current has a magnitude exceeding a quarter of the wave velocity in still water, i.e. $U < -c_0/4$, then no solution of equation (3.89) is possible. At the critical point, $U = -c_0/4$ and $c = c_0/2$ while the local group velocity $V = c/2 = -U$. Thus the local group velocity is equal and opposite to the current velocity and no wave energy can be propagated against the current. The waves would, in fact, steepen and break before the limiting velocity was reached.

The change in wave height can be obtained from the principle of conservation of wave action, defined by $E/\sigma$. In the present case the principle leads to the equation

$$E(U + \frac{1}{2}c)c = \text{const.} = \frac{1}{2}E_0 c_0^2 \tag{3.90}$$

where $E$ and $E_0$ are the energy per unit area of the waves in the presence and absence of the current respectively. Since

$$E = \frac{1}{2}g\rho a^2, \quad E_0 = \frac{1}{2}g\rho a_0^2$$

where $a$ and $a_0$ are the corresponding wave amplitudes,

$$\frac{a}{a_0} = \frac{c_0}{[c(c+2U)]^{1/2}} \tag{3.91}$$

With an opposing current, $U < 0$, it is seen that the amplitude increases and approaches infinity as the velocity $U$ approaches $-c/2$, the limit found above. If the depth is shallow ($h < \lambda/2$), equations (3.87) and (3.90) are still valid, but $c$ and $c_0$ must be obtained from the equation involving $\tanh \kappa h$.

In a more general case, the waves may approach the current at an angle and the current velocity may vary across it. Fig. 3.22 illustrates the case of waves travelling at an angle $\theta_0$ to the $y$ axis meeting a current $U(y)$, the velocity of which varies in the $y$ direction. In this case the waves may be refracted as well as undergo changes in velocity and wavelength. Let $\kappa_0$, $c_0$ and $\theta_0$ be the values of wavenumber, wave velocity and angle to the $y$ axis where $U = 0$ and $\kappa$, $c$ and $\theta$ be the corresponding values where the current has a finite value $U$. Applying the same principles to this case, we have

$$\kappa \sin \theta = \kappa_0 \sin \theta_0 \tag{3.92}$$

$$\kappa (c + U \sin \theta) = \kappa_0 c_0 = \sigma . \tag{3.93}$$

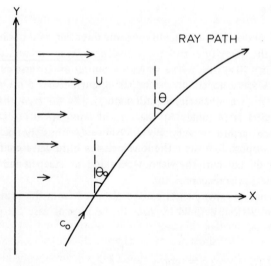

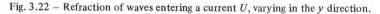

Fig. 3.22 – Refraction of waves entering a current $U$, varying in the $y$ direction.

Assuming that the waves are in deep water, equation (3.88) holds. Then from (3.88), (3.92) and (3.93), it may be shown that

$$\frac{c}{c_0} = \frac{1}{1 - (U/c_0) \sin \theta_0} \tag{3.94}$$

$$\frac{\kappa}{\kappa_0} = [1 - (U/c_0) \sin \theta_0]^2 \tag{3.95}$$

$$\sin \theta = \frac{\sin \theta_0}{[1 - (U/c_0) \sin \theta_0]^2} \tag{3.96}$$

Since $\sin \theta$ cannot exceed unity, there is an upper limit to $U$ for which a solution exists, i.e.

$$\frac{U}{c_0} \leqslant \frac{1 - (\sin \theta_0)^{1/2}}{\sin \theta_0} . \tag{3.97}$$

At this limit $\sin \theta = 1$, so that $\theta = \pi/2$ and the waves are totally reflected by the current.

If the current is in the opposite direction, i.e. $U < 0$, there is no limit on its magnitude but as $U \to -\infty$, $\kappa$ becomes very large and the angle $\theta$ approaches zero. In other words, the wavelength becomes very small and the direction of propagation of the waves is nearly normal to the current.

The change in wave height may be shown to be given by

$$\frac{a}{a_0} = \left(\frac{E}{E_0}\right)^{1/2} = \left(\frac{\sin 2\theta_0}{\sin 2\theta}\right)^{1/2} \tag{3.98}$$

As in the previous case considered, in shallow water the appropriate equation for the wave velocity $c$ must be used in place of (3.88) and equations (3.94) onwards will be modified.

When a spectrum of waves encounters a current, the various components must be considered separately, since the changes depend on the velocity $c_0$ in still water, which is a function of frequency. The waves of shorter wavelength will be affected to a greater extent. If the wave spectrum enters an adverse current, either head-on or obliquely, the shorter waves may reach breaking point producing a very choppy sea. The longer waves, although modified, may be able to pass through the current without breaking so that the wave field emerging on the far side will appear smoother.

### 3.6.5 Dissipation of wave energy

The effect of molecular viscosity on wave motion has been shown to be negligible except for very short waves. In the presence of an oil slick, the effect of viscosity is concentrated in a very thin surface layer and its effect on capillary waves is increased, thus contributing to the calming of the sea surface.

Breaking acts as a dissipating mechanism in both deep and shallow water and influences the form of the wave spectrum, as described in section 3.4.2. When waves leave the generating area and travel as swell through a region of light winds there is very little dissipation of energy. The changes which occur in wave height and the wave spectrum arise from the geometrical spreading of the waves and the different group velocity of various components.

When swell enters shallow water and the wave motion becomes appreciable at the sea bed, bottom friction becomes effective as a dissipating agency. Its effect may be represented by a quadratic law similar to that considered in the cases of tidal currents and storm surges, i.e.

$$\tau_b = k\rho \, |U_b| \, U_b$$

where $U_b$ is the velocity just above the bottom boundary layer and $k$ is a friction coefficient. In the case of waves alone, $U_b$ represents the orbital velocity just above the bed. If the waves are superposed on tidal or other currents, $U_b$ must be taken as the resultant velocity in calculating the rate of dissipation.

In the JONSWAP observations, referred to in section 3.4.3, the energy of swell approaching the line of stations from the west was attenuated by a factor varying between 0.2 and 0.7 and averaging 0.5, over a distance of 160 km. The corresponding friction coefficient, assuming the quadratic law to apply, would average $k = 0.015$. A strong tidal modulation would be expected in the rate of attenuation but this was not observed and there was some doubt whether bottom friction could be regarded as the major dissipating process (Hasselmann *et al.*, 1973).

### 3.6.6 Changes in wave form

It has been shown already that, in applying wave theory, the finite depth of water must be taken into account when it is less than half a wavelength, i.e. $h < \lambda/2$. As the depth becomes shallower the amplitude $a$ of the waves may no longer be small compared with the depth of water. When the depth is less than $\lambda/10$ the Stokes theory becomes unsatisfactory, even with the higher approximations for finite amplitude waves taken into account. An alternative theory of waves of finite height in shallow water was developed by Korteweg and De Vries in 1895. In these waves, known as cnoidal waves, the profile is given in terms of elliptic functions and their properties depend on the ratio $a/h$ as well as the ratio $h/\lambda$. Observations have shown that cnoidal waves are a better representation than Stokes waves when $h < \lambda/10$. The waves have sharp crests and flat troughs which become flatter as the ratio $a/h$ increases.

In very shallow water cnoidal waves approach asymptotically the solution known as a 'solitary wave'. The wave consists essentially of a crest, raised above the still water level, which advances without any preceding or following trough. As the wave passes a fixed point the water level rises and falls and a finite mass of water is displaced in the direction of propagation. The profile of the wave, taking the origin under the crest, is given by

$$\zeta = a \operatorname{sech}^2 \frac{1}{2} \frac{x}{b} \tag{3.99}$$

where $a$ is the elevation of the crest and $b$ is given by

$$b^2 = \frac{h^2 (h + a)}{3a} \tag{3.100}$$

$b$ is a measure of the horizontal extent of the wave, which cannot properly be said to have a wavelength. The velocity of propagation of the crest is given by

$$c = [g(h + a)]^{1/2} \tag{3.101}$$

The basic theory of cnoidal waves and solitary waves was reproduced in the book by Defant (1961, vol. II) and is also discussed by Wood and Fleming (1981).

## 3.7 WAVE BREAKING

In an unbroken wave the forward orbital velocity at a crest is less than the velocity of propagation. If the velocity of a water particle at the crest exceeds the velocity of propagation it will break away from the wave profile. A patch of water thus spills over at the crest, forming a turbulent wake which, if sufficiently intense, will entrain air bubbles and lead to the formation of 'whitecaps' or 'white horses'. The wave does not necessarily collapse as a whole but, having lost energy at its crest, travels on at a lower amplitude.

It has been shown theoretically that Stokes waves of finite amplitude would reach the breaking point when the ratio height/wavelength reached 1/7. The crest would then form a cusp with an angle of 120° between the tangents to the two faces. This is too idealised a picture of how a wave breaks in practice, but it gives a reasonably good estimate of the steepness of a breaking wave. In nature there are two main sets of conditions in which waves break: the first is when wind is blowing over the waves in deep water and the second is when waves arrive at the shore over a sloping bottom.

When wind is blowing over the waves in a generating area, energy is being fed continuously into the waves and the shorter wave components reach their maximum height and break. The effect of this process on the form of the wave spectrum has been described in section 3.4.2. Breaking does not take place uniformly at all crests in the wave field. Transient breaking of larger scale waves occurs when an individual wave crest moves into a region where the energy density is locally high. An example is that of a wave crest moving forward, with its phase velocity, into the centre of a wave group moving with the group velocity. The wave would tend to break at its crest and continue to move towards the front of the group with a decreasing amplitude. The breaking of short waves has been shown to be strongly influenced by the existence of a drift current within a thin surface boundary layer. Where a wide range of wavelengths is present, the conditions often lead to the breaking of short waves on the crests of the longer waves. Waves travelling beyond the generating area may be caused to steepen and break by an opposing wind or by encountering an adverse current, as discussed in section 3.6.4.

When waves enter shallow water over a shoaling bottom their wavelength is reduced and their height is increased, as described in section 3.6, with a resulting increase in steepness. When the waves advance to a depth which is between 1 and 1.5 times their height, they have usually reached the state at which the forward particle velocity at the crest is equal to the wave velocity and they break. The changing shape adopted by a wave as it breaks varies considerably and types of breakers described as 'spilling', 'plunging' or 'surging' have been distinguished. The exact ratio of water depth to wave height at which breaking occurs and the way in which the wave breaks depend on the deep water steepness of the waves and the slope of the beach. The term 'surf' is used collectively to describe the region of breaking waves along a beach and the surging up the beach of the broken water from the waves.

### 3.8   WAVE SET-UP AND ITS EFFECTS

The occurrence of mass transport is one way in which the passage of waves through a region of sea may affect the mean conditions: in that case the mean velocity. There are other ways in which mean properties, such as the mean water level or mean current, can be influenced by waves. One effect, which can be predicted theoretically, is a lowering of mean surface level as a group of high waves passes a given point. This has been observed as the phenomenon of 'surf beats' which has been found on certain wave records. Their period is that of the wave groups, which may be of the order of 2 minutes corresponding, perhaps, to groups having an average of 10 waves of 12 s period.

It may also be shown theoretically and has been observed that a steady train of waves approaching the shore over a sloping bottom gives rise to a lowering of the mean level as the breaker zone is approached. Inshore of the breaker zone the mean level rises steeply as far as the highest point on the beach reached by the waves. This can be attributed to the mass transport of water shorewards by the breaking waves. Assuming that, inshore of the breaking point, the wave amplitude $a$ is proportional to the depth of water $h$, i.e.

$$a = \alpha h$$

where $\alpha$ is a function of the bottom slope and varies between 0.3 and 0.6, then it may be shown that

$$\frac{\partial \overline{\zeta}}{\partial x} = -\frac{3}{2}\alpha^2 \frac{\partial h}{\partial x} \qquad (3.102)$$

where $\overline{\zeta}$ is the mean elevation of the sea surface above its level in the absence of waves.

The increase in mean level produced in this way is known as 'wave set-up'. As a consequence of the surface slope, a return flow seawards is produced having an average velocity $U$ given by

$$U = -\frac{1}{2}\alpha^2 \sqrt{gh} \; . \qquad (3\,103)$$

This seaward flow, against the incoming waves, would be evenly distributed along the beach if the waves and the beach conditions were uniform along it. In practice the return flow tends to be concentrated in narrow seaward flowing currents known as 'rip currents'. Once such a current starts to flow at a particular position, it tends to reduce the wave action at that part of the beach, enabling the rip current to develop further. A rip current is typically only a few tens of metres wide, with a seaward velocity up to 3 m s$^{-1}$ or even 5 m s$^{-1}$ in severe storm conditions, and extending out to sea for several hundred metres. Rip currents are most strongly developed on long, exposed sandy beaches. The currents may be spaced up to several hundred metres apart, drawing in water which flows parallel to the shore in the spaces between them.

When waves approach the shore obliquely, the discharge of broken water on the beach gives rise to a longshore current at the top of the breaker zone, in the direction of the wave component parallel to the shore. The accumulated volume of flow is reduced at intervals by water drawn into the rip currents and carried out to sea. The pattern of longshore currents and rip currents on a beach has an important influence on the movement of beach material and the formation of features such as offshore bars.

A fuller theoretical treatment of the effects of waves in shallow water and on beaches is given by LeBlond and Mysack (1978) while the engineering aspects are dealt with by Wiegel (1954) and by Wood and Fleming (1981). Each of these books gives numerous references to original papers.

# 4

# Wind-driven currents and surges

## 4.1 INTRODUCTION

The most obvious effect of wind stress on the sea is the generation of waves, which has been considered in Chapter 3. As well as the oscillatory wave motion, the wind also produces a steady movement of the surface layer of water in the same general direction as the wind and this movement is communicated to layers below the surface by internal shear stresses. The surface current is of direct relevance to the drift of floating matter such as an oil slick or sewage solids. Below the surface the velocity of the wind-induced current varies with depth, usually decreasing in speed and rotating in direction. The effect of the current on a floating object of several metres draught, such as a drifting buoy or ship, depends on the averaged current to that depth and may differ significantly from that of the surface current itself.

In the proximity of a land barrier, the bodily movement of water will be restricted, leading to a piling-up of water and the development of surface slopes which may extend away from the coast over a wide area of sea. The surface slopes give rise to horizontal pressure gradients in the water and these in turn generate currents which are superimposed on the initial wind drift. The slope-currents may oppose the current driven directly by the wind stress and cause a reversal of current at depth. Thus in the case of a wind blowing towards the head of a gulf, a two-layer flow may develop, with the upper layer moving in the direction of the wind while the lower layer forms a compensating flow in the opposite direction. Near the head of the gulf there would be a sinking of surface water to maintain the continuity of the circulation.

The Coriolis acceleration, arising from the earth's rotation, begins to influence the water as soon as it is set in motion and, except in very restricted areas, it has a significant effect on the resultant motion and distribution of surface slopes. The overall result induced by the wind is thus a distribution of surface elevations superimposed on the normal tides and of currents which, in general, vary in speed and direction with depth as well as from place to place.

The general scheme of this chapter is to start by considering empirical results on the surface currents induced by the wind and some of their effects. A dynamical approach is then adopted, in which the wind stress is included in the equations governing the water movements.

The pioneering work in this field was that due to Ekman, from 1902 onwards, who considered both steady and transient currents in deep water, well away from land, and then extended his work to allow for shallow water and surface slopes due to coastal boundaries. A summary is given of Ekman's results and some modifications which lead to better agreement with observations, particularly in the surface layer.

The latter part of the chapter is devoted to the study of storm surges, in which the emphasis is on the changes of sea level arising from a given distribution of atmospheric pressure and wind stress. As in the case of tides, there is an intimate relation between elevations and currents so that both must be treated together, even if the currents are not of direct practical concern. The basic equations of motion are given and some general results are described. The analysis of sea level data in order to extract the surge from the tide is outlined and examples are given of the types of storm surge which occur in various parts of the world. The forecasting of storm surges is usually done by means of mathematical models and a simplified account is given of the way in which such models are formulated and operated.

## 4.2 SURFACE CURRENT DUE TO THE WIND

An estimate of the movement of the surface water for a given wind speed and direction is required for practical purposes such as forecasting the movement of an oil slick. Many observations of surface drift have been made over the years with drift cards or other objects floating in the top few centimetres of the sea. The results have been expressed in terms of the wind factor, defined as the ratio of surface current to wind speed measured at a standard height, and the deviation of the current direction from the wind direction. The results of individual investigations have varied to some extent but may be summed up by saying that the surface current is approximately in the same direction as the wind and has a speed of approximately 3% of the wind speed measured at a height of 10 m above the sea surface. Some observations have shown the current to deviate a few degrees to the right of the wind in the northern hemisphere and to the left the southern hemisphere, but the deviation has seldom exceeded $10°$. The results of experiments have been confirmed by the observed movements of oil slicks themselves. An analysis of the movement of slicks from the *Torrey Canyon,* which went aground off Lands End, at the south-west extremity of England in March 1967, indicated a wind factor of 3.4%, with the movement in the direction of the wind. More recent data have not led to significantly different results.

The drift of the surface layer of water is made up of two components: a wind-driven current generated by the stress of the wind on the sea surface, which is Eulerian in the sense that it could be measured by a current meter in a fixed position, and the Lagrangian drift due to wave motion, known as the Stokes drift. The Stokes drift occurs because the orbits of the water particles are not closed, with the result that after the passage of each wave there is a net movement of water in the forward direction. For a uniform train of waves of height $H$ and period $T$ in deep water. the surface drift is given by equation (3.40) of Chapter 3, which may be written

$$\bar{u} = \frac{2\pi^3 H^2}{gT^3} .$$
(4.1)

Thus waves with a period $T$ of 5 s and a height $H$ of 3 m would produce a surface drift of about 45 cm s$^{-1}$. When a spectrum of waves is present, the significant wave height $H_s$ and period $T_s$ may be inserted in the equation to estimate the magnitude of the Stokes drift. A more accurate determination can be made by using the properties of the wave spectrum. This was done by Kenyon (1969) who took the empirical wave spectrum of Pierson and Moskowitz (1964) for a fully developed sea. He found that the Stokes drift was about 1.6% of the wind speed and increased linearly with it. In shallow water the rate might be reduced but it seems possible that up to one-third or even a half of the observed surface drift could be attributed to the Stokes drift associated with the waves.

The wind-driven current decreases rapidly with depth below the surface. It is only in recent years that it has been possible to make reliable measurements with current meters within a few metres of the sea surface. Measurements from a surface-following data buoy, moored in a position off the east coast of England, indicated that the current at 3 m depth was about 0.9% of the wind speed (Collar and Vassie, 1978). Later measurements in a more open position, 200 km from the nearest land and in a depth of 170 m, showed a current at 3 m of about 0.75% of the wind speed. The variation of a wind-driven current with depth is considered more fully in section 4.4.2.

The Stokes drift due to a uniform wave train is attenuated below the surface according to the factor $\exp(-4\pi z/\lambda)$ where $z$ is the depth below the surface and $\lambda$ is the wavelength. For $T = 5$ s the wavelength $\lambda$ in deep water would be 39 m and the attenuation factor for $z = 3$ m would be 0.38, so that a drift velocity of 45 cm s$^{-1}$ would be reduced to 17 cm s$^{-1}$ at 3 m. In the case of a fully developed wave spectrum, Kenyon (1969) showed that the rate of attenuation is highly dependent on the wind speed. At a depth of 5 m, the Stokes drift is reduced to 0.05, 0.15 and 0.25 of the surface value for wind speeds of 10, 15 and 20 m s$^{-1}$ respectively.

## 4.3 THE STRESS OF THE WIND ON THE SEA SURFACE

The wind blowing over the sea exerts an effective tangential stress on the surface.

If the processes acting on the wave-covered surface are considered in detail, it is probable that much of the stress is contributed by normal pressures on the deformed sea surface. From the point of view of the wind-driven current, however, we consider the shearing stress in the air above the sea to be communicated to the layer of water below the surface, without considering in detail what happens at the surface itself. A proportion of the wind stress is used directly in generating the surface waves and some of the wave momentum is probably passed on to the drift current by breaking waves. The corresponding stress will be included in the effective tangential stress due to the wind. The wave field also reacts on the stress by determining the effective roughness of the sea surface. These various effects are assumed to have been taken into account in defining the effective tangential stress of the wind on the sea surface, denoted by $\tau_s$.

In specifying the stress $\tau_s$, it is usually assumed that it acts in the direction of the wind relative to the sea surface and that its magnitude is proportional to the square of the wind speed relative to the sea surface. Thus

$$\tau_s = C_D \rho_a W^2 \qquad (4.2)$$

where $W$ is the wind speed measured at a given height, usually taken as 10 m, above the sea surface, $\rho_a$ is the density of the air and $C_D$ is a drag coefficient. The value of $C_D$ depends on (a) the height at which $W$ is measured, (b) the stability of the lowest few metres of the atmosphere and (c) the roughness of the sea surface, as affected by waves. The value of $C_D$ also depends on $W$ itself: in other words the dependence of $\tau_s$ on $W$ is not strictly quadratic.

There is considerable evidence that the velocity profile of the wind in the boundary layer above the sea surface follows the logarithmic law, mentioned in section 2.8.3 in connection with the bottom boundary layer in a tidal current. In the case of the wind, the velocity $W$ at a height $z$ above the surface is given by

$$W = \frac{W_*}{k_0} \log_e \frac{z}{z_0} \qquad (4.3)$$

where $W_*$ is the friction velocity, related to the stress $\tau_s$ by

$$\tau_s = \rho_a W_*^2 \qquad (4.3a)$$

$z_0$ is the roughness length and $k_0$ is von Kármán's constant, usually taken as 0.41. If measurements of the wind speed are made at several heights, $W_*$ and $z_0$ can be calculated. This method has been widely used to determine the wind stress and hence the drag coefficient $C_D$.

From (4.2) and (4.3a), it is seen that

$$W_* = C_D^{1/2} W_{10} \qquad (4.4)$$

where $W_{10}$ is the wind speed measured at a height of 10 m and $C_D$ is the corresponding drag coefficient.

A large number of determinations by various authors of the wind stress over the sea surface, under conditions of neutral stability, was reviewed by Garratt (1977) and Fig. 4.1, showing the drag coefficient $C_{DN}$ under neutral conditions as a function of wind speed $W_{10}$, measured at a height of 10 m, is based on his paper. The points corresponding to the individual determinations and their standard errors, which were given by Garratt, are not reproduced in Fig. 4.1. It is seen that the coefficient $C_{DN}$ increases from approximately $1.1 \times 10^{-3}$ at a wind speed of 5 m s$^{-1}$ to $1.4 \times 10^{-3}$ at 10 m s$^{-1}$ and $2.0 \times 10^{-3}$ at 20 m s$^{-1}$. For higher wind speeds the coefficient increases almost linearly with wind speed and reaches $3.2 \times 10^{-3}$ at a wind speed of 40 m s$^{-1}$.

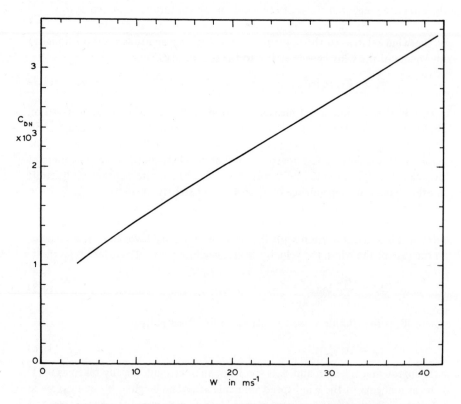

Fig. 4.1 – Drag coefficient $C_{DN}$, in neutral stability, as a function of wind speed.

Table 4.1 gives the value of $C_{DN}$ at a series of values of wind speed $W_{10}$ and the corresponding shear stress $\tau_s$ in N m$^{-2}$ (newtons per square metre). The density of the air $\rho_a$ has been taken as 1.25 kg m$^{-3}$, corresponding to a typical pressure and temperature at sea level.

**Table 4.1** — Drag coefficient and surface stress as a function of wind speed.

| Wind speed $W_{10}$ (m s$^{-1}$) | Drag coefficient $C_{DN} \times 10^3$ | Surface stress $\tau_s$ (N/m$^{-2}$) | Friction velocity $W_*$ (m s$^{-1}$) | Roughness length $z_0$ (mm) |
|---|---|---|---|---|
| 5 | 1.11 | 0.034 | 0.17 | 0.04 |
| 10 | 1.45 | 0.18 | 0.38 | 0.21 |
| 15 | 1.77 | 0.50 | 0.63 | 0.59 |
| 20 | 2.07 | 1.03 | 0.91 | 1.2 |
| 25 | 2.36 | 1.84 | 1.21 | 2.2 |
| 30 | 2.65 | 3.0 | 1.55 | 3.5 |
| 35 | 2.95 | 4.5 | 1.98 | 5.3 |
| 40 | 3.25 | 6.5 | 2.28 | 7.7 |

When the lower layer of the atmosphere is stably stratified the drag coefficient is somewhat reduced but there are few reliable measurements available and it is not possible to give a useful quantitative expression of the effect.

The stress $\tau_s$ on the sea surface is frequently represented by the friction velocity $W_*$, given by

$$\tau_s = \rho_a W_*^2 .$$ (4.3a)

Thus from equation (4.2),

$$W_* = C_{DN}^{1/2} W_{10} .$$ (4.4a)

Another quantity of interest in considering the profile of wind velocity above the surface and also the current profile just below the surface is the roughness length $z_0$. In flow over a solid boundary $z_0$ is related to the geometrical roughness of the surface and it may be expected that over the sea surface it is related in some way to the wave form, although the physical meaning is not clear. In his review of shear stress determinations, Garratt (1977) showed that the relation between $C_{DN}$ and $W_{10}$ was consistent with the following relation between $z_0$ and $W_*$, suggested by Charnock (1955):

$$z_0 = \frac{\alpha_1 W_*^2}{g}$$ (4.5)

where $\alpha_1$ is a constant, found by Garratt to be 0.0144. In Table 4.1 the corresponding values of $W_*$ and $z_0$ are given for a series of values of $W_{10}$.

Several investigators have found evidence that, at a given wind speed $W_{10}$, the roughness length $z_0$ and hence also the drag coefficient $C_{DN}^{\wedge}$ vary with the state of the sea surface and the wave spectrum. In a developing sea, the peak of the spectrum occurs at a higher frequency and the values of $z_0$ and $C_{DN}$ are higher than when the sea has become fully developed, for the same wind speed. Workers with storm surge models have often found it necessary to use higher drag coefficients than those derived from other air—sea interaction experiments. It has been suggested that this is because storm surges are being generated in the early stages of a storm, while the waves are still being developed and have not reached a saturated wave spectrum. Taking this effect into account, the drag coefficient applicable to a developing storm surge might be up to about 50% higher than that given by Fig. 4.1 or Table 4.1.

## 4.4 DYNAMICAL APPROACH

### 4.4.1 Ekman's theory

The important role of the Coriolis effect on wind-driven currents was first pointed out by Nansen and was expressed quantitatively by Ekman in a paper published in 1905. Ekman's theoretical treatment, which in some respects is still valid today, is described in textbooks of dynamical oceanography, such as Pond and Pickard (1978) or Neumann and Pierson (1966), and only a summary of the results will be given here.

### A. *Pure wind drift in homogeneous water*

It is assumed that the wind exerts a shearing stress on the sea surface which is communicated to the water below by turbulent shear stresses. The sea surface is assumed to remain horizontal.

### (a) STEADY STATE SOLUTION

(i) In deep water the wind-driven current is limited to a surface layer, of depth $D$, which is of the order of 10 to 100 m and is small compared with the total depth of water. The total transport of water in a column extending from the surface to depth $D$ is at right angles to the direction of the wind stress: to the right in the northern hemisphere and to the left in the southern hemisphere. The volume transport, per unit length in the direction of the wind, is given by

$$T = \frac{\tau_s}{\rho f} \tag{4.6}$$

where $\tau_s$ is the wind stress per unit area of surface, $\rho$ is the density of the water and $f$ is the Coriolis parameter, $2\,\omega \sin \phi$. Thus the 'Ekman transport', as it is called, depends only on the wind stress and the latitude. It is independent of the depth $D$ or the detailed nature of the turbulent shear stresses in the water.

In order to calculate the variation of velocity with depth, it is necessary to relate the shearing stress to the velocity gradient. If $\tau_x$, $\tau_y$ are the components of shearing stress at depth $z$, they are related to the velocity components $u$, $v$ by

$$\tau_x = \rho\,N_z \frac{\partial u}{\partial z}\,, \quad \tau_y = \rho\,N_z \frac{\partial v}{\partial z}\,. \tag{4.7}$$

If the coefficient of eddy viscosity $N_z$ is assumed to be independent of $z$, an analytical solution can be obtained; the so-called 'Ekman spiral'. According to this solution, the surface current is in a direction $45°$ to the right of the wind, in the northern hemisphere, and the current vector rotates further to the right with increasing depth below the surface. The magnitude of the current vector decreases exponentially with depth. At a depth $z = -D$, where $D$ is given by

$$D = \pi \left( \frac{2 N_z}{f} \right)^{1/2} \tag{4.8}$$

the current is in the opposite direction to the surface current and has a magnitude $u_s \exp(-\pi) = 0.043\, u_s$, where $u_s$ is the surface current. Since the current below this depth is small, the depth $D$ defined as above is described as the 'depth of frictional influence' or 'Ekman depth'.

The surface current $u_s$ is related to the wind stress $\tau_s$ by

$$u_s = \frac{\tau_s}{\rho (fN_z)^{1/2}} = \frac{\sqrt{2\pi}\tau_s}{\rho fD} \tag{4.9}$$

and thus depends on the eddy viscosity.

In fact there is no way of predicting $N_z$ from first principles but a knowledge of the surface current as related to the surface stress enables $N_z$ and hence the Ekman depth $D$ to be estimated. In this way, making use of observations of surface wind-driven currents, determined mainly from their effect on the drift of ships, the following equations for $u_s$ and hence $N_z$ and $D$ in terms of the wind speed $W$ have been derived (Pond and Pickard, 1978):

$$u_s = \frac{0.0127 W}{(\sin \phi)^{1/2}} \tag{4.10}$$

for $\phi$ greater than $10°$ from the equator and $W > 6\ \text{m s}^{-1}$

$$D = \frac{4.3 W}{(\sin \phi)^{1/2}} \text{ in } m \text{ if } W \text{ in m s}^{-1} \tag{4.11}$$

$$N_z = 1.37 W^2 \quad \text{in cm}^2\,\text{s}^{-1} \text{ if } W \text{ in m s}^{-1}. \tag{4.12}$$

(ii) In shallow water the current is assumed to be zero at the bottom, i.e. $u = v = 0$ at $z = -h$ where $h$ is the depth of water. This leads to a distorted Ekman spiral, the character of which depends on the value of $h/D$. In general the surface current deviates from the wind direction by an angle smaller than the $45°$ applicable in deep water. In very shallow water, if $h/D$ is of order 0.1, the surface current is almost in the direction of the wind and the variation of direction with depth is small.

## (b) TRANSIENT STATE

If a wind stress is applied suddenly to water previously at rest and is then maintained at a constant value, the surface current flows initially in the direction of the wind and is confined to a very shallow layer. As time goes on the surface current vector turns to the right (in the northern hemisphere) and the current extends to greater depth. The steady state, represented by the Ekman spiral, is approached in a time of the order of a pendulum day, given by $2\pi/\omega \sin \phi$, which is equal to a sidereal day divided by the sine of the latitude. This is approximately 24 hours at the poles, 27.7 hours at latitude 60°, 48 hours at latitude 30° and becomes very large near the equator.

### B. *Pure slope currents in homogeneous water*

Surface slopes can arise from the piling up of water, by wind stress or varying atmospheric pressure, at a coastal boundary. They can also arise, even in an unbounded sea, by a non-uniform wind field so that the Ekman transport forms a convergence or divergence with a corresponding rise or fall in sea level. A surface slope produces a horizontal pressure gradient which, in homogeneous water, is uniform with depth. This sets up a current which, in the steady state and in the absence of friction, is in geostrophic balance and is at right angles to the gradient. In the northern hemisphere a geostrophic current flows with the surface rising to the right of it and in the southern hemisphere to the left.

If the sea surface has an elevation $\zeta$ above a reference level, then the components of slope in the $x$ and $y$ directions respectively will be $\partial\zeta/\partial x$ and $\partial\zeta/\partial y$ and the components $u$, $v$ of geostrophic current will be given by

$$u = -\frac{g}{f}\frac{\partial\zeta}{\partial y}, \qquad v = \frac{g}{f}\frac{\partial\zeta}{\partial x}. \tag{4.13}$$

In the presence of friction an inverted Ekman spiral in a bottom layer is superimposed on the geostrophic flow so as to make the resultant current zero at the bottom. In shallow water the bottom Ekman depth, associated with the inverted spiral, may be greater than the depth of water and the whole water column will then be affected by friction. The current, even at the surface, will no longer flow at right angles to the gradient but will have a down-slope component.

### C. *Wind drift combined with slope currents*

### (a) STEADY STATE

The two horizontal components of velocity, $u$ and $v$, may be expressed as

$$u = u_1 + u_2 + u_3, \qquad v = v_1 + v_2 + v_3 .$$

where     $u_1, v_1$ represent the surface Ekman spiral,

               $u_2, v_2$ represent the geostrophic slope current

and       $u_3, v_3$ represent the bottom Ekman spiral.

If the flow is bounded by a straight coast and the $y$-axis is taken parallel to the coast, then

$$\int_0^{-h} u \, dz = 0$$

perpendicular to the coast.

For a given wind stress and prescribed bottom conditions, the above condition determines the slope of the sea surface.

### (b) TRANSIENT STATE
For a wind stress which is suddenly applied and then maintained constant, the current in the surface layer builds up in a time of the order of a pendulum day. The slope builds up more slowly, at a rate depending on the depth of water and the width of the zone affected and it may take a number of days for the steady state to be approached.

### D. *Non-homogeneous water*
The above features are modified if the water is stably stratified, as it is in a number of coastal areas, particularly in the summer months. In the first place the vertical eddy viscosity is reduced and the surface Ekman spiral is confined to a shallower depth. The total transport remains the same so the speed of the surface layer current may be expected to increase. In the second place, the horizontal pressure gradient associated with a surface slope is no longer independent of depth and the corresponding geostrophic flow may vary with depth. The flow need not, in fact, extend to the bottom and in that case the bottom Ekman spiral will not occur.

### 4.4.2 Modifications to Ekman's theory
Ekman's result for the total transport in a wind-driven surface layer which does not extend to the bottom, given by equation (4.6), is universally valid as it is independent of the value of eddy viscosity. The details of the variation of current with depth, the Ekman spiral, depend on the eddy viscosity being constant with depth and they are modified if the eddy viscosity varies with depth. There is evidence from measurements of flow near a solid boundary and from the distribution of wind velocity in the atmospheric boundary layer, above either a land or sea surface, that the effective eddy viscosity is very small near the boundary and increases linearly with distance from it. Thus, if $z$ is distance from the boundary, one may take

$$N_z = k_0 u_* z \tag{4.14}$$

where $u_*$ is the friction velocity given by

$$u_* = (\tau_s/\rho)^{1/2} \tag{4.15}$$

and $k_0$ is von Kármán's constant, numerically equal to 0.41.

In the case of the atmospheric boundary layer above the sea surface, $\rho$ is replaced by $\rho_a$, the density of the air, and $u_*$ becomes $W_*$, the friction velocity of the wind. We are now concerned with conditions in the water boundary layer below the surface, so that $\rho$ is taken as the density of the water and $u_*$ is the friction velocity in the water. Assuming that the stress $\tau_s$ is the same on both sides of the interface,

$$u_* = (\rho_a/\rho)^{1/2} W_*$$

and if $\rho_a = 1.25$ kg m$^{-3}$ and $\rho = 1025$ kg m$^{-3}$, then $u_* = 0.035 \, W_*$.

When the Coriolis effect can be neglected, the above expression for $N_z$ is consistent with the logarithmic velocity profile within the constant stress layer, i.e. the layer adjacent to the boundary within which the stress does not change appreciably with distance. In this case the equation of steady motion in the layer immediately below the sea surface, measuring $z$ downwards, may be written

For $z > 0$,

$$\tau_s = -\rho \, N_z \frac{\partial u}{\partial z} . \tag{4.16}$$

Thus

$$\rho u_*^2 = -\rho \, k_c u_* z \frac{\partial u}{\partial z}$$

$$\frac{\partial u}{\partial z} = -\frac{u_*}{k_0 z}$$

Hence

$$u = -\frac{u_*}{k_0} \ln z + \text{const.}$$

If we apply the boundary condition that $u = u_s$ at $z = z_0$, then

$$u = u_s - \frac{u_*}{k_0} \ln \frac{z}{z_0} . \tag{4.17}$$

In this equation, $z_0$ is the 'roughness length' characteristic of the sea surface in the conditions under consideration.

In general, however, the Coriolis effects can not be neglected when considering wind-driven currents and the problem is to solve the equations of motion, including the Coriolis terms, with an eddy viscosity given by equation (4.14) in the vicinity of the surface, although it may approach a constant value at greater depths. Several researchers have tackled this problem and we will refer, in particular, to the treatment of Madsen (1977). His solution for the wind-driven current in deep water showed that the surface current vector deviated from the wind by only about $10°$, instead of $45°$ as in Ekman's theory, and decreased in magnitude more rapidly with depth.

Figure 4.2, taken from Madsen's paper, shows the current vector and its variation with depth, as determined above, and the Ekman solution for comparison. If $u_s$ is the magnitude of the surface current vector, Madsen showed that

$$u_s = 25\, u_* \text{ approximately}$$

although the factor of proportionality varied to some extent with the wind speed $W_{10}$ and the roughness length $z_0$.

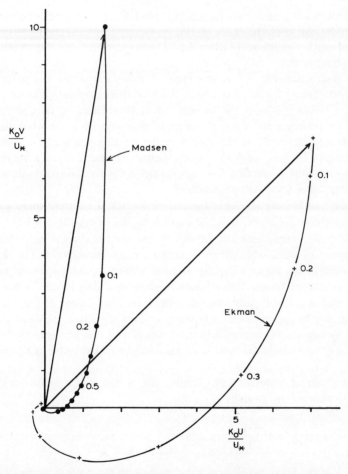

Fig. 4.2 – Variation of current with depth in a wind-driven current in deep water. Madsen's solution is compared with the classical Ekman spiral. The numbers marked on the curves are values of $(z/D)^{1/2}$, where $D$ is the Ekman depth. From Madsen (1977), by courtesy of the American Meteorological Society.

The scale length $L_E$ representing the thickness of an Ekman layer, as given by Madsen and other workers, is;

$$L_E = 0.4 \frac{u_*}{f} \qquad (4.18)$$

where $f$ is the Coriolis parameter. With $u_* = 0.035 W_*$ and $f = 1.458 \times 10^{-4} \sin \phi \, s^{-1}$.

$$L_E = 96 \frac{W_*}{\sin \phi} . \qquad (4.19)$$

From Table 4.1 it is seen that for a wind speed $W_{10}$ of the order of 15 m s$^{-1}$ in mid-latitudes, $L_E$ is of the order of 100 m. Equations (4.18) and (4.19) may be compared with equations (4.8) and (4.11) respectively for the depth $D$ in Ekman's treatment.

In constructing Fig. 4.2 it was assumed that $L_E = D$ for the purposes of comparison. Taking $L_E$ or $D$ as 100 m, it is seen from the figure that, at a depth of 1 m, in Madsen's result the current would be reduced to only about one-third of its surface value while the angle of deviation from the wind direction would increase from 9° to 25°. At 4 m the corresponding figures would be approximately 0.27 $u_s$ and 35°. These figures represent a much more rapid change with depth in the first few metres than in the Ekman spiral solution and are in better agreement with observations.

In the first few metres below the surface, in fact, the current speed given by Madsen's solution follows closely the logarithmic law of equation (4.17).

Madsen also considered the growth of the surface current produced by a sudden onset of wind which then remained steady. As shown in Fig. 4.3, the surface drift builds up very rapidly and has almost reached a steady state in about 3 pendulum hours. This is much more rapidly than in the Ekman spiral solution with a uniform eddy viscosity, which required a time of the order of a pendulum day to approach a steady state. Below the surface, in Madsen's solution, the steady state is approached more slowly and it is probable that for the Ekman layer as a whole the time scale may still be of the order of a pendulum day.

In the case of water of finite depth, one would expect a bottom Ekman layer of thickness $L_{EB}$, given by

$$L_{EB} = 0.4 \frac{u_{*B}}{f} \qquad (4.20)$$

where $u_{*B}$ is the friction velocity corresponding to the bottom stress. Near the bottom the eddy viscosity would be given by

$$N_z = k_0 u_{*B} z_B \qquad (4.21)$$

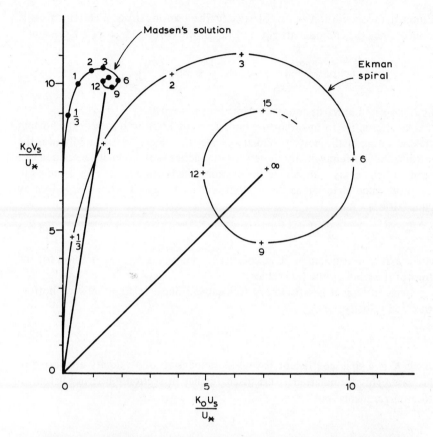

Fig. 4.3 — Development of a surface drift current with time. Madsen's solution is compared with the Ekman spiral solution. The figures represent time in pendulum hours after the application of a steady wind stress. From Madsen (1977), by courtesy of the American Meteorological Society.

where $z_B$ is measured upwards from the bottom, and the magnitude of the velocity would follow the logarithmic law. If the total depth $h$ were large compared with $L_E + L_{EB}$, distinct surface and bottom Ekman layers would occur, separated by a mid-depth layer of frictionless geostrophic flow. If the water were shallower so that $h$ was comparable with, or less than $L_E + L_{EB}$, the two Ekman layers would overlap. Madsen indicated the method of solution in this case but did not give any results.

### 4.4.3 Bottom boundary conditions
In Ekman's treatment of currents in shallow water he assumed a 'no slip' boundary condition at the bottom, i.e. at the bottom

$$u_b = v_b = 0 \ .$$

Although this condition does not specify the bottom stress, a certain stress is implied, since the components $\tau_{bx}$ and $\tau_{by}$ of the bottom stress $\tau_b$ are given by

$$\tau_{bx} = \rho N_z \left(\frac{\partial u}{\partial z}\right)_{z=-h} , \qquad \tau_{by} = \rho N_z \left(\frac{\partial v}{\partial z}\right)_{z=-h}$$

if $z$ is measured upwards and the bottom is at $z = -h$.

An alternative form of bottom boundary condition is to specify the bottom stress in terms of the bottom velocity. Since the velocity varies rapidly near the bottom, the 'bottom velocity' is defined in practice as the velocity measured at a standard height, say 1 m, above the bottom. The bottom stress $\tau_b$ is assumed to act in the same direction as the bottom velocity $U_b$ and is often related to it by a quadratic law, i.e.

$$\tau_b = k\rho |U_b| U_b \tag{4.22}$$

where $k$ is a dimensionless drag coefficient analogous to that defined for the stress of the wind on the sea surface.

In some cases it is satisfactory to assume a linear relation between bottom stress and velocity, i.e.

$$\tau_b = K\rho U_b \tag{4.23}$$

where $K$ is a drag coefficient having the dimension of a velocity applicable to this case. This formulation is discussed further in section 4.6.2, in relation to storm surge calculations.


## 4.5 STORM SURGES

### 4.5.1 Definition

A storm surge is defined as a disturbance of sea level, relative to that due to tides alone, produced by meteorological causes. The height of surge is given by:

Surge height = recorded level − tidally predicted level.

A surge may be either positive or negative, i.e. the actual sea level may be either higher or lower than that expected from tidal predictions. The time scale of a storm surge may range from a few hours to several days. A surge of several days' duration could be identified by subjecting the sea level data to a low-pass numerical filter which would eliminate oscillations of frequencies within the diurnal, semidiurnal and higher harmonic tidal bands. This procedure, however, would eliminate surge components on a time scale of less than a day, including changes in the amplitude and phase of the tidal constituents which can arise from interactions between surge and tide. The alternative is to subtract the predicted tide from the recorded levels directly.

### 4.5.2  Basic dynamical equations
The equations governing the dynamics of storm surges are similar to those given in section 2.3.1 for tides, including the frictional terms arising from shear stresses across horizontal planes. Taking the same rectangular coordinate system with the $z$-axis directed vertically upwards and retaining the horizontal gradients of atmospheric pressure $p_a$, these equations are

$$\frac{Du}{Dt} - fv = -\frac{1}{\rho}\frac{\partial p_a}{\partial x} - g\frac{\partial}{\partial x}(\zeta - \bar\zeta) + \frac{1}{\rho}\frac{\partial \tau_x}{\partial z} \qquad (4.24)$$

$$\frac{Dv}{Dt} + fu = -\frac{1}{\rho}\frac{\partial p_a}{\partial y} - g\frac{\partial}{\partial y}(\zeta - \bar\zeta) + \frac{1}{\rho}\frac{\partial \tau_y}{\partial z} \qquad (4.25)$$

for momentum in the $x$ and $y$ directions, with the continuity equation

$$\frac{\partial u}{\partial x} + \frac{\partial v}{\partial y} + \frac{\partial w}{\partial z} = 0 \; . \qquad (4.26)$$

By integrating through a vertical column from the bottom $z = -h$ to the surface $z = \zeta$ and defining the components $U$, $V$ of the volume transport by

$$U = \int_{-h}^{\zeta} u \, dz \qquad V = \int_{-h}^{\zeta} v \, dz \qquad (4.27)$$

the depth-integrated equations may be written as

$$\frac{\partial U}{\partial t} + \frac{\partial}{\partial x}\left(\frac{U^2}{h + \zeta}\right) + \frac{\partial}{\partial y}\left(\frac{UV}{h + \zeta}\right) - fV = -\frac{(h + \zeta)}{\rho}\frac{\partial p_a}{\partial x} - $$

$$g\,(h + \zeta)\frac{\partial}{\partial x}(\zeta - \bar\zeta) + \frac{\tau_{sx} - \tau_{bx}}{\rho} \; . \qquad (4.28)$$

$$\frac{\partial V}{\partial t} + \frac{\partial}{\partial x}\left(\frac{UV}{h + \zeta}\right) + \frac{\partial}{\partial y}\left(\frac{V^2}{h + \zeta}\right) + fU = -\frac{(h + \zeta)}{\rho}\frac{\partial p_a}{\partial x} - $$

$$g\,(h + \zeta)\frac{\partial}{\partial y}(\zeta - \bar\zeta) + \frac{\tau_{sy} - \tau_{by}}{\rho} \qquad (4.29)$$

$$\frac{\partial U}{\partial x} + \frac{\partial V}{\partial y} + \frac{\partial \zeta}{\partial t} = 0 \; . \qquad (4.30)$$

In these equations the elevation $\zeta$, the velocity components $u$, $v$ and the transport components $U$, $V$ refer to the resultant values due to the tidal constituents and the meteorological effects. In coastal waters of limited extent the direct effects of the tide-generating potential, represented by $\bar\zeta$, can often be neglected. The tangential shearing stress of the wind on the sea surface is represented by the components $\tau_{sx}$ and $\tau_{sy}$ while $\tau_{bx}$ and $\tau_{by}$ represent the components of stress at the bottom.

### 4.5.3 Steady state solutions for a narrow channel

The special case of a narrow channel with sides parallel to the $x$-axis is considered first, so that it is assumed that $V = 0$ and that the variation of $\zeta$ across the channel is small compared with the variation along it. To get an idea of the elevations to be expected, we will consider the effects of atmospheric pressure and wind stress separately.

(a) *Atmospheric pressure effect only*
Neglecting the acceleration terms, the $\bar{\zeta}$ term and the $\tau_{sx} - \tau_{bx}$ term, equation (4.28) reduces to

$$\frac{\partial \zeta}{\partial x} = -\frac{1}{g\rho}\frac{\partial p_a}{\partial x} . \tag{4.31}$$

If $\Delta\zeta$ and $\Delta p_a$ represent changes over a finite horizontal distance $\Delta x$, this gives

$$\Delta\zeta = -\frac{1}{g\rho}\Delta p_a . \tag{4.32}$$

Thus an increase in atmospheric pressure is accompanied by a decrease in sea level. This is the 'inverted barometer effect'. If atmospheric pressure is expressed in millibars then it is seen that a 1 mb fall in pressure corresponds to about 1 cm rise in sea level.

This result is often generalised to apply to a larger area of sea, over which it is assumed that the average pressure and sea level remain constant. If an atmospheric disturbance, such as a depression, occurs over a part of this area, then equation (4.32) should also apply to the change in sea level $\Delta\zeta$ due to a change in atmospheric pressure $\Delta p_a$ with time. It is assumed here that the change occurs sufficiently slowly for a steady state to be achieved. In the case of a fast moving disturbance this will not be the case and the inverted barometer law is only a rough guide.

(b) *Wind stress effect only*
In this case equation (4.28) reduces to

$$\frac{\partial \zeta}{\partial x} = \frac{\tau_{sx} - \tau_{bx}}{g\rho\,(h + \zeta)} . \tag{4.33}$$

For a channel closed at one end, such as a gulf, the longitudinal transport $U = 0$ in the steady state. In the case of a wind blowing towards the head of the gulf, as in Fig. 4.4, there will still be a surface flow in the direction of the wind

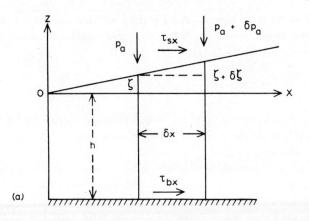

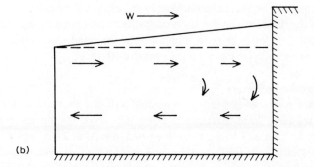

Fig. 4.4 — Storm surge in a gulf: (a) surface slope related to wind stress and atmospheric pressure; (b) pattern of currents.

with a compensatory flow in the lower layer and sinking of water near the head. It may be shown that in these conditions the bottom stress lies between zero and $-\tau_{sx}/2$, so that equation (4.33) may be written

$$\frac{\partial \zeta}{\partial x} = C \frac{\tau_{sx}}{g\rho\,(h + \zeta)} \tag{4.34}$$

where $1 < C < 1.5$. In practice, $C$ is likely to be nearer 1 than 1.5.

If the elevation $\zeta$ remains small compared with the mean depth of water $h$, equation (4.34) is simplified to

$$\frac{\partial \zeta}{\partial x} = C \frac{\tau_{sx}}{g\rho h}\,. \tag{4.35}$$

For a wind of 20 m s$^{-1}$ it is shown in section 4.3 that the stress $\tau_s$ would be of the order of 1 N m$^{-2}$. For a depth $h = 50$ m and taking $g = 9.8$ m s$^{-2}$, $\rho = 1025$ kg m$^{-3}$, $C = 1$, equation (4.35) gives

$$\frac{\partial \zeta}{\partial x} = 2.0 \times 10^{-6} \text{ approximately} .$$

Thus over a distance of 500 km, the level would rise by 1 m. The slope is inversely proportional to the depth of water so that it would be correspondingly greater in shallower water.

Although equation (4.35) was derived for the special case of a wind blowing along a narrow gulf, it can provide a useful indication of the elevation to be expected at a coast due to a steady wind of a given strength. It has been found to apply in the North Sea, for example, to the surge elevation observed at the southern end at the peak of a surge due to northerly winds, when the acceleration terms in equations (4.28) and (4.29) become small.

A comparison of the elevation due to the shearing stress of the wind with that due to the direct atmospheric pressure effect, estimated by equation (4.32), indicates that for depressions in mid-latitudes the wind stress effect is usually an order of magnitude greater than the pressure effect.

### 4.5.4 Propagation of surges
A disturbance of sea level which is generated within a localised area of sea will tend to travel away from that area as a free long wave. On the continental shelf this is likely to be a Kelvin wave, as described in section 2.3.5, which will travel with the velocity $c = (gh)^{1/2}$. A moving meteorological system will produce forced waves and resonance may occur, giving an increased amplitude of surge, if the speed of travel of the system approximates to the free wave velocity. Usually the speed of travel of meteorological systems is of the order of $10 - 15$ m s$^{-1}$ and is slower than the Kelvin wave velocity, as indicated in Table 4.2, except in very shallow water. Surges generated in deep water at the edge of a continental shelf may thus travel across the shelf and affect sea level at the coast in advance of the arrival of the system, assuming that their propagation is similar to that of a Kelvin wave.

Table 4.2 — Velocity of Kelvin waves.

| Depth (m) | 10 | 20 | 40 | 60 | 80 | 100 | 200 |
|---|---|---|---|---|---|---|---|
| Velocity (m s$^{-1}$) | 9.9 | 14.0 | 19.8 | 24.2 | 28.0 | 31.3 | 44.3 |

### 4.5.5 Occurrence of storm surges
From the dynamical principles discussed above, storm surges may be expected to occur along coasts bounding areas of shallow water which are affected by the

passage of storms. This is indeed the case as is shown by the areas where storm surges, sometimes having disastrous effects, are experienced. In North America surges are of frequent occurrence in the Gulf of Mexico and along the east coast of USA, in both cases associated with the passage of hurricanes. On the opposite side of the North Atlantic, surges occur in the North Sea and the Baltic Sea. The Pacific coasts of Japan and other countries of eastern Asia are affected by surges produced by the passage of typhoons. In the Indian Ocean the Bay of Bengal is particularly seriously affected and disastrous flooding has occurred on a number of occasions: in 1970 a surge 7 m high, driven inland by a cyclone, caused the deaths of more than 300,000 people. Surges of considerable magnitude can also be generated in large inland bodies of water and have occurred in Lake Okeechobee, Florida, Lake Erie and Lake Michigan.

As an example of a hurricane surge on the east coast of USA, Fig. 4.5(a) shows the track of hurricane 'Carol' on 29–31 August, 1954. The track ran parallel to the coast, passing close to Cape Hatteras at 22.00 hr on 30 August, until it passed over the eastern end of Long Island and crossed the coast of Connecticut at New London at about 09.00 on 31 August. Surge heights, extracted from tide gauge records at a number of locations, are shown plotted against time in Fig. 4.5(b). A noteworthy feature at Atlantic City and Sandy Hook is the gradual rise in sea level before the arrival of the storm followed by an oscillatory response after the passage of its centre. At Montauk, Long Island, there was a single sharp peak reaching 7 ft (2.1 m), while at Woods Hole, Massachusetts, the level rose to 8 ft (2.4 m) above its predicted value before the tide gauge was put out of action. This example is one of a number of surges described by Redfield and Miller (1957).

The surge produced by a hurricane in the Gulf of Mexico on 26–28 June 1957 is illustrated in Fig. 4.6, taken from Neumann and Pierson (1966, page 372). The centre crossed the coast about a third of the distance between Galveston and Eugene Islands at 08.00 hr on 27 June. The surge level curves for Freeport and Galveston show that the rise of level before the arrival of the centre of the hurricane, when the wind was blowing towards the coast, was followed by a fall to below the predicted value when the wind turned to blow away from the coast in the rear of the storm. This feature did not appear in the curve for Eugene Islands, to the right of the track of the hurricane where the wind continued to blow towards the shore.

The North Sea storm surge for 31 January–1 February, 1953, which caused serious flooding and loss of life in the Netherlands and eastern England is illustrated in Figs. 4.7 and 4.8, taken from Heaps (1967). Figure 4.7 shows the weather chart for 06 hr on 1 February 1953 with the track of the depression during the previous 48 hours superimposed. The principal cause of the surge was the deep depression which travelled eastwards to the north of the British Isles and then south-eastwards into the North Sea. The northerly winds to the west of the depression were accentuated by the developing ridge of high pressure

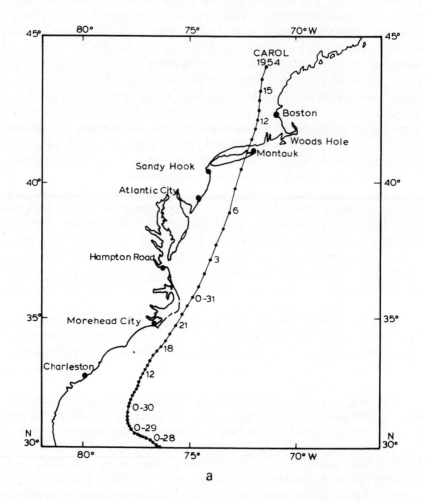

a

Fig. 4.5 – Hurricane 'Carol' off the east coast of USA in August 1954. (a) Track of the hurricane: hourly positions of the storm centre are marked. (b) Surge levels in feet recorded by tide gauges at the positions marked in (a). The arrows denote the time of nearest approach of the centre, with the distance in nautical miles and direction of the tide gauge from the storm track. From Redfield and Miller (1957), by courtesy of the American Meteorological Society.

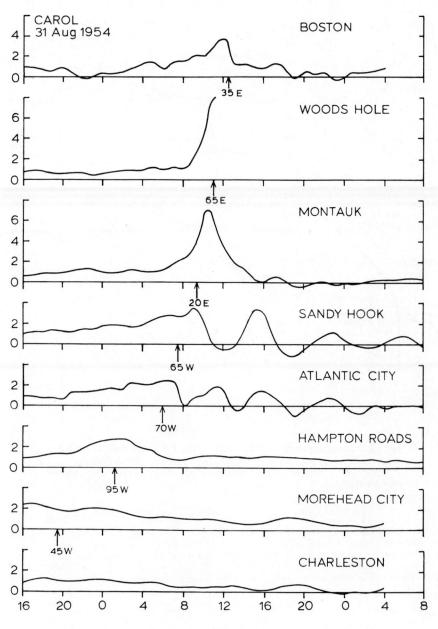

b

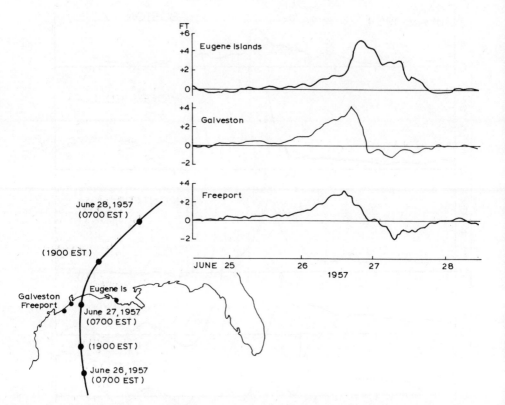

Fig. 4.6 – Hurricane in the Gulf of Mexico, June 1957. The track of the hurricane is shown in the lower part of the figure. The upper part shows the surge recorded at three coastal positions. From Neumann and Pierson (1966), by courtesy of Prentice-Hall, Inc.

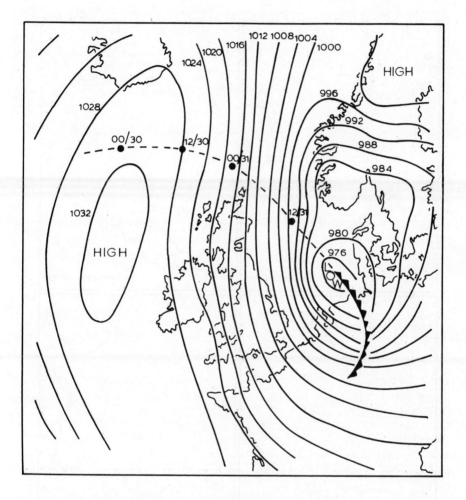

Fig. 4.7 – North Sea surge, 1953: weather chart for 1 February 1953 showing track of the depression. From Heaps (1967), by courtesy of George Allen & Unwin.

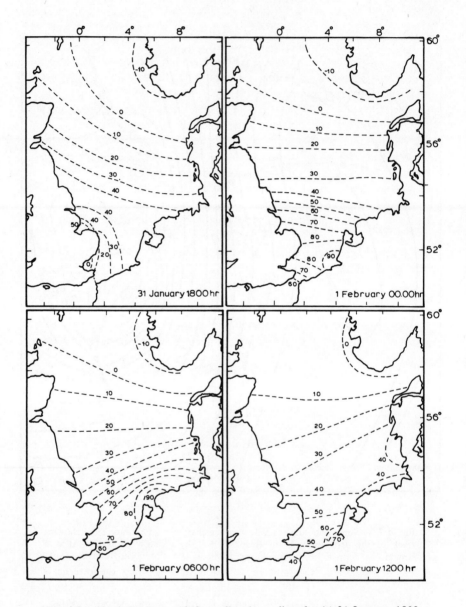

Fig. 4.8 – North Sea surge, 1953: co-disturbance lines for (a) 31 January, 1800 hr, (b) 1 February, 0000 hr, (c) 1 February, 0600 hr, (d) 1 February, 1200 hr. From Heaps (1967), by courtesy of George Allen & Unwin.

further to the west. The water levels are illustrated, in this case, by the charts of co-disturbance lines shown in Fig. 4.8 for four times at 6-hour intervals. The co-disturbance lines, in units of 0.1 ft (3 mm), are based on the surge heights extracted from tide gauge records at ports around the North Sea, but their actual course across the open sea is largely conjectural. The maximum surge travelled around the southern part of the North Sea in a counter-clockwise direction, the highest elevations on the east coast of England occurring at about 00 hr on 1 February while the peak of the surge reached the Netherlands coast about 06 hr on the same day. The surge then travelled northwards along the west coast of Denmark.

Many similar analysis of storm surges have been carried out for various areas and used in studies of such aspects as the mode of generation by atmospheric pressure and wind stress, the propagation of a surge as a progressive wave and the generation of resonant oscillations characteristic of the sea areas concerned. The sets of data obtained in these studies have played an essential role in the development of numerical methods of forecasting, as described in the following section.

## 4.6 METHODS OF FORECASTING STORM SURGES
### 4.6.1 Empirical and mathematical methods
Two stages are involved in forecasting the occurrence and magnitude of a storm surge:

(1) Knowing or forecasting the pressure and wind fields over the sea;
(2) Forecasting their effect on the elevation of sea level and possibly on currents.

The first is a meteorological problem which will not be considered further here. In the second stage the first step is to convert the data on wind speed and direction to the distribution of shearing stress on the sea surface. The physical processes involved in the response of the sea to the atmospheric pressure and shear stress fields are known and the dynamics are expressed in the equations already given. There are a number of constants or coefficients which are not known from first principles, however, and have to be determined empirically or derived in some other way. These include the drag coefficients relating to surface and bottom stress and the method of specifying the internal shear stresses, which usually involves a coefficient of effective eddy viscosity. Analytical solution to the equations may be found in some relatively simple cases and these are useful in bringing out basic features. More complex cases, involving the actual geometry of a sea area and stress distributions varying in space and time, have to be treated numerically. An indication of the methods of solution employed is given in section 4.6.3.

Storm surge warning services involving forecasting in real time have been set up in a few cases and use the principles described above. In other cases a real-time forecasting service for a particular sea area is not attempted but a knowledge of what surges would occur in various meteorological conditions is required. A suitable model may be developed, using the same principles, and tested by 'hindcasting', i.e. calculating the response of the sea to a set of meteorological conditions which occurred in the past and comparing the model results with actual observations for the same period.

(a) *Empirical methods*

Prior to the development of numerical models, empirical methods were devised for forecasting the surge level at a particular coastal location by correlating it with meteorological conditions over an area of sea. As an example, a formula was obtained for the surge height at Southend, at the mouth of the Thames estuary, in terms of northerly and easterly pressure gradients over the North Sea (Heaps, 1967). A term was added representing the surge observed nine hours earlier at Dunbar, on the east coast of Scotland. This term was to allow for the effect of an external surge, if present, generated outside the North Sea which is known to travel southwards along the east coast of Great Britain at a rate equivalent to that of a Kelvin wave. In a formula of this type the coefficients of the correlation terms are derived from an analysis of previous observations and are not related explicitly to the physical processes involved.

(b) *Mathematical methods*

The methods of studying or forecasting storm surges now in use usually employ a suitable model to which the basic equations given above may be applied. The model may be two-dimensional, using the depth-integrated equations, or three-dimensional retaining the variation of velocity with depth. Two-dimensional models may be classified as linearised, involving several approximations, or non-linear using the full equations. Linearised models have the advantage that the tidal and surge components may be treated separately and then added linearly to give the resultant elevations and currents. It is also possible to calculate the response of the sea to different types of meteorological disturbance and then form a linear combination of the effects. In many cases the linearised models give an adequate representation of conditions but this is not always the case. In shallow water areas, where the tidal amplitude or surge height is not small compared with the depth of water and bottom friction effects are considerable, there is a significant interaction between tide and surge and misleading results may be obtained unless the non-linear terms are retained.

### 4.6.2 Linearised equations for depth-integrated flow

The equations (4.28) and (4.29) for depth-integrated flow may be linearised if it is assumed that

    (1) the elevation $\zeta$ remains small compared with the undisturbed depth of water $h$,

(2) the convective acceleration terms are negligible compared with the $\partial U/\partial t$, $\partial V/\partial t$ terms;

(3) the components of bottom stress can be linearly related to the components of integrated transport $U$ and $V$.

As discussed earlier, the bottom stress $\tau_b$ may be related to the resultant bottom current $U_b$ by the quadratic law

$$\tau_b = k\rho \,|U_b|\,U_b$$

as in equation (4.22), where $k$ is a drag coefficient and $U_b$ is measured at a standard height, usually taken as 1 m, above the bottom. If $U_b$ has components $u_b, v_b$ in the $x$ and $y$ directiosn respectively, then

$$U_b^2 = u_b^2 + v_b^2$$

and $\qquad \tau_{bx} = k\rho\,|U_b|\,u_b \;, \qquad \tau_{by} = k\rho\,|U_b|\,v_b \;.$ $\qquad\qquad$ (4.36)

Linearising the bottom stress in the depth-integrated equations involves replacing equation (4.36) by

$$\tau_{bx} = \lambda\rho U \;, \qquad \tau_{by} = \lambda\rho V \qquad\qquad (4.37)$$

where $\lambda$ is a coefficient having the dimensions of velocity.

The linearisation may be justified in a simple way if the tidal currents are strong, and the surge current may be regarded as a small perturbation (Bowden, 1953). If, for example, one may represent the current by

$$U_b = U_0 + C_b \cos \sigma t$$

where $U_0$ is a steady component and $C_b$ is the amplitude of a tidal constituent of angular frequency $\sigma$, then it may be shown that

$$|U_b|\,U_b = a_0 + a_1 \cos \sigma t + a_2 \cos 2\sigma t + \ldots$$

where, if $C_b \gg U_0$,

$$a_0 \approx \frac{4}{\pi} C_b U_0 \;, \qquad a_1 \approx \frac{8}{3\pi} C_b^2 \;.$$

Then $\qquad \tau_b = K_0' \rho U_0 + K_1' \rho C_b \cos \sigma t$, approximately

where $\qquad K_0' = \dfrac{4}{\pi} k C_b$ and $K_1' = \dfrac{8}{3\pi} k C_b \;.$

In this equation the bottom stress is still expressed in terms of the bottom velocity constituents. In order to relate it to the depth-mean velocity it is necessary to assume a constant ratio of bottom velocity to depth-mean velocity. This is a reasonable approximation for the tidal constituent but is more difficult to justify for the surge constituent since, in some cases, the bottom flow may be in the opposite direction to the surface flow. This assumption is necessary, however, in order to justify linearisation and in that case we may take

$$\tau_{bx} = K\rho\bar{u} \, , \quad \tau_{by} = K\rho\bar{v}$$

for the bottom stress associated with the surge current, where

$$K = A\,k\,\bar{C}$$

$\bar{C}$ is the depth-mean amplitude of the tidal current and $A$ is a factor of order unity which allows for the ratio of bottom velocity to depth-mean velocity and includes the factor $4/\pi$. As a numerical example, if $k = 2.5 \times 10^{-3}$ and $\bar{C} = 1$ m s$^{-1}$ then $K \approx 0.25$ cm s$^{-1}$.

The linearised equations are derived from equations (4.28), (4.29) and (4.30) by

(1) neglecting $\zeta$ relative to $h$;
(2) neglecting the second-order acceleration terms;
(3) setting $\tau_{bx} = \lambda\rho U$, $\tau_{by} = \lambda\rho V$

where $\lambda = K/h \approx k\bar{C}/h$,

Then

$$\frac{\partial U}{\partial t} + \lambda U - fV = -\frac{h}{\rho}\frac{\partial p_a}{\partial x} - gh\frac{\partial \zeta}{\partial x} + \frac{\tau_{sx}}{\rho} \tag{4.38}$$

$$\frac{\partial V}{\partial t} + \lambda V + fU = -\frac{h}{\rho}\frac{\partial p_a}{\partial y} - gh\frac{\partial \zeta}{\partial y} + \frac{\tau_{sy}}{\rho} \tag{4.39}$$

$$\frac{\partial U}{\partial x} + \frac{\partial V}{\partial y} + \frac{\partial \zeta}{\partial t} = 0 \, . \tag{4.40}$$

In these equations the tide-generating potential term in $\bar{\zeta}$ has been neglected. The surface shear stress components are derived from the wind field and are in general functions of $x$ and $y$. The coefficient $\lambda$, which depends on the tidal current amplitude and the depth $h$, is also a function of $x$ and $y$.

### 4.6.3 Analytical and numerical solutions

(a) *Analytical solutions*

A number of analytical solutions have been obtained for areas of simple geometrical shape, e.g. a shelf adjacent to a straight coast, a closed basin or a channel closed at one end. The wind stress has usually been assumed to be applied suddenly and then maintained at a constant value. Various solutions of this type were reviewed by Welander (1961). Such studies are valuable in showing the essential effects produced by characteristic distributions of wind. In some cases actual regions may be approximated by geometrical areas and the analytical solutions applied but the results can be expected to be only partly quantitative.

An example of an investigation using analytical solutions is that by Heaps (1965) dealing with storm surges on a continental shelf. A shelf of uniform width and depth was assumed, bounded by a straight coast on one side and connected with an infinitely deep ocean on the other as in Fig. 4.9. A moving wind field was applied and the following cases considered:

(1) the response on the shelf to an input surge from the ocean, specified by $\zeta = f(t)$ at $x = l$;

(2) the generation of a surge on the shelf by a steady wind stress suddenly created;

(3) the elevations at the coast produced by a wind field with a moving boundary.

The model results were applied to surges affecting the west coast of the British Isles. It was shown that these surges were generated mainly by the wind fields, associated with moving depressions, acting on the shelf to the south of Ireland. In two cases considered, surges recorded at Milford Haven, in South Wales, could be reproduced satisfactorily in this way.

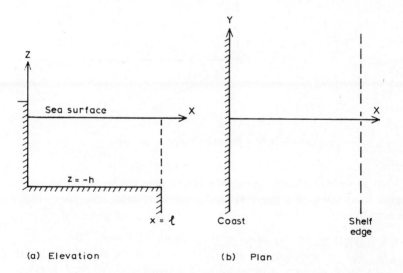

Fig. 4.9 – Continental shelf of uniform width and depth, as used in the Heaps (1965) model.

(b) *Numerical solutions*

For detailed studies of surges in a particular region numerical models are more suitable. The region can be represented by a network of elementary areas which approximate to the actual coastline at a boundary and which use the actual depths of water in the offshore areas. Finite difference models have been developed for this purpose from about 1955 onwards and more recently finite element methods have also been used.

An important point in formulating a numerical model is the specification of appropriate boundary conditions. The coast is usually represented as a vertical wall with the condition that transport normal to it, denoted by $V_n$, is zero. Thus if the normal to the coast is inclined at an angle $\alpha$ to the $x$-axis, as in Fig. 4.10, the condition is:

$$V_n = U \cos \alpha + V \sin \alpha = 0 . \tag{4.41}$$

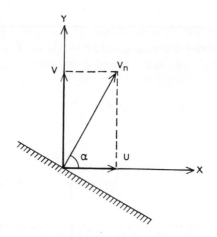

Fig. 4.10 – Boundary condition at a coast.

At an open boundary, represented by a straight line separating the modelled region from the open ocean, there are several alternative conditions which may be applied:

(a) the elevation may be assumed to be zero, i.e. $\zeta = 0$;
(b) the elevation may be prescribed, e.g. from the distribution of atmospheric pressure or by an assumed external surge, i.e. $\zeta (x, y, t)$ is given on the boundary;
(c) the normal transport may be prescribed, i.e.

$$V_n = U \cos \alpha + V \sin \alpha = F (x, y, t); \tag{4.42}$$

(d) the derivative of the transport normal to the boundary may be assumed to be zero, i.e.

$$\partial V_n / \partial y_n = 0 ;$$

(e) the 'radiation condition' may be applied, stating that any energy reaching the boundary from inside the model travels outwards as a progressive wave, without reflection.

This can be expressed as

$$V_n = (gh)^{1/2}\zeta \tag{4.43}$$

which is a special case of the more general condition:

$V_n = A\zeta$ where $A$ is an admittance coefficient.

No attempt is made here to discuss the finite difference formulation of the equations and the numerical methods of solution. For information on these reference should be made to the review by Welander (1961) and to the original publications which are cited below.

### (c) Examples of finite difference models

1. A continental shelf model, approximating to the area off the east coast of USA, was used by Jelesnianski (1965) to study the storm surges induced by a tropical storm impinging on the shelf. Since the build-up phase of the surge was of primary interest, a linearised model without bottom friction was employed. Across the deep sea boundary, as at $x = l$ in Fig. 4.9, the condition $\zeta = 0$ was applied, while across the boundaries of varying depth, running across the shelf, it was assumed that $\partial V/\partial y = 0$. The effects of both atmospheric pressure gradients and wind stress were investigated. The response to the pressure gradients was found to be static in deep water, i.e. according to the inverted barometer law, but to give an elevation at the coast of up to three times the static value in the case of a storm approaching at 30 m.p.h. (13.5 m s$^{-1}$). The effect was greater when the scale of the storm was smaller than the dimensions of the shelf. In considering the wind stress effect the rate of movement of the storm was less important. Allowing for the inflow of wind across the isobars produced a significant increase in the computed height of the surge.

2. A two-dimensional model of a sea area, described by Heaps (1969), was formulated in such a way that particular coastal and open sea boundaries could be specified as required. The model was linearised and depth-integrated but used polar coordinates, so that it could be applied to larger sea areas for which rectangular coordinates would not be adequate. The specification of the model and its boundary conditions and the method of solution were described in detail. Heaps applied the model to the North Sea and adjacent waters of the continental shelf of north-west Europe and tested it on three major storm surges which had occurred between 1956 and 1962. The finite difference grid used in one form of the model is shown in Fig. 4.11. The computed curves of surge height against time at a number of ports were compared with those derived from records of sea level and were found to agree to a good approximation. The model also

enables charts of 'co-disturbance lines', joining positions with the same elevation at a given time, to be constructed.

Similar linearised depth-integrated models have been developed by other workers and have been used for the study of tides and storm surges in a number of areas.

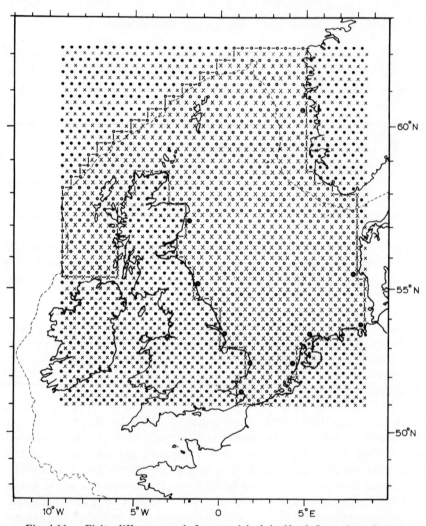

Fig. 4.11 – Finite difference mesh for a model of the North Sea and northern shelf areas, with the Strait of Dover closed. The elevation is computed at points marked by circles and the current components at points marked by crosses. – o – o – denotes an open boundary and – × – × – a closed boundary; – – – – 100 fathom contour; ◎ point at which calculated elevations are compared with elevations derived from observations at a nearby port. From Heaps (1969), by courtesy of The Royal Society.

### 4.6.4 Non-linear effects on depth-integrated flow

When the elevation of the water surface is no longer small compared with the depth of water, the effects of the non-linear terms in the equations of motion become significant, so that to obtain sufficiently accurate results the full equations (4.28) and (4.29) must be used rather than the linearised equations (4.38) and (4.39). In general terms the non-linear effects arise from

(1) the quadratic law of friction;
(2) the height of surge $\zeta$ becoming comparable with $h$;
(3) the advective acceleration terms becoming significant relative to $\partial U/\partial t$ and $\partial V/\partial t$.

It appears that in a particular region, the terms usually become important in the above order as the elevation increases.

The bottom friction terms in (4.28) and (4.29) are given by

$$\frac{\tau_{bx}}{\rho} = \frac{k(U^2 + V^2)^{1/2}U}{(h + \zeta)^2} \quad , \quad \frac{\tau_{by}}{\rho} = \frac{k(U^2 + V^2)^{1/2}V}{(h + \zeta)^2} \quad .$$

The linearised equations (4.38) and (4.39) are thus replaced by the non-linear equations:

$$\frac{\partial U}{\partial t} + \frac{\partial}{\partial x}\left(\frac{U^2}{h + \zeta}\right) + \frac{\partial}{\partial y}\left(\frac{UV}{h + \zeta}\right) + \frac{k(U^2 + V^2)^{1/2}U}{(h + \zeta)^2} - fV$$

$$= -\frac{(h + \zeta)}{\rho}\frac{\partial p_a}{\partial x} - g(h + \zeta)\frac{\partial \zeta}{\partial x} + \frac{\tau_{sx}}{\rho} \quad (4.44)$$

$$\frac{\partial V}{\partial t} + \frac{\partial}{\partial x}\left(\frac{UV}{h + \zeta}\right) + \frac{\partial}{\partial y}\left(\frac{V^2}{h + \zeta}\right) + \frac{k(U^2 + V^2)^{1/2}V}{(h + \zeta)^2} + fU$$

$$= -\frac{(h + \zeta)}{\rho}\frac{\partial p_a}{\partial y} - g(h + \zeta)\frac{\partial \zeta}{\partial y} + \frac{\tau_{sy}}{\rho} \quad .$$

$$(4.45)$$

The continuity equation is unchanged, so that

$$\frac{\partial U}{\partial x} + \frac{\partial V}{\partial y} + \frac{\partial \zeta}{\partial t} = 0 \text{ as in equation (4.40)}$$

In the non-linear equations above $\zeta$, $U$ and $V$ refer to the elevation and transport components due to the tide and surge combined, since it is no longer possible to deal with them separately.

The interaction of tide and surge in the Thames estuary and southern North Sea was studied by Banks (1974), using a combined model which coupled a two-dimensional non-linear model of the Southern Bight of the North Sea with a one-dimensional model of the Thames estuary. The results confirmed the following conclusions, which had earlier been made tentatively on empirical grounds.

(1) A surge peak in the Thames estuary, occurring near high water of the semidiurnal tide, is decreased in magnitude by the tide-surge interaction but a peak occurring on the rising tide is increased.

(2) A surge rising to a maximum before high water and then remaining steady is transformed into two peaks, one before and one after high water.

(3) The degree of interaction between tide and surge increases with distance upstream from the mouth of the estuary.

The interaction in the same area was considered further by Prandle (1975) who also investigated its effect on the operation of the Thames barrier, which has been built to prevent flooding in the London area due to surge action. The barrier will normally lie flat on the sea bed but will be raised on the rising tide when a surge is forecast.

The interaction over a wider area of the southern North Sea was investigated by Prandle and Wolf (1978) who used two similar non-linear models concurrently, one simulating the tidal propagation and the other the surge propagation. It was possible to introduce perturbation terms to represent the influence in either model of sea levels and velocities computed by the other. When the conditions of the surge of 31 January–2 February 1953 was examined by this method, it was found that the interaction in the southern North Sea arose primarily from the quadratic friction term and developed rapidly in the coastal region from Lowestoft southwards to the Thames estuary, where the water velocities were high. Changes in water level can develop rapidly in time, as a result of the interaction, and may be localised in space. On a time scale of several days a systematic perturbation of the tidal regime took place. Thus the amphidromic system in the Southern Bight was displaced to the west of its normal position and the cotidal lines were rotated in an anti-clockwise direction, the system returning to normal at the end of the surge event.

A non-linear model of the whole north-west European continental shelf has been used in conjunction with an atmospheric weather prediction model to provide real-time predictions of storm surges in the North Sea (Flather, 1979). The 10-level atmospheric model was developed by the British Meteorological Office for weather forecasting and in this application it provides the distribution of atmospheric pressure and surface wind. From these the pressure gradient and wind stress terms are derived and used as inputs to the sea model. After testing the system by hindcasting previous surges, it was run on a routine basis to provide real-time storm surge forecasts for the east and west coasts of the British Isles during the winter of 1978–79. Figure 4.12 shows the grid network of the sea model with the grid points of the atmospheric model, at which the meteorological data were specified, superimposed on it.

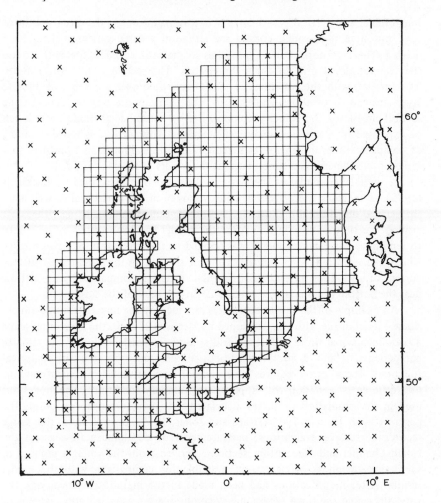

Fig. 4.12 – Finite difference mesh of the continental shelf sea model with grid points (X) of the 10-level model of the atmosphere. From Flather (1979), by courtesy of Elsevier Scientific Publishing Co.

### 4.6.5 Three-dimensional models

Two-dimensional models give the depth-integrated transport of water but are unable to provide any information on how the current varies with depth. In some cases a knowledge of the current profile may be needed in order to assess the effect of current surges on structures or on the movement of bed material. If bottom friction is important, its effect cannot be adequately estimated without knowing the current velocity near the bottom, which may be quite different from that near the surface. In an estuary a two-dimensional model using longitudinal and vertical coordinates, while averaging across the estuary, is often used but in a more open coastal sea situation a three-dimensional model is needed. There are three basic approaches to the problem. The first is to extend the computational grid to three dimensions. The second is to form a multi-layer model, with the equations of motion averaged over a number of discrete layers instead of over the whole depth. The third approach is to represent the vertical profile of the velocity components by a number of modes, which can be expressed by a series of analytical functions. This method is less demanding of computer time, in general, as it reduces the three-dimensional problem to a series of two-dimensional computations, the results of which are added.

A three-layer model of the German Bight has been described by Backhaus (1979). It includes the effects of eddy viscosity in the horizontal as well as in the vertical direction and allows for the drying-out of sandbanks near the coast around the time of low water. After the model had been tested by its ability to reproduce the tidal regime, it was applied to the simulation of a storm surge which had occurred on 3 January 1976. It showed an inward-directed surface current of up to four times the normal tidal current, accompanied by an outflow near the bottom of comparable magnitude, at the peak of the surge.

An example of the third approach is provided by the linearised three-dimensional model of the Irish Sea developed by Heaps (1974). In the horizontal plane a two-dimensional finite difference grid is used. The distribution of the velocity components, $u$ and $v$, in the vertical is represented by a series of analytical functions. The solution requires the evaluation of eigenvalues and eigenfunctions of a differential equation with appropriate boundary conditions. The model was used in the simulation of surges associated with two severe storms during the period 10–18 January 1965 (Heaps and Jones, 1979). In addition to tide gauge records of surface evaluations, measurements of depth-mean flow across the North Channel and three other sections, derived from the voltages induced in submarine telephone cables, were available for comparison with the model results. After modifications had been made in the methods of specifying the wind stress and the open sea boundary conditions, a reasonably good agreement between the simulated and observed values of elevations and depth-mean currents was obtained. The model indicated some interesting differences between surface and bottom currents but unfortunately there were no current meter observations during the period with which these could be compared.

### 4.6.6 Other developments

The use of finite difference dynamical models to study tides and storm surges was initiated by Hansen in 1948 and has been widely developed by a number of workers. A disadvantage of a rectangular grid of uniform mesh size, as in Fig. 4.11, is its rather crude representation of the bounding coastlines. It is at the coast and in bays or inlets that surge effects are often of most interest and it is desirable to be able to represent conditions there more accurately. One solution which has been adopted is to use a system of nested grids, with a smaller mesh size near the coast and a larger size over the open sea part of the model. Conditions at the junction of the grids have to be suitably matched. An alternative approach is to use a conformal transformation to convert irregularly shaped areas into a rectangular grid. A method of this type was described by Reid *et al.* (1977) and applied to an area of the Gulf of Mexico in the vicinity of Galveston, extending from the coast to the 200-m depth contour. The area is first mapped in orthogonal curvilinear coordinates which are transformed to a rectangular grid with varying mesh sizes. The elemental areas are then 'stretched' in such a way that the computation is actually performed in a rectangular grid of uniform spacing.

The finite element method has the advantage of not being constrained to a uniform mesh but of being able to cover an area with a mosaic of triangular elements of varying dimensions. It is able to approximate closely to the form of the coastline with small elements while using larger elements in the open sea part of the area. The finite element method, however, is more expensive in computer time since it requires matrix inversion at every time step. A scheme which appears to combine the advantages of both the finite element and finite difference methods is the irregular grid finite difference technique described by Thacker (1979). This uses a mosaic of triangular areas, similar to a finite element grid, but the computation is carried out by finite difference methods.

Surge forecasting services for regions in danger of flood damage have been in operation for many years. In his review article, Heaps (1967) referred to surge forecasts for the North Sea coasts of Great Britain, Germany and the Netherlands, at Atlantic City and in New York Bay, USA, in Lake Erie and along the Japanese coast. In most cases empirical methods of surge prediction, as mentioned in section 4.6.1 above, have been used in conjunction with weather forecasts. Theoretical considerations, based on solutions of the hydrodynamical equations, have been used to supplement the empirical methods in some cases. The combination of atmospheric and sea area models to provide numerical forecasts of surges on the east and west coasts of Great Britain, referred to in section 4.6.4, appears to be the first operational use of models for this purpose. Work on the development of similar systems is being undertaken in West Germany, the Netherlands and Belgium.

# 5

# Coastal upwelling

---

## 5.1 INTRODUCTION: CHARACTERISTIC FEATURES OF UPWELLING

Upwelling is the term used to describe the processes which cause the upward movement of water from depths of the order of 100 to 300 m into the surface layer. Since the temperature in the sea usually decreases with depth, the up-welled water will be colder than the surface water which it displaces. Very often it has higher concentrations of nutrient salts (nitrate, phosphate and silicate) than the surface water, which may have been depleted of nutrients by the growth of phytoplankton. Regions of upwelling are usually, therefore, regions of high biological productivity. The enhanced growth of phytoplankton can support a greater zooplankton concentration which in its turn can maintain fish populations. Most of the important fisheries of the world ocean are found, in fact, in regions of upwelling.

Although upwelling also occurs in certain areas of the open ocean, we are concerned here with upwelling over the continental shelf. Usually this is induced by the wind acting under suitable conditions although the occurrence of up-welling in some areas does not appear to be due to the local wind. If a wind is blowing in the northern hemisphere with a coast to the left of the direction towards which it is blowing, then the Ekman transport, being to the right of the wind, will carry surface water away from the coast. The same situation arises in the southern hemisphere if the wind blows with a coast on its right-hand side. In either case, continuity of flow is maintained by water rising near the coast to replace the surface water which is moving offshore. The essential steps in the process may be described as follows, with reference to Fig. 5.1, which is drawn for the northern hemisphere.

(1) The wind-induced Ekman transport in the surface layer is away from the coast and upwelling occurs near the coast to preserve continuity. An onshore movement of water occurs at some depth below the surface.

(2) Under the action of the wind, the sea level at the coast is lowered, giving rise to a slope of the sea surface, upwards in the offshore direction. This produces a geostrophic flow parallel to the coast, with the

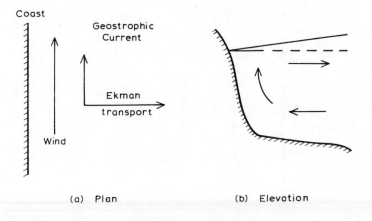

Fig. 5.1 – Ekman transport and coastal upwelling.

surface rising to the right of the current so that the geostrophic component of flow is in the direction of the wind.

(3) In water of uniform density, a frictionless geostrophic flow is independent of depth so that, unless the surface has a gradient parallel to the
coast, there will be no flow perpendicular to the coast at mid-depth.
The return flow necessary to compensate for the surface layer Ekman
transport would take place in a bottom Ekman layer. If there is a slope
parallel to the coast, however, upward in the direction of the wind,
there will be a component of geostrophic flow onshore at all depths. In
the surface layer this will reduce somewhat the offshore Ekman transport but below the surface layer it will provide an onshore compensatory flow. In general a bottom Ekman layer will still occur but it will
contribute only a fraction of the onshore flow.

(4) In stratified water, geostrophic flow can vary with depth, so that the
onshore flow may vary and need not extend to the bottom. In that case
a bottom Ekman layer would not be necessary.

In this chapter the simple Ekman–Sverdrup model of upwelling will be outlined first as a background to a description of the observed features of upwelling.
More sophisticated models will then be considered and the extent to which they
account for the observations will be discussed.

## 5.2 EKMAN–SVERDRUP MODEL OF UPWELLING

### 5.2.1 Basic theory

The case of a steady wind blowing parallel to a straight coast, on its left-hand
side in the northern hemisphere, will be considered. Axes are taken, as in Fig. 5.2,

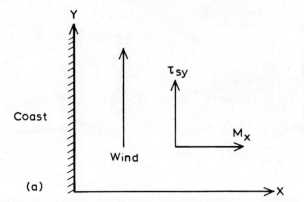

(a)

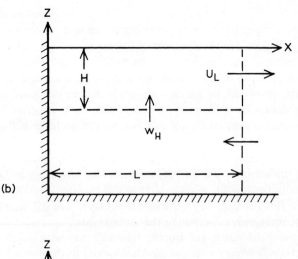

(b)

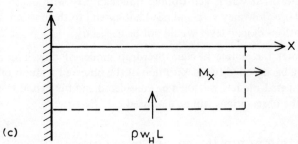

(c)

Fig. 5.2 – Simple model of upwelling: (a) plan, (b) and (c) elevations perpendicular to the coast.

with the $y$-axis along the coast and the $x$-axis perpendicular to it. Let the stress of the wind, which is blowing in the $y$-direction, be denoted by $\tau_{sy}$. Then, from equation (4.6) of Chapter 4, the mass transport offshore in the surface Ekman layer is given by

$$M_x \equiv \int_{-D}^{0} \rho u \, dz = \frac{\tau_{sy}}{f} \tag{5.1}$$

where $f$ is the Coriolis parameter, the $z$-axis is positive upwards and $D$ is the depth of the Ekman layer.

From the equation of continuity

$$\frac{\partial u}{\partial x} + \frac{\partial v}{\partial y} + \frac{\partial w}{\partial z} = 0$$

and assuming that conditions are uniform parallel to the coast, so that $\partial v/\partial y = 0$, we have

$$\frac{\partial u}{\partial x} = -\frac{\partial w}{\partial z} . \tag{5.2}$$

Across a vertical plane at a distance $L$ from the coast, as in Fig. 5.2(b), where $L$ is sufficiently large for the direct influence of the coast to be negligible,

$$u_L = -\int_{0}^{L} \frac{\partial w}{\partial z} \, dx . \tag{5.3}$$

The mass transport across the vertical plane at $x = L$ taken down to a depth $H$ is given by

$$M'_x = \int_{-H}^{0} \rho u_L \, dz = -\int_{-H}^{0} \int_{0}^{L} \rho \frac{\partial w}{\partial z} \, dx \, dz \tag{5.4}$$

Now $$\int_{-H}^{0} \frac{\partial w}{\partial z} \, dz = w_0 - w_H$$

where $w_0$ and $w_H$ are the vertical velocities at the surface and at depth $H$ respectively. Assuming $w_0 = 0$,

$$M'_x = \int_{0}^{L} \rho w_H \, dx . \tag{5.5}$$

If $H \geqslant D$, where $D$ is the depth of the Ekman layer,

$$M'_x = M_x .$$

To obtain an approximate estimate of the vertical velocity $w_H$ at the base of the upwelling layer, we assume that $w_H$ is uniform from $x = 0$ to $x = L$. Then, as in Fig. 5.2(c),

$$\rho w_H L = M_x = \frac{\tau_{sy}}{f} \, . \tag{5.6}$$

If we assume a wind stress of 0.2 N m$^{-2}$, which corresponds to a wind speed of about 10 m s$^{-1}$ (see Table 4.1 of Chapter 4), then at latitude $\phi = 30°$, where $f = \omega = 7.29 \times 10^{-5}$ s$^{-1}$,

$$M_x = 2.75 \times 10^3 \text{ kg m}^{-1} \text{ s}^{-1}$$

If $L = 50$ km and $\rho = 1.025 \times 10^3$ kg m$^{-3}$, then

$$w_H = 5.4 \times 10^{-5} \text{ m s}^{-1} = 4.6 \text{ m per day} \, .$$

### 5.2.2 Major upwelling regions

Although the occurrence of an offshore Ekman transport is only the first stage in the development of an upwelling situation, it is a useful index of regions where upwelling is likely to occur and its possible strength. Wooster and Reid (1962) computed $M_x$ from equation (5.1), using mean values of wind stress over 5-degree squares adjacent to the west coasts of continents. The computed values were consistent with the known upwelling regions of the world and indicated the seasonal variations to be expected.

The main regions in which coastal upwelling occurs, either seasonally or throughout the year, are as follows:

| | | |
|---|---|---|
| North Atlantic: | Canary Current region: | 10°–40°N |
| South Atlantic: | Benguela Current region: | 5°–30°S |
| North Pacific: | California Current region: | 25°–45°N |
| South Pacific: | Peru Current region: | 5°–45°S |
| Indian Ocean: | off the coasts of Somalia and Arabia during the south-west monsoon. | |

Seasonal variations in upwelling occur, associated with changes in the wind regime. On the eastern side of the North Atlantic, for example, the southern limit of coastal upwelling is determined by the tropical front which moves from about 10°N in winter to 20°N in summer (Wooster et al., 1976). Off the coasts of Senegal, Gambia and Mauritania, in latitude 12–20°N, upwelling occurs during the period January to May. Between 20° and 25°N, in the Cap Blanc area, there is strong upwelling throughout the year. From 25° to 43°N, including the coastal areas of Morocco and Portugal, upwelling occurs mainly in the summer months, particularly from June to October. In the other main upwelling areas upwelling is usually strongest in the spring or summer months, but the southern part of the Peru Current region is an exception with the strongest upwelling occurring in the winter.

The Ekman transport method has also been used to calculate daily and weekly indices of upwelling activity. The wind speed and direction for this purpose were estimated from synoptic charts of surface atmospheric pressure.

## 5.3 OBSERVATIONS OF UPWELLING

### 5.3.1 General features

Observations which provide evidence of coastal upwelling include, firstly, surveys of sea surface temperature which indicate the areas of cold upwelled water. Vertical profiles of temperature, salinity and nutrients, from which the distribution of properties in sections perpendicular to the coast can be plotted, enable the presence of upwelling and the depth from which it occurs to be inferred. Measurements of currents, by drifting drogues or by current meters used from a ship or from moored buoys, show the components of flow normal to and parallel to the coast, at various depths. Techniques are not yet available for measuring directly the vertical movements of water, which have to be inferred from the change in depth of isopycnals with time or from horizontal currents, applying considerations of continuity. A good review of the state of knowledge up to the time it was written was given by Smith (1968).

A number of features appear to be common to all upwelling areas, although significant variations do occur. Figure 5.3 represents the main features of upwelling in the Benguela Current, off the south-west coast of Africa, based on a diagram given by Hart and Currie (1960). The following points may be noted:

(1) The offshore Ekman transport in the surface layer is directed to the left of the wind, as this region is in the southern hemisphere.

(2) Upwelling occurs near the coast and also above the edge of the continental shelf.

(3) The isothermal and isopycnal surfaces rise towards the coast.

(4) The upwelled water spreads offshore in a coastal zone and then shows a tendency to sink at a convergence over the outer shelf.

(5) Where sinking occurs, a frontal zone develops between the coastal and oceanic surface water. The front follows a sinuous course, indicating the presence of eddies between the upwelled coastal water and oceanic surface water.

(6) There is a northerly (equatorward) flow on the shelf, parallel to the coast.

(7) A southerly (poleward) deep counter current develops over the upper continental slope.

(8) Alongshore variations occur in the upwelling processes and upwelling does not necessarily take place uniformly along the coast.

These features, which are illustrated by the Benguela Current upwelling region, are fairly typical of other upwelling areas as well but variations occur

from one region to another or from time to time, even in the same area. For
example, the offshore frontal zone may vary in intensity, or may not occur at
all, depending on the properties of the upwelled water and the extent to which
they are modified by solar heating and exchanges with the atmosphere. The
two-cell type of offshore-onshore circulation, shown in Fig. 5.3, may be replaced by a one-cell circulation. The poleward undercurrent may vary in position,
flowing along the shelf or on the continental slope and its intensity may be
variable. Off north-west Africa, where there is a broad continental shelf, the
undercurrent is found on the slope and does not appear to occur on the shelf
(Hughes and Barton, 1974). Off the Oregon coast, where the shelf is narrower,
the undercurrent frequently extends on to the shelf and it appears to be a
permanent feature on the narrow shelf off the coast of Peru. On some occasions
the 'undercurrent' appears to extend to the surface and give a surface flow
against the wind. This occurs quite frequently off Peru, as mentioned in section
5.3.4.

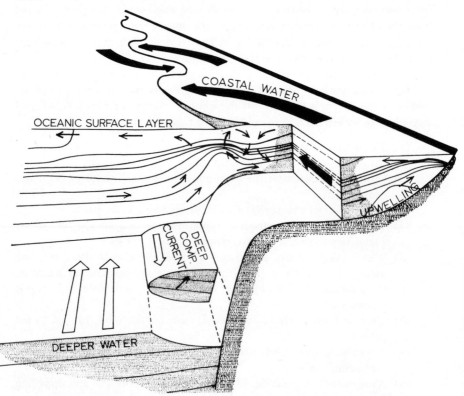

Fig. 5.3 – Schematic diagram of circulation during upwelling in the Benguela
Current region: many of the features shown occur also in other upwelling regions.
From Hart and Currie (1960) by courtesy of the Institute of Oceanographic
Sciences.

### 5.3.2 Time-dependent nature of upwelling

It is unusual for a steady state of upwelling to be maintained for any considerable length of time. Since wind is usually the primary cause of upwelling, the occurrence of a period of strong winds in the right direction may be expected to initiate an upwelling event, which will build up towards a steady state if the wind persists, and then decay following a cessation or weakening of the wind. Starting from a relatively calm period, with the isothermal and isopycnal surfaces in the water over the shelf approximately horizontal, the onset of upwelling will be shown by a rise of the isopycnals towards the surface. The rate of rise of the isopycnals is often identified with the rate of upwelling, or vertical velocity of the water. Such an estimate is a lower limit, in fact, since it disregards diffusive processes which may cause heating of the upwelling water as it rises, by the conduction of heat downwards from the surface. Over a period of two or three days, however, the effects of diffusive processes are probably slight.

The development of an upwelling event of the coast of Oregon, USA, induced by northerly winds during July 1973, was described by Halpern (1976). Fig. 5.4(a), taken from this paper, shows the variation of temperature with time at a station on the shelf, for a series of depths from the surface to 23.6 m. Prior to 11 July the temperature was about 15.5°C at the surface, decreasing with depth to about 9°C at 23 m. Between 11 and 13 July the surface temperature dropped by about 6°C to 9.5°C and that at 23 m by 1°C to 8°C. The temperature of the whole surface layer remained low until 15 July and then rose rapidly over the next two days. The spatial structure of the event is illustrated in Fig. 5.4(b), showing the density $\sigma_t$ in a sequence of vertical sections across the shelf. In the first three of these diagrams the isopycnals near the surface, such as that for $\sigma_t = 24.5$, remain almost horizontal. In the last two sections, on 12 and 13 July, those for 24.5, 25.5 and 26.0 reach the surface. The estimated vertical velocities of the 25.5 and 26.0 isopycnals, shown in the inset diagrams reach 1 to $2 \times 10^{-2}$ cm s$^{-1}$ near the coast.

An upwelling season consists of a series of such events and a number of observational studies of individual events have been made in different areas. In the north west African region, Barton et al. (1977) found that the onset and development of an event followed a complex pattern. Upwelled water appeared first over the inner shelf but the centre of upwelling migrated to the shelf break over a period of several days. Development continued while the strength of the wind was maintained and conditions gradually relaxed following a decrease in the wind.

### 5.3.3 Spatial variations

An example of the local variability of upwelling within a general area is given in Fig. 5.5. This shows the distribution of sea surface temperature along the coast of Peru, between 5°S and 18°S, from a quasi-synoptic survey by a fleet of fishing vessels on 28–30 May 1974 (from Zuta et al., 1978). The area of upwelling along the coast is shown by the reduced temperatures compared with

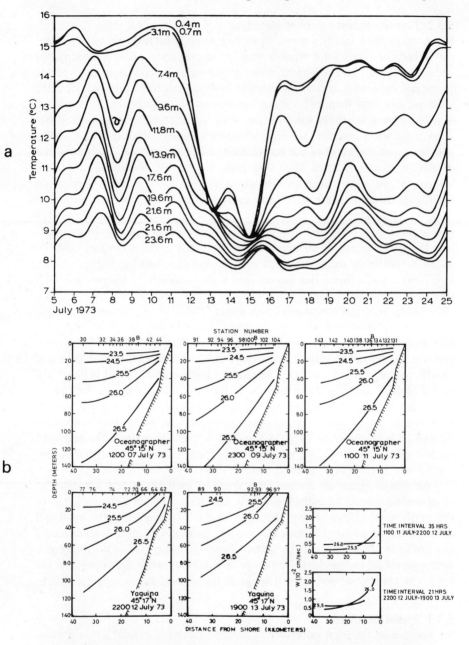

Fig. 5.4 – Changes during a coastal upwelling event off Oregon in July 1973:
(a) temperature time-series measurements at a number of depths at Station B,
5–25 July. Note the reduction in temperature throughout the upper layer from
11 to 16 July. (b) Sequence of sections perpendicular to the coast, showing
changes in density $\sigma_t$ during the event. The position of Station B is marked.
The inset diagram, bottom right, shows the estimated vertical velocity of selected
$\sigma_t$ surfaces during two successive time intervals. From Halpern (1976), by courtesy of Pergamon Press.

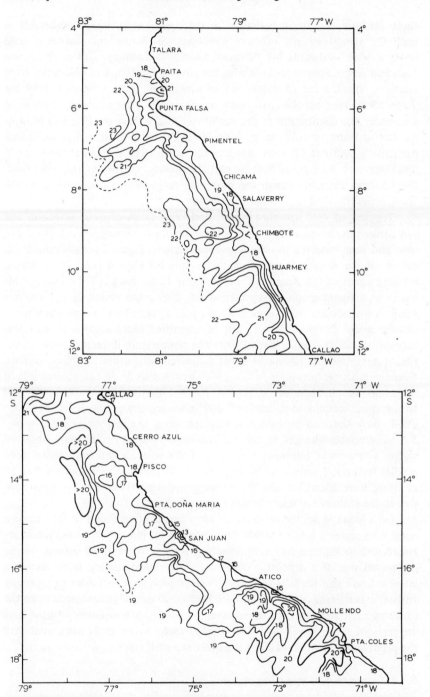

Fig. 5.5 – Synoptic chart of sea-surface temperature off Peru, from Eureka 29 survey, 28–30 May 1974: (a) northern part, (b) southern part. From Zuta, Rivera and Bustamente (1978), by courtesy of Springer-Verlag.

those offshore, but the temperature in the coastal zone varies considerably in both the alongshore and offshore directions. Six prominent tongues of cold water extend westwards off Pimentel, Chimbote-Huarmay, Callao, Pisco, San Juan and Atico, apparently indicating the advection offshore of cold water from relatively small areas of more intense upwelling. These tongues extend for 70 to 130 miles from the coast, with warmer water between them, resulting in a meander-like distribution of the isotherms. As a further result of this process, patches of warm or cold water, from 10 to 30 miles in diameter, are found, particularly south of 12°S, as shown in Fig. 5.5(b). The alongshore variations in upwelling may be due, at least in part, to inhomogeneities in the wind field. Deep valleys cutting through the mountain range, which runs parallel to the coast, cause the wind to be intensified locally.

Tongues of cold upwelled water, projecting in an offshore direction and sometimes interleaved with tongues of warmer water moving towards the coast, have also been observed in other upwelling regions. Figure 5.6 shows the distribution of sea surface temperature in an area off Cape Town, South Africa, forming a part of the Benguela Current region (from Bang, 1973). This chart is based on a thermograph survey carried out during the period 20–28 January 1968. A meandering front, separating the cold upwelled water from the warmer oceanic water further offshore, can be identified extending for at least 100 miles to the north-west of Cape Point. The temperature difference between the two water masses is unusually large, compared with other upwelling regions. Near the coast temperatures of 10–14°C occurred while on the oceanic side of the front the temperature exceeded 20°C. Following this survey, repeated temperature sections to a depth of 200 m during the period 5–10 February 1968 were obtained by bathythermograph along the line marked AB in Fig. 5.6. Appreciable changes in the surface temperature patterns were observed within a few hours following a reversal of the wind. Within the frontal zone smaller features, described as 'mixing cells', from 2 to 5 miles across and 5 to 20 m deep, were identified and it was suggested that they played a significant part in the exchange of water masses across the front.

On a larger scale, the intensity of upwelling is often found to vary along a coast on a scale of tens to hundreds of kilometres. In some cases the variations are related to topography, with upwelling tending to be more intense on the downwind side of a cape or promontory. Theoretical studies, to be discussed later, indicate that features of bottom topography, such as a ridge or a canyon with its axis running offshore, are more likely than coastal irregularities to be the cause of such variations. In other cases the alongshore variation of upwelling appears not to be linked with topographic features but to be associated with the propagation of an event along the coast as a shelf wave.

### 5.3.4 Comparison of upwelling regions

The coastal upwelling regions which have been studied most intensively are those

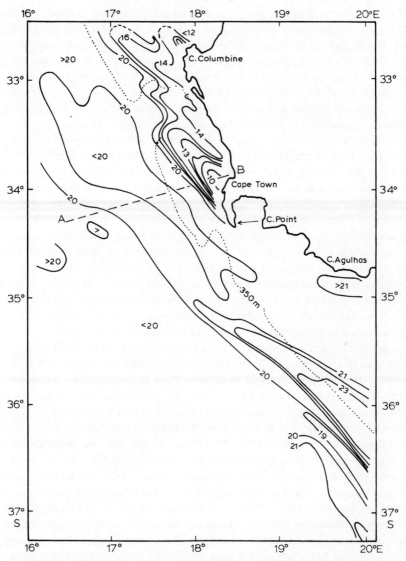

Fig. 5.6 – Sea surface temperature off Cape Town, 20–28 January 1968, from surface thermograph records. From Bang (1973), by courtesy of *Tellus*.

off the Oregon coast, north-west Africa and Peru. In each region a favourable local wind appears to be the primary cause of upwelling but the response varies to some extent with the topography of the continental shelf and with the degree of stratification in the water. Off north-west Africa the shelf is fairly broad and shallow with an abrupt transition to a steep continental slope, while off Oregon the shelf is narrower with a more gradual change in slope. The shelf off Peru is narrow with a steep continental slope. The stratification, as shown by the vertical gradient of density, is typically less intense off north-west Africa and Peru than off Oregon. Observations made at different times in each region have shown considerable variation in the upwelling response, so that it is difficult to generalise about differences between the regions. On the whole the upwelling phenomena off Oregon and north-west Africa appear to have much in common, although it is possible to pick out some differences (Huyer, 1976).

The upwelling off the coast of Peru shows some significant differences from the other two regions. The upwelled water comes from a depth of about 70 m in the offshore water, whereas in both the other regions it often comes from as deep as 200 m. The wind speed appears to be less variable in the Peru region and as a result the upwelling does not seem to be so clearly separated into a series of identifiable events. Another difference is that off Peru the mean surface current is often in the opposite direction to the wind which is causing the upwelling. Over a six month period, March–September 1976, Brink *et al.* (1978) found the alongshore current between $12°$ and $16°$S to be consistently towards the south, although the wind was blowing towards the north and active upwelling was taking place. Fluctuations in the alongshore current were poorly correlated with those in the wind at the beginning of the period but the correlation was increased later as the mean wind speed gradually increased.

Another feature of the Peru region, particularly in the northern part, is the large year to year variation in the effects of upwelling, associated with El Niño Between January and March in most years there is an intrusion southwards of warm equatorial water, poor in nutrients, into the coastal zone displacing the cold Peru Current water. Usually this intrusion extends only a few degrees south of the equator but in some years it extends further, sometimes to $12°$S, with disastrous consequences. In the absence of the cold, nutrient-rich water, biological productivity is greatly reduced and catches in the Peruvian anchovy fishery fall catastrophically. There are also climatic changes, with heavy rainfall along a normally desert coastal strip. From observations it appears that the change in character of the surface water near the coast is not necessarily due to a cessation of upwelling but to a change in the source of upwelled water, as a result of the southward intrusion of water of equatorial origin. The occurrence of El Niño has been the subject of a number of investigations and it appears not to be a local phenomenon but to be associated with ocean-wide fluctuations in the wind regime and current systems across the whole width of the equatorial Pacific Ocean.

Although coastal upwelling is usually induced by local winds, there are some regions where significant upwelling occurs which cannot be explained in this way. In the Gulf of Guinea, off the coasts of Nigeria, Ghana and the Ivory Coast, upwelling occurs seasonally from July to September, with a decrease in the sea surface temperature and a marked increase in biological productivity. During the other nine months of the year a warm surface mixed layer, extending to a depth of 30–40 m, is separated by a sharp· thermocline from the cold water below. With the onset of upwelling the thermocline rises, bringing to the surface cold water, rich in nutrients, usually found at 60–100 m. The upwelling does not appear to be correlated with any change in the wind. The fall in temperature measured at Tema harbour, Ghana, in the summer of 1974, was associated with a lowering of séa level, giving support to the idea, which has been proposed, that the upwelling is induced by some type of long wave motion propagated into the area from further west in the equatorial Atlantic Ocean (Houghton and Mensah, 1978).

Most of the observations described in this section have been concerned with the physical processes involved in bringing water from greater depths into the surface layer. After the water reaches this layer its temperature may be changed by the flux of heat through the sea surface and its salinity by evaporation or precipitation. Such changes may be detected by comparing the temperature–salinity relationship, as shown on a T–S diagram, of the upwelled water with that of the source water from which it originated. The concentrations of nutrient salts, such as nitrate, phosphate and silicate, will be changed by the growth of phytoplankton in the euphotic zone and subsequently by regeneration processes in the deeper part of a water column. These processes are of prime interest in relation to the biological productivity of the area and its value as a fishery resource. A number of papers dealing with these various aspects are published in a book edited by Boje and Tomczak (1978).

## 5.4 MATHEMATICAL MODELS OF UPWELLING

### 5.4.1 Homogeneous water

Unless the water is stratified, so that upwelling brings to the surface water of different characteristics from that otherwise found there, the occurrence of upwelling is of little practical interest. In studying the dynamics of the process, however, homogeneous models have proved to be useful as the water movements are often governed primarily by wind stress and surface slopes. The Ekman–Sverdrup model, which does not allow explicitly for frictional effects in the water, has been described above. The next stage is to include vertical and horizontal frictional terms in the equations of motion.

With axes as in Fig. 5.2, the steady state equations, including constant coefficients of eddy viscosity, $N_H$ in the horizontal and $N_v$ in the vertical directions, and assuming the $v$-component of velocity to be uniform in the $y$-direction, may be written:

$$-fv = -g\frac{\partial \zeta}{\partial x} + N_H \frac{\partial^2 u}{\partial x^2} + N_v \frac{\partial^2 u}{\partial z^2} \left.\right\} \tag{5.7}$$

$$fu = -g\frac{\partial \zeta}{\partial y} + N_H \frac{\partial^2 v}{\partial x^2} + N_v \frac{\partial^2 v}{\partial z^2} \left.\right\} \tag{5.8}$$

$$\frac{\partial u}{\partial x} + \frac{\partial w}{\partial z} = 0 \ . \tag{5.9}$$

In equations (5.7) and (5.8), $\zeta$ represents the elevation of the sea surface. Two length scales $D_H$ and $D_v$ may be defined by the equations

$$D_H = \left(\frac{N_H}{f}\right)^{1/2} , \quad D_v = \left(\frac{N_v}{f}\right)^{1/2} \tag{5.10}$$

$D_v$ corresponds to the Ekman layer depth and $D_H$ is an analogous horizontal mixing length.

Hidaka (1954) obtained an analytical solution to a model governed by equations (5.7), (5.8) and (5.9) but with the additional assumption that the water surface had no slope parallel to the coast, so that in (5.8) the $-g \ \partial\zeta/\partial y$ term was zero. He also assumed an infinitely deep ocean and a constant wind stress acting over the area extending from the coast to a distance $2\pi D_H$. The most significant features of the solution are:

(a) The offshore mass transport takes place in a surface layer of thickness $D_v$;

(b) Upwelling takes place within a zone adjacent to the coast of width $D_H$;

(c) The ratio of vertical to horizontal velocity is that of $D_v$ to $D_H$, i.e.

$$\frac{w}{u} = \frac{D_v}{D_H} = \left(\frac{N_v}{N_H}\right)^{1/2} \tag{5.11}$$

If $N_v/N_H \sim 10^{-6}$, which is a reasonable order of magnitude, and $u \sim 1 \ \mathrm{cm \ s^{-1}}$, then $w \sim 10^{-3} \ \mathrm{cm \ s^{-1}}$. Also $D_H/D_v \sim 10^3$, so that if $D_v \sim 20 \ \mathrm{m}$, then $D_H \sim 20 \ \mathrm{km}$.

A more complete analysis of the steady state, homogeneous water model was given by Garvine (1971), who retained the $\partial\zeta/\partial y$ term and considered water of uniform depth $H$ which was large compared with $D_v$. Including a finite $\partial\zeta/\partial y$ term led to the following significant differences compared with Hidaka's solution:

(i) The onshore transport of water below the surface Ekman layer can be uniformly distributed with depth: there is no need for a bottom Ekman layer. Beyond a narrow coastal boundary layer, the frictional terms on the right-hand side of equation (5.8) may be neglected, leaving the geostrophic balance:

$$fu = -g \frac{\partial\zeta}{\partial y} \tag{5.12}$$

(ii) Outside the coastal boundary layer, the net transport offshore across any vertical section parallel to the coast is zero so that

$$\int_{-H}^{0} \rho u \ \mathrm{d}z = 0 \ . \tag{5.13}$$

In the surface layer the offshore Ekman transport is $M_x = \tau_{sy}/f$ while the transport due to geostrophic flow throughout the depth is, from equation (5.12),

$$- \int_{-H}^{0} \rho \, \frac{g}{f} \frac{\partial \zeta}{\partial y} \, dz = - \frac{\rho g H}{f} \frac{\partial \zeta}{\partial y} \; .$$

Inserting these values in equation (5.13) gives the surface gradient, which is

$$\frac{\partial \zeta}{\partial y} = \frac{\tau_{sy}}{\rho g H} \tag{5.14}$$

(iii) Further analysis showed that, in the conditions postulated by Garvine,

$$\int_{-H}^{0} v \, dz = 0 \; . \tag{5.15}$$

This means that below the surface current parallel to the coast, in the direction of the wind, there must be a compensating undercurrent flowing in the opposite direction.

Taking the wind stress $\tau_{sy} = 0.2$ N m$^{-2}$, as in the earlier example, a water depth $H = 100$ m, $g = 9.8$ m s$^{-2}$ and $\rho = 1{,}025$ kg m$^{-3}$, equation (5.14) gives the longshore slope as $2 \times 10^{-7}$ approximately, i.e. 2 cm in 100 km. In latitude $30°$, so that $f = 7.29 \times 10^{-5}$ s$^{-1}$, equation (5.12) gives the onshore flow, uniform with depth, as $u = 2.7$ cm s$^{-1}$. If the offshore Ekman transport is confined to the upper 20 m, the average offshore velocity in this layer would be about 11 cm s$^{-1}$.

In a later paper Garvine included the effect of depth varying in the offshore direction.

## 5.4.2 Two-layer models

The simplest way to take into account the vertical variation of density, which is a feature of any real upwelling region, is to postulate a two-layer model, in which each layer is of uniform density. Such models have played a useful part in the development of upwelling theory, particularly in studying the transient state during the early stages of an upwelling event.

The equations of momentum balance and continuity are written down for each layer, allowing for vertical movement of the interface between them. In general, a shearing stress across the interface can be included. Usually conditions in a vertical section, normal to a straight coastline running north–south, are considered. The velocity field is assumed to be independent of the $y$-coordinate (parallel to the coast) but a longshore slope of the surface is included. A general treatment by this method was given by Yoshida (1967), who derived both transient and steady state solutions.

As an example of a two-layer model, we will consider a quasi-steady state solution, valid for a time of the order of a day, during which the movement of the interface is small. A vertical section, normal to the coast, on a flat, wide shelf is taken, as in Fig. 5.7. The upper and lower layers are of density $\rho_1$ and $\rho_2$ respectively and their thicknesses $h_1$ and $h_2$ are functions of the offshore coordinate $x$. The velocity components are $u_1, v_1$ and $u_2, v_2$ in the two layers.

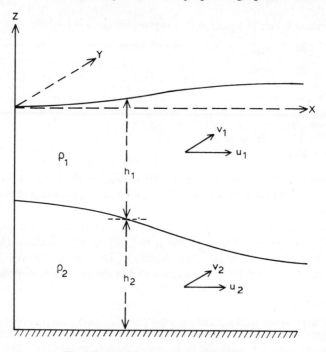

Fig. 5.7 — Two-layer model of upwelling.

The momentum equations for the upper layer are

$$fv_1 = g \frac{\partial}{\partial x}(h_1 + h_2) \tag{5.16}$$

$$fu_1 = -g \frac{\partial}{\partial y}(h_1 + h_2) + \frac{\tau_{sy}}{\rho_1 h_1} + N_H \frac{\partial^2 v_1}{\partial x^2} \tag{5.17}$$

and for the lower layer

$$fv_2 = g \frac{\partial}{\partial x}(h_1 + h_2) - g' \frac{\partial h_1}{\partial x} \tag{5.18}$$

$$fu_2 = -g \frac{\partial}{\partial y}(h_1 + h_2) + N_H \frac{\partial^2 v_2}{\partial x^2} \tag{5.19}$$

where $\qquad g' = \dfrac{\rho_2 - \rho_1}{\rho_2} g$ $\hfill$ (5.20)

$\tau_{sy}$ is the wind stress on the surface and $N_H$ is the coefficient of horizontal eddy viscosity.

The horizontal shear stress terms are important only within a distance of the coast given by

$$D_H = \left(\frac{N_H v_1}{f u_1}\right)^{1/2} \hspace{3cm} (5.21)$$

where $v_1$ is determined by equation (5.16) and $u_1$ by the Ekman transport. With typical numerical values, $D_H$ is of the order of 5 km.

Further offshore, equations (5.17) and (5.19) lead to the following equations for the offshore transport in the two layers

$$\rho_1 u_1 h_1 = \frac{\tau_{sy}}{f} - \frac{\rho_1 g h_1}{f} \frac{\partial}{\partial y}(h_1 + h_2) \hspace{2cm} (5.22)$$

$$\rho_2 u_2 h_2 = -\frac{\rho_2 g h_2}{f} \frac{\partial}{\partial y}(h_1 + h_2) \hspace{2cm} (5.23)$$

Equation (5.22) gives a reduced Ekman transport offshore, which is less than the pure Ekman value because of the alongshore surface gradient. Equation (5.23) gives the return flow shoreward in the lower layer, which is balanced geostrophically by the alongshore gradient. A small alongshore pressure gradient, of the order of a few centimetres per 1000 km, appears to play an essential part in coastal upwelling.

By considering the vorticity of the flow over the whole upwelling area, it may be shown that a coastal jet, flowing in the direction of the wind, develops in the upper layer and a counter jet, flowing in the opposite direction, in the lower layer. If the wind stress curl vanishes over the upwelling region, it may be shown that the vertically integrated alongshore transport is zero, so that

$$v_1 h_1 + v_2 h_2 = 0 . \hspace{3cm} (5.24)$$

From equations (5.16), (5.18), and (5.24) it follows that

$$v_1 = \frac{g'}{f} \frac{h_2}{(h_1 + h_2)} \frac{\partial h_1}{\partial x} \hspace{2.5cm} (5.25)$$

$$v_2 = -\frac{g'}{f} \frac{h_1}{(h_1 + h_2)} \frac{\partial h_1}{\partial x} . \hspace{2.5cm} (5.26)$$

Several scales representative of coastal upwelling may be derived from the two-layer model and these will be quoted, without going into further details of the solutions. The appropriate scale for width of the upwelling zone is the Rossby baroclinic radius of deformation which, for the two-layer model, is given by

$$\lambda = \frac{1}{f} \left( \frac{g' H_1 H_2}{H_1 + H_2} \right)^{1/2} \tag{5.27}$$

where $g'$ is given by equation (5.20), while $H_1$ and $H_2$ are the undisturbed thicknesses of the two layers, $H_1 + H_2$ being the total depth of water.

The time scale for the interface to reach the surface, starting from the horizontal, is given by

$$T = \frac{\rho_1 H_1 \lambda f}{\tau_{sy}} \tag{5.28}$$

A typical value of the vertical velocity is given by

$$W = \frac{\tau_{sy}}{\rho_1 \lambda f} \tag{5.29}$$

To obtain numerical estimates, we may take $\tau_{sy} = 0.1$ N m$^{-2}$, $H_1 = 50$ m, $H_2 = 150$ m, $g = 9.8$ m s$^{-2}$, $\rho_1 = 1{,}025$ kg m$^{-3}$, $\rho_2 = 1{,}026$ kg m$^{-3}$ and latitude 30° so that $f = 7.29 \times 10^{-5}$ s$^{-1}$. Then $g' = 9.55 \times 10^{-3}$ m s$^{-2}$ and from (5.27) the baroclinic radius of deformation, $\lambda$, is 8.2 km. From (5.28) the time $T$ taken for the interface, initially at 50 m, to reach the surface is 85 hours, about three-and-a-half days. A typical vertical velocity, during this initial stage, while the interface is rising, is given by (5.29) as $W = 1.6 \times 10^{-2}$ cm s$^{-1}$.

If the surface layer thickness is small compared with that of the lower layer, i.e. $H_1 \ll H_2$, it is seen from (5.27) that

$$\lambda \approx \frac{1}{f} (g' H_1)^{1/2} \tag{5.30}$$

For the numerical values of $f$ and $g'$ given above and with $H_1 = 50$ m, this gives a baroclinic radius of deformation of 9.5 km approximately. The corresponding vertical velocity, from (5.29), with $\tau_{sy} = 0.1$ N m$^{-2}$ as before, would be $1.4 \times 10^{-2}$ cm s$^{-1}$ approximately.

### 5.4.3 Continuously stratified models

The next stage in the refinement of a model of upwelling is to allow for the density to vary continuously with depth, as in the real sea. An analytical study of a model of this type was described by Allen (1973) and similar concepts formed the basis of the numerical model of Hamilton and Rattray (1978).

The following parameters which are relevant to this type of model may be defined:

(a)  The Brunt–Väisälä frequency $N$, given by

$$N^2 = -\frac{g}{\rho}\frac{\partial \rho}{\partial z} \tag{5.31}$$

where $z$ is measured upwards. $N$ may be regarded as a measure of the density gradient.

(b)  The Rossby radius of deformation $R$, given by

$$R = \frac{Nh}{f} \tag{5.32}$$

where $h$ is the depth of water. Upwelling occurs mainly within a distance $R$ from the coast. The parameter $R$ is analogous to the baroclinic radius of deformation $\lambda$, defined above for the two-layer model.

(c)  The Ekman number $E_v$, given by

$$E_v = \frac{N_v}{fh^2} \tag{5.33}$$

where $N_v$ is the coefficient of vertical eddy viscosity. (Note that $N_v$ is not to be confused with $N$, the Brunt–Väisälä frequency.)

The basic equations of the model, taking rectangular axes as before, with the $x$-axis perpendicular to the coast, the $y$-axis parallel to the coast and the $z$-axis vertically upwards are

$$\frac{\partial u}{\partial t} - fv = -\frac{1}{\rho}\frac{\partial p}{\partial x} + N_H\frac{\partial^2 u}{\partial x^2} + N_v\frac{\partial^2 u}{\partial z^2} \tag{5.34}$$

$$\frac{\partial v}{\partial t} + fu = -\frac{1}{\rho}\frac{\partial p}{\partial y} + N_H\frac{\partial^2 v}{\partial y^2} + N_v\frac{\partial^2 v}{\partial z^2} \tag{5.35}$$

$$\frac{\partial u}{\partial x} + \frac{\partial w}{\partial z} = 0 \tag{5.36}$$

with the following equation for the conservation of density:

$$\frac{\partial \rho}{\partial t} + u\frac{\partial \rho}{\partial x} + w\frac{\partial \rho}{\partial z} = K_H\frac{\partial^2 \rho}{\partial x^2} + K_v\frac{\partial^2 \rho}{\partial z^2} \tag{5.37}$$

where $K_H$ and $K_v$ are the coefficients of horizontal and vertical diffusion of density respectively. In these equations it is assumed that $N_H, N_v, K_H$ and $K_v$ are all independent of position.

The pressure $p$ is given by the equation

$$p = p_a + g\rho_0\zeta - g\int_0^z \rho \, dz \qquad (5.38)$$

where $p_a$ is the atmospheric pressure, $\rho_0$ is the density of the surface water and $\zeta$ the elevation of the surface. By differentiating equation (5.38), the values of $\partial p/\partial x$ and $\partial p/\partial y$ for use in equations (5.34) and (5.35) can be obtained.

The analytical solutions obtained by Allen will not be described here, but on the basis of them it is possible to formulate a conceptual model having the following features:

(1) Upwelling events, lasting for a period of several days to one or two weeks, are superimposed on a quasi-steady state circulation which is subject to seasonal variations.

(2) In the quasi-steady state circulation, there is offshore flow in a surface Ekman layer. Below this layer there is an onshore flow which is in geostrophic balance with an alongshore pressure gradient. The onshore flow is not necessarily uniform with depth but may have a baroclinic component. In relatively shallow water on the shelf, the onshore flow tends to become concentrated in a bottom Ekman layer.

(3) In a wind-generated upwelling event the following features may be distinguished.

   (i) The surface layer flow and Ekman transport is developed first, on a time-scale of order $f^{-1}$, i.e. in about a day. The onshore flow, below the Ekman layer, is initially almost uniform with depth.

   (ii) The spin-up time for the development of (a) the slope of the sea surface, which is lowered at the coast, (b) the alongshore current and (c) the bottom Ekman layer is on a time-scale $E_v^{-1/2} f^{-1}$ which is typically of the order of 3 days.

   (iii) The vertical upwelling movement of water takes place within a zone adjacent to the coast of width equivalent to the Rossby radius of deformation. It is accompanied by a bending of the isopycnal surfaces upwards towards the coast and the resulting pressure gradients cause an increase in the alongshore current leading to the development of a coastal jet.

   (iv) Horizontal diffusion of density and momentum becomes significant on a time scale $T_H$ given by

$$T_H = \frac{h^2 N^2}{f^2 K_H} \qquad (5.39)$$

$T_H$ is typically of the order of 25 days.

(4) When the wind ceases to blow, or weakens significantly, reverse changes occur in the water movements:

   (i) The surface Ekman drift stops almost immediately and reverses, becoming onshore at the surface and offshore below the surface layer.

   (ii) The alongshore current and the flow in the bottom Ekman layer relax more slowly.

   (iii) The slope of the isopycnal surfaces also relaxes more slowly.

The numerical model of Hamilton and Rattray (1978) allowed for the depth of water to vary across the shelf and included vertical eddy coefficients of viscosity and diffusion which were functions of the local Richardson number. A number of spin-up experiments, with a wind stress applied suddenly at time $t = 0$, demonstrated quantitatively the features shown in Allen's model. A sloping shelf was found to intensify flow in the bottom Ekman layer and could produce secondary cross-shelf circulations, depending on the values of the eddy coefficients. The model was also applied to an upwelling event off north-west Africa and the computed current and density fields were in reasonable agreement with those observed, considering the simplifications made in the model.

### 5.4.4 Other aspects of modelling

Many models of upwelling, including those described in the previous section, have been two-dimensional in that they have assumed wind stress, flow conditions and the density distribution to be uniform in a direction parallel to the coast. A number of theoretical workers from Yoshida (1967) onwards, however, have considered the effect of including a wind stress which varies with position along the coast, as well as with time, in a two-layer model. They have shown that the vertical movements of the interface and the patterns of flow in the two layers can be interpreted as the generation and propagation of internal Kelvin waves. Such waves travel along the shelf with the coast on the right of the direction of propagation in the northern hemisphere. Thus in the case of a northerly wind blowing along a coast on the eastern side of an ocean, the occurrence of upwelling at a particular position is influenced by the wind stress at earlier times at positions nearer the equator, as well as by the local wind. If the slope of the bottom in the offshore direction is taken into account, continental shelf waves may also be generated. The development with time of equatorward flow in the upper layer and poleward flow in the lower is also reproduced by these models. By extending the model to include developments after the interface reaches the surface, Suginohara (1977) was able to simulate the formation of a front and a two-cell circulation, normal to the coast, as found in some observations.

Observations of currents in a particular section normal to the coast rarely show a balance between the offshore Ekman transport and the onshore compensating flow. The natural inference is that the balance is maintained by horizontal convergence or divergence of flow resulting from variations in the alongshore direction. This feature can be reproduced in models which include an alongshore variation in bottom topography. The numerical two-layer model of Peffley and O'Brien (1976) included a smoothed representation of the bottom topography off a length of the Oregon coast. The results showed that variations in bottom topography were more important than coastline irregularities in determining the alongshore changes in upwelling. In general a mass balance was not established in a section normal to the coast. In the case of a submarine ridge running offshore, for example, there was a net transport offshore to the north (upwind) of the ridge and onshore to the south (downwind) of it.

# 6

# Density currents and salinity distribution

## 6.1 INTRODUCTION

### 6.1.1 Transition from estuary to coastal water

Along many coasts there is an influx of river water, producing a zone of low salinity water which mixes gradually with that of higher salinity further ashore. The mixing of river water and sea water usually starts in estuaries and gives rise to characteristic patterns of estuarine circulation and salinity distribution. The presence of a density gradient, with the density increasing from the river end to the mouth of an estuary, produces pressure gradients within the water. These in turn tend to produce a seaward flow of low salinity water in an upper layer with an upstream flow of higher salinity water below it. Tidal currents, if present, tend to cause vertical mixing between the two layers, reducing the salinity difference.

It is the interaction between processes arising from the river discharge on one hand and the tidal currents on the other, which leads to the occurrence of a series of types of estuary circulation, described in detail in textbooks such as those of Dyer (1973) and Officer (1976). At one extreme is the salt wedge estuary, in which the influence of river discharge is dominant and fresh water flows out of the estuary as a surface layer above an intruding wedge of sea water. At the other extreme, when the tidal currents are dominant, the water is almost completely mixed vertically and there is little variation in current with depth. In the intermediate case of a partially mixed estuary there is a gradual increase of salinity from surface to bottom, with a net seaward flow (averaged over a tidal period) in the upper layer and an upstream flow below it.

If the depth of water varies across the estuary with, for example, a deep channel in the centre and shallower water at the sides, the upstream flow is often confined to the deep channel with seaward flow extending to the bottom in the shallower parts of the cross-section. Across the estuary there will be a transverse slope of the isohaline and ispycnal surfaces arising from the Coriolis effect. with the surfaces sloping downward to the right, looking towards the sea, in the northern hemisphere and to the left in the southern hemisphere. The upper layer of outflowing water will, therefore, be deeper on the right-hand side and shallower on the left. In a sufficiently wide estuary, in fact, the interface between the outflowing and inflowing layers may reach the surface so that on the left hand side, in the northern hemisphere, the upstream flow reaches the surface.

Where a salt wedge estuary or a highly stratified estuary opens out into the sea, the low salinity water flowing out as a surface layer usually forms a pronounced plume, which can be traced for a considerable distance out to sea. Some examples will be described later. The plume is often separated from the surrounding water by a narrow region of high density gradient, known as a front, which is associated with a local pattern of water movements, giving a convergence zone at the surface. In the case of other estuaries, where considerable mixing with sea water takes place in the estuary itself, the salinity of the water leaving the mouth does not differ so much from that of the coastal water and a distinctive plume is not formed. The mixing of estuarine and offshore water then takes place by the action of turbulent diffusion, probably associated with horizontal eddies in the tidal or wind-driven currents.

### 6.1.2 Interaction between salinity distribution and currents

In the coastal area, as in an estuary, the density-driven circulation is largely determined by the distribution of salinity. This is itself influenced by the currents and the effects of turbulent mixing in the vertical and horizontal directions. There is, therefore, an interaction between the currents and the salinity distribution and to treat this mathematically the equations of momentum balance and salt balance should be solved simultaneously. In a narrow estuary, where the horizontal current is constrained to flow parallel to the axis of the estuary and Coriolis effects can be neglected, the equations can be solved without difficulty in many cases. A number of analytical solutions are given in the book by Officer (1976). Off an open coast, however, Coriolis effects cannot be neglected and the horizontal current is essentially two-dimensional. It becomes much more difficult to derive analytical solutions to the simultaneous equations, even in apparently simple cases. An approach often adopted, therefore, is to assume the density distribution to be known from observations and to calculate the current distribution which arises from it.

In this chapter the main features of plumes and fronts will be considered first. The density-driven current off a straight coast, assuming the density distribution to be known, will then be treated. Some useful results on the mixing of water in a coastal area or on a continental shelf may be obtained by considerations of continuity alone and examples of these will be given. We will then return to the question of treating the density distribution and currents as a single interacting system and discuss attempts to deal with this problem.

## 6.2 PLUMES OF LOW SALINITY WATER

### 6.2.1 General features

The surface layer of low salinity water flowing out from an estuary often forms a distinct plume, which can be traced over a wide area of the continental shelf. In some cases, as at the mouth of a salt wedge estuary, the upper layer is divided by a sharp halocline from the higher salinity coastal water below it. Because of the lower density of the plume water, its free surface is above the level of the surrounding sea water. The resulting pressure gradients cause a lateral spreading of the plume over the ambient sea water, accompanied by a thinning in its vertical extent. A sharp front often separates the plume from the surrounding water. The main driving force in the equations of motion for water in the plume is the pressure gradient, arising from the buoyancy of the low salinity water. The other forces which may play a significant part are friction at the interface with the lower layer, possibly accompanied by entrainment, vertical turbulent stresses and horizontal turbulent stresses. In general the Coriolis effect should be considered and in some cases, particularly near the edge of the plume, the inertial acceleration terms may be significant. It becomes difficult to include all these effects in a dynamical treatment and usually one or two effects are assumed to be dominant.

Other estuaries, although not of the salt wedge type, are partially stratified and are characterised by a two-layer flow at the mouth. The rate of transport of outflowing low salinity water in the upper layer and of inflowing higher salinity water below may each be an order of magnitude or more greater than the discharge of fresh water into the estuary. In these cases the outflowing surface layer water may spread as a plume over a wide area of sea.

In a third type of estuary vertical mixing within the estuary or at its mouth may weaken the two-layer structure to such an extent that the water is practically homogeneous. Spreading into the coastal water then takes place mainly by horizontal turbulent mixing. It is still possible for sharp transitions or fronts to occur between the coastal water and that further offshore. In all cases the movement and dispersion of plumes as they move away from the estuary mouth are dependent to a large extent on the winds and currents which are present on the continental shelf.

### 6.2.2 Examples of plumes

A good example of a salt wedge estuary is that of the River Mississippi. Under low discharge conditions the salt wedge extends for more than 300 km upstream in the main channel but at very high discharges it is pushed completely out of the estuary. The river water leaving the mouth spreads as a plume over the shallow water of the delta on to the continental shelf of the Gulf of Mexico. The behaviour of the plume, with its load of suspended sediment, has been the subject of a number of investigations, including that of Wright and Coleman

(1971) who gave a theoretical treatment, which is mentioned later. The spreading river water has a considerable influence on the coastal band of water out to the edge of the continental shelf, as marked by the 200 m contour which, in the region of the delta, is about 50 km from the coast.

The Columbia River flows into the Pacific Ocean as the boundary between the states of Washington and Oregon, USA. Its estuary is partially mixed as a result of a high river discharge averaging 7,300 $m^3$ $s^{-1}$, combined with strong tidal currents. The outflowing upper layer forms a plume of relatively low salinity water which can be distinguished over a large area of the adjacent ocean. The behaviour of the plume depends largely on the wind and wind-driven currents and shows a seasonal variation. In the winter the prevailing winds are from the south and there is a northward flow of coastal water. As shown in Fig. 6.1(a), the plume turns to the north on leaving the river mouth and is held to the coast as it spreads northward, gradually becoming dispersed. In summer the winds are from the north and there is a southward surface current, with an Ekman component in the offshore direction. The plume moves westward from the mouth and spreads to the south-west. The surface layer of low salinity water is perceptible over a large area, as shown in Fig. 6.1(b) taken from a paper by Duxbury (1965). Because of wind-induced upwelling off the Oregon coast, the plume water is separated from the coast by a band of colder, more saline water. Bottom drifter experiments near the mouth of the Columbia River have indicated a movement of bottom water towards the mouth and into the estuary, below the surface outflow.

Another example of a river plume, the behaviour of which is largely determined by wind conditions, is that of the Hudson River flowing into the New York Bight. In light winds the low salinity plume tends to meander across the open waters of the Bight, with rather diffuse boundaries, whereas in stronger winds it hugs the coast to the north or south of the mouth, depending on the wind direction. Figure 6.2, taken from Bowman (1978) shows the plume held to the coast of New Jersey as it moves southward under the influence of northerly winds. A number of studies of the Hudson River plume, in relation to its influence on pollution and sedimentation, have been made.

The River Amazon has such a high rate of discharge, averaging $175 \times 10^3$ $m^3$ $s^{-1}$, that in spite of considerable tidal movements, no penetration of sea water into the estuary occurs. The water leaving the mouth is completely fresh but intense mixing with sea water takes place in a region of shallow water just outside the mouth. The mixed water, still of relatively low salinity, then spreads as a surface layer parallel to the coast, in a northwesterly direction, merging with the Guiana Current. The low salinity water can be identified as far as 1,000 km from the river mouth (Gibbs, 1970).

These examples serve to indicate both the common features of plumes of estuary water spreading in the open sea and also the variations which occur due to different local conditions and changing wind regime.

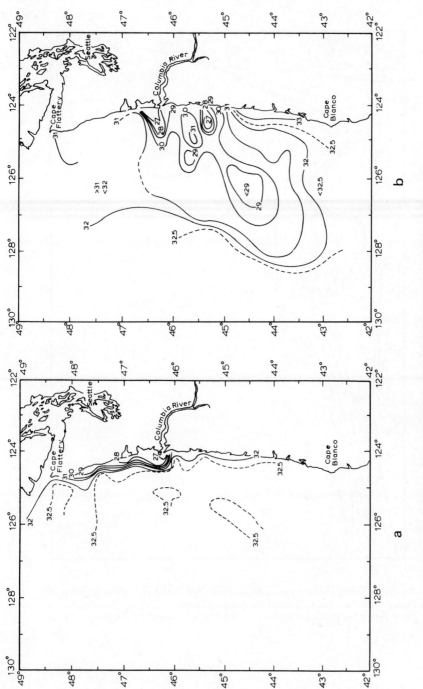

Fig. 6.1 – Surface salinity in the region affected by the Columbia River discharge: (a) winter, (b) summer. From Duxbury (1965), by courtesy of the Marine Technology Society, Washington, D.C.

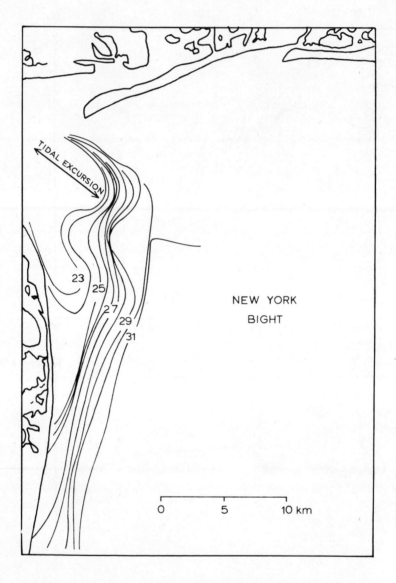

Fig. 6.2 – Surface salinity in the New York Bight, 19 August 1976, showing the plume from the River Hudson discharge. Contours show the salinity in $^o/_{oo}$. From Bowman (1978), by courtesy of the Elsevier Scientific Publishing Company.

### 6.2.3 Dynamics of plumes

Various theoretical treatments have been given for the spreading of a plume of lower density water over a body of denser water. The primary driving force for the spreading is the buoyancy of the plume water which causes its free surface to be above the level of the surrounding denser water. The elevation of the free surface gives rise to horizontal pressure gradients which produce the spreading of the plume as it moves over the underlying water. If there is no significant mixing of water across the interface, the plume necessarily becomes thinner in its vertical extent as it spreads laterally.

A simple steady state theory of a plume of river water entering the sea off a straight coast was given by Takano in 1954 and was reproduced in the books of Defant (1961) and Officer (1976). It is assumed that the only force acting in addition to the pressure gradient is horizontal eddy viscosity. It is assumed further that there is a constant rate of discharge of water from the river mouth, that there is no mixing across the interface between the plume and the underlying water, and that the velocities are sufficiently low for the inertial acceleration terms to be negligible. If the Coriolis acceleration is neglected, the solution for the thickness of the plume shows that it is symmetrical about the extension of the river axis out to sea.

In particular the plume is bounded laterally by the branches of the hyperbola

$$y^2 = x^2 + l^2$$

as shown in Fig. 6.3(a), where the origin of coordinates is at the centre of the river mouth, the $x$-axis is directed along the extension of the river axis, the $y$-axis is along the coast and $2l$ is the width of the river at its mouth. The relative depth of the plume varies as shown by the dotted lines in Fig. 6.3(a), decreasing laterally away from the $x$-axis. The form of the plume is independent of the magnitude of the coefficient of horizontal eddy viscosity, $N_h$, which is assumed not to vary with position.

When the Coriolis effect is taken into account, the plume is no longer symmetrical about the $x$-axis but deviates to the right in the northern hemisphere, as shown in Fig. 6.3(b), the extent of the deviation being dependent on the parameter $R$, given by

$$R = \frac{fl^2}{N_h} .$$

In several cases of observed plumes, their form has appeared to be similar to that given by Takano's solution, but the extent of their deviation has been found to correspond to values of $N_h$ of order $10^8$ cm$^2$ s$^{-1}$, which is about two orders of magnitude higher than values derived for coastal waters in other ways. This discrepancy suggests that the processes which have been neglected, such as entrainment or interfacial friction, may have been significant so that their neglect would lead to spuriously high values of horizontal eddy viscosity. A further

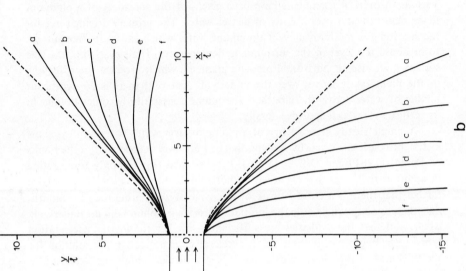

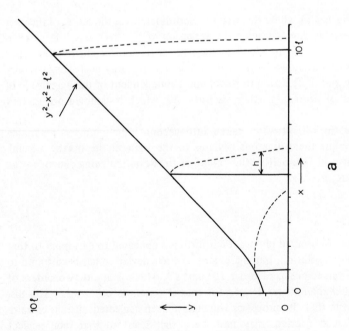

Fig. 6.3 – Spreading of the plume from a river discharge: (a) Coriolis effect neglected, (b) Coriolis effect taken into account. The lines a, b, c, d, e and f correspond to values of $500R = 1, 2, 4, 8, 16$, and $32$ respectively. From Takano
(1954, 1955), by courtesy of The Oceanographical Society of Japan.

point is that Takano's theory assumes the water over which the plume spreads is at rest. If there is a current flowing parallel to the coast it will cause a deviation of the plume towards the down-current direction which may predominate over that due to the Coriolis effect alone.

A different theoretical approach was used by Wright and Coleman (1971) in their treatment of the spread of water from the South Pass distributary of the Mississippi into the Gulf of Mexico. They assumed that entrainment of sea water upwards through the base of the plume predominated over lateral mixing. The spreading of the plume then depended on two parameters only: (1) the relative density difference between the plume and underlying water, given by

$$\gamma = \frac{\rho_2 - \rho_1}{\rho_1}$$

where $\rho_1$ and $\rho_2$ are the densities of the plume and underlying water respectively; (2) the densimetric Froude number given by

$$F_i = \frac{U}{(\gamma g H)^{1/2}}$$

where $U$ is the mean velocity in the upper layer and $H$ is the depth to the interface.

The free surface of the plume is at a height $\Delta\zeta$, given by $\Delta\zeta = \gamma H$, above the level of the surrounding water and the rate of lateral flow, away from the centre line of the plume, is given by $V_b = (2g\gamma Z)^{1/2}$, where $Z$ is the distance above the interface.

At the mouth of the South Pass, $F_i$ is found by observations to be near its critical value of unity. As $H$ decreases with lateral expansion of the plume, $F_i$ becomes supercritical, leading to the formation of internal waves on the interface and entrainment of denser water into the plume. This results in a reduction of the mean velocity and an increase in the density of the plume water. The upward entrainment velocity, according to an equation given earlier by Keulegan, is

$$U_e = 3.5 \times 10^{-4} (U - 1.15 U_c)$$

where $U_c$ is a threshold velocity. In this case $U_c$ was taken to be given by $U_c = (\gamma g H)^{1/2}$. Using these concepts, equations were derived from which the changes in breadth $b$, thickness $H$, velocity $U$, relative density $\gamma$ and internal Froude number $F_i$ could be calculated. At the mouth of South Pass the breadth was 240 m, the thickness of the plume 1 to 2 m, the velocity 0.8 to 1.2 m s$^{-1}$ and $\gamma$ from 0.014 to 0.020, with $F_i$ between 0.8 and 1.2. At a distance from the mouth equal to 8 times its breadth, the width of the plume had increased by a factor of between 6 and 8 and its thickness had decreased by a factor of 4.

A more general theoretical model for the flow of estuary water over an adjacent shelf was described by Beardsley and Hart (1978). This is a two-layer model, driven by a seaward flux of water in the upper layer and a shoreward flux in the lower layer, which allows for friction at the interface and at the bed, includes the Coriolis effect and variable bottom topography but neglects lateral friction. Analytical solutions were found for the streamlines of flow, given certain distributions of bottom topography, but they are too complicated to be reproduced here. With the lower layer at rest, the Coriolis effect causes the upper layer flow to deviate to the right on leaving the mouth of the estuary, as in Takano's solution. When flow in the lower layer is included, however, the deviation in the upper layer may be to the left because of the influence of the slope of the interface. Solutions were given for estuary flow into a current flowing alongshore as well as into a sea with no mean current. The model predictions were compared with current observations in the vicinity of the Hudson estuary outflow to the New York Bight and at the mouth of Chesapeake Bay. In the latter case the spreading of the outflowing water in the upper layer was shown to be accompanied by an inflow towards Chesapeake Bay in the lower layer, drawn from a width of about 30 km of the continental shelf.

## 6.3 FRONTS

Fronts occur on a wide range of scales, starting with those formed within an estuary between inflowing river water and the estuary water. On a rather larger scale are the fronts bordering plumes entering the open sea, as described above. Other fronts are found on the continental shelf, separating a zone of coastal water from oceanic water or a stratified water mass from one which is vertically mixed. Fronts also occur on a larger scale in the deep ocean, between water masses of different properties.

The essential feature of a front bordering a plume is the density difference between the water on the two sides of it but other features are often present, enabling it to be detected visually. There is often a colour difference between the water masses, arising from a greater concentration of phytoplankton or suspended particles in one than in the other. The front itself is frequently marked by a line of foam or of floating debris. The various indications of the position of a front do not always coincide exactly. Figure 6.4, taken from Bowman and Iverson (1978), shows how the foam line, the detritus line and the colour line may become separated. The foam line is located at the surface convergence, the detritus line where buoyant objects are trapped by currents moving in opposite directions at the surface and near the interface and the colour front where the upwelled light undergoes a distinct spectral shift in the region of the steeply descending isopycnals. Since the slope of the front is probably of order $10^{-2}$, the three lines may be separated by several tens of metres. The colour change, or in some cases a change in surface roughness and hence in optical reflectivity, enables the front to be detected by aerial photography or by remote sensing from a satellite.

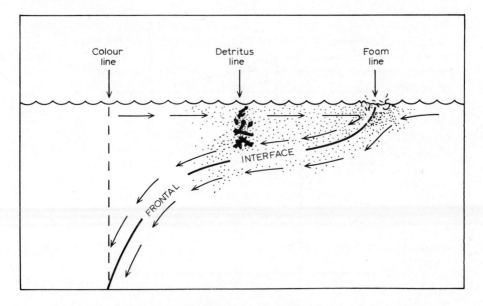

Fig. 6.4 – Schematic cross-section of a shallow front, showing the visual indications of the front. From Bowman and Iverson (1978), by courtesy of Springer-Verlag.

The various features of a front are determined by the pattern of currents in its vicinity. The following simplified treatment of the dynamics of a front follows that of Officer (1976, page 133) or that of Model 2 of Bowman and Iverson (1978). A front cannot remain stationary relative to the underlying water but will advance across it at a velocity $c$ given by

$$c = (\gamma g \bar{h})^{1/2} \tag{6.1}$$

where $\gamma = (\rho_2 - \rho_1)/\rho_2$ as before and $\bar{h}$ is a depth characteristic of the upper layer. It is possible to find a steady state solution for the velocities in the two layers, however, relative to the moving front.

Let axes be taken as in Fig. 6.5, with origin at the front, the $x$-axis perpendicular to the front, the $y$-axis along it and the $z$-axis vertically upwards. Let $\rho_1$ and $\rho_2$ be the density in the upper and lower layer respectively, $\zeta_1$ the elevation of the free surface and $\zeta_2$ that of the interface so that $\zeta_1 - \zeta_2$ is the total depth of the upper layer ($\zeta_2$ is negative). The cross-frontal velocities are $u_1$ and $u_2$ in the upper and lower layers respectively.

Coriolis effects and inertial acceleration terms are neglected. Internal friction is parameterised by a constant eddy viscosity $N_z$ in the upper layer and it is assumed that there is no entrainment between the two layers.

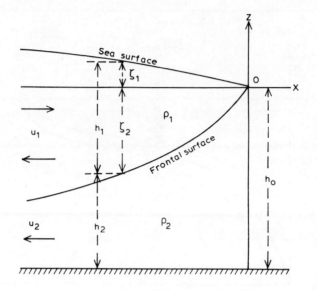

Fig. 6.5 – Coordinate system for cross-frontal circulation.

In a steady state, the equations of motions in the cross-frontal direction in the two layers are

$$\frac{\partial p_1}{\partial x} = \rho_1 N_z \frac{\partial^2 u_1}{\partial z^2} \tag{6.2}$$

$$\frac{\partial p_2}{\partial x} = \rho_2 N_z \frac{\partial^2 u_2}{\partial z^2} \tag{6.3}$$

where the pressures $p_1$ and $p_2$ are given from the hydrostatic equation by

$$p_1 = g\rho_1(\zeta_1 - z) \tag{6.4}$$

$$p_2 = g\rho_1(\zeta_1 - \zeta_2) + g\rho_2(\zeta_2 - z) . \tag{6.5}$$

If $h_1$ and $h_2$ denote the thicknesses of the two layers and $h_0$ the depth of water, as in Fig. 6.5, the continuity equations for the two layers are

$$\int_{-h_1}^{0} u_1 \, dz = 0 \tag{6.6}$$

$$\int_{-h_0}^{-h_1} u_2 \, dz = q = \text{constant} . \tag{6.7}$$

In these equations it is assumed that $\zeta_1 \ll \zeta_2$, so that in the limits of integration $\zeta_1$ is taken as zero and $\zeta_2$ as $-h_1$. Equation (6.6) expresses the condition that there is no net integrated flow in the upper layer perpendicular to the front. If the front is advancing with velocity $c$ over water initially at rest, then $q = -ch_0$.

In order to simplify the solution, it will be assumed that the thickness of the upper layer is only a small fraction of the total depth and that the velocity is practically uniform with depth in the lower layer. It will also be assumed that the stress at the interface may be related to the velocity in the lower layer (relative to the moving front) by a quadratic law with a friction coefficient $k$.

The boundary conditions may then be taken as follows:

(i) at $z = 0$,  $\dfrac{\partial u_1}{\partial z} = 0$

assuming no surface stress,

(ii) at $z = -h_1$,  $u_1 = u_2$

assuming no slip at the interface,

(iii) for $z < -h_1$,  $u_2 = $ constant,

(iv) at $z = -h_1$,  $\rho_1 N_z \dfrac{\partial u_1}{\partial z} = k\rho_2 u_2^2$ .

The solution for the velocities $u_1$ and $u_2$ is

$$u_1 = U_s \left(1 - 3\frac{z^2}{h_1^2}\right) \tag{6.8}$$

$$u_2 = -2U_s$$

where     $$U_s = \frac{3\rho_1 N_z}{2\rho_2 k h_1} \tag{6.9}$$

Thus the velocity at the interface is in the opposite direction to the surface velocity and has twice its magnitude.

The form of the interface, represented by $\zeta_2(x)$, is given by

$$x = -\frac{k\gamma g \zeta_2^4}{36 N_z^2} \tag{6.10}$$

for $x < 0$.

The slope of the interface, as given by equation (6.10), becomes infinite at the front, $x = 0$. A more realistic solution, giving a finite slope at the front, may be obtained by including the advective acceleration terms in the momentum equation. A schematic diagram of the frontal interface and the velocity profiles in the vicinity of the front is given in Fig. 6.6.

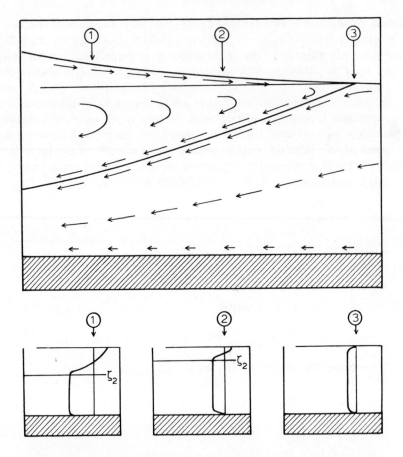

Fig. 6.6 – Schematic diagrams of velocity streamlines and cross-frontal velocity profiles at three selected positions. From Bowman and Iverson (1978), by courtesy of Springer-Verlag.

As a numerical example we may take $\rho_1 = 1{,}000$ kg m$^{-3}$, $\rho_2 = 1{,}020$ kg m$^{-3}$, corresponding to a plume of fresh water spreading over sea water of salinity $26^\circ/_{oo}$ approximately, so that $\gamma = 2 \times 10^{-2}$. Then with $g = 9.80$ m s$^{-2}$ and $\bar{h} = 1$ m, equation (6.1) gives the velocity of advance of the front as $c = 0.44$ m s$^{-1}$. If the front is advancing into water which is at rest, the velocity in the lower layer, assumed to be much deeper than the upper layer, will be $u_2 = -0.44$ m s$^{-1}$ approximately. In the upper layer, the surface velocity, from equation (6.8) will be $U_s = 0.22$ m s$^{-1}$, relative to the advancing front. With $U_s = 0.22$ m s$^{-1}$ and $h_1 = 1$ m, equation (6.9) indicates that $N_z/k \cong 0.15$ m$^2$ s$^{-1}$, implying a relationship between the eddy viscosity in the upper layer and the coefficient of interfacial friction. If $k = 2 \times 10^{-3}$, then $N_z$ would be $3 \times 10^{-4}$ m$^2$ s$^{-1} = 3$ cm$^2$ s$^{-1}$, which does not seem unreasonable.

## 6.4 DYNAMICS OF DENSITY-DRIVEN CURRENTS

### 6.4.1 Flow off a straight coast

The idealised case of flow bounded by a straight coast, as in Fig. 6.7, is considered. The $x$-axis is taken perpendicular to the coast, the $y$-axis along the coast and the $z$-axis vertically upwards. As a result of a uniform influx of river water from the coast, it is assumed that the density of the water increases in the offshore direction, the isopycnals running parallel to the coast. It is assumed that at any position the water column is vertically well mixed. Conditions are assumed to be uniform in the $y$-direction, so that $\partial/\partial y = 0$ for any variable.

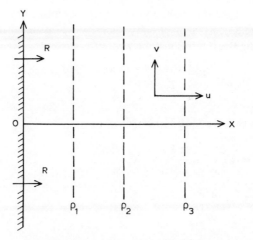

Fig. 6.7 – Density current off a straight coast: coordinate system.

Then the basic equations of motion for a steady state are

$$fv = \frac{1}{\rho}\frac{\partial p}{\partial x} - \frac{1}{\rho}\frac{\partial \tau_x}{\partial z} \tag{6.11}$$

$$fu = \frac{1}{\rho}\frac{\partial \tau_y}{\partial z} \tag{6.12}$$

$$\frac{1}{\rho}\frac{\partial p}{\partial z} + g = 0 \tag{6.13}$$

$$\frac{\partial u}{\partial x} + \frac{\partial w}{\partial z} = 0 \tag{6.14}$$

Equations (6.11) and (6.12) include shearing stresses across horizontal planes but shearing stresses across vertical planes are neglected.

If $\zeta$ is the elevation of the free surface and $p_a$ is the atmospheric pressure, equation (6.13) gives

$$p = p_a + g\rho \, (\zeta - z) \tag{6.15}$$

since $\rho$ is independent of $z$. If the atmospheric pressure $p_a$ is uniform over the area, then it follows from (6.15) that

$$\frac{\partial p}{\partial x} = g\rho \frac{\partial \zeta}{\partial x} + g \, (\zeta - z) \frac{\partial \rho}{\partial x} \; .$$

If $\zeta$ is small, $(\zeta - z)$ in the above equation may be replaced by $-z$.

Introducing a coefficient of eddy viscosity $N_z$, assumed to be independent of $z$, the shearing stress terms may be written

$$\tau_x = \rho N_z \frac{\partial u}{\partial z} \qquad \tau_y = \rho N_z \frac{\partial v}{\partial z} \; .$$

Then equations (6.11) and (6.12) become

$$fv = g \frac{\partial \zeta}{\partial x} - \frac{gz}{\rho} \frac{\partial \rho}{\partial x} - N_z \frac{\partial^2 u}{\partial z^2} \tag{6.16}$$

$$fu = N_z \frac{\partial^2 v}{\partial z^2} \; . \tag{6.17}$$

It is convenient to represent the current by the complex variable

$$W = u + iv$$

where $i = \sqrt{-1}$, so that $u$ is the real part and $v$ is the imaginary part of $W$. Then equations (6.16) and (6.17) may be combined as

$$fW = i \left( g \frac{\partial \zeta}{\partial x} - \frac{g}{\rho} \frac{\partial \rho}{\partial x} z - N_z \frac{\partial^2 W}{\partial z^2} \right) \tag{6.18}$$

Since this equation is linear, the solution may be written

$$W = W_1 + W_2 + W_3$$

where $\qquad W_1 = \dfrac{ig}{f} \dfrac{\partial \zeta}{\partial x}, \qquad W_2 = - \dfrac{ig}{\rho f} \dfrac{\partial \rho}{\partial x} z$

$$\frac{\partial^2 W_3}{\partial z^2} - \frac{if}{N_z} W_3 = 0 \; .$$

Thus

$$u_1 = u_2 = 0$$

$$v_1 = \frac{g}{f}\frac{\partial \zeta}{\partial x}, \quad v_2 = -\frac{g}{\rho f}\frac{\partial \rho}{\partial x}z \tag{6.19}$$

and $W_3$ has the solution

$$W_3 = Ae^{\alpha z} + Be^{-\alpha z} \tag{6.20}$$

where $\qquad \alpha = (1+i)\frac{\pi}{D}, \quad D = \pi\left(\frac{2N_z}{f}\right)^{1/2}$ $\tag{6.21}$

and $A$ and $B$ are constants.

$W_1$ represents a gradient current, proportional to the slope of the surface and independent of $z$, $W_2$ represents a density current, proportional to the density gradient and varying linearly with $z$, while $W_3$ is an Ekman spiral type of solution.

*Boundary conditions*

The boundary conditions to be satisfied are:

(i) At the surface, $z = 0$, the shear stress is assumed to be zero, so that

$$N_z\frac{\partial W}{\partial z} = 0 \ .$$

(ii) At the bottom, $z = -h$, either (a) there is no slip, i.e. $W = 0$, or (b) the shear stress is assumed to be proportional to the bottom current, i.e.

$$\tau_b = \rho N_z\frac{\partial W}{\partial z} = K\rho W_b \tag{6.22}$$

where $\tau_b$ is the bottom stress, $W_b$ the bottom current and $K$ is a friction coefficient with the dimensions of velocity. The assumption of a linear friction relation may be justified if, for example, the density-driven current is superimposed on a tidal current of much larger amplitude. This case is similar to that of a storm surge current superimposed on a tidal current, as discussed in Section 4.6.2. It is shown that $K = Ak\bar{C}$, where $k$ is the friction coefficient in the quadratic law, $\bar{C}$ is the depth-mean amplitude of the tidal current and $A$ is a factor of order one.

(iii) The total transport offshore, at any value of $x$, should equal the rate of discharge of fresh water from the coast. Thus if $R$ is the rate of influx per unit length of coastline,

$$\int_{-h}^{0} u \, dz = R \tag{6.23}$$

### 6.4.2 Solution for frictionless flow

Firstly, we will look at the case of negligible internal friction, so that we can take $N_z = 0$ and hence $W_3 = 0$. Then, from equation (6.19),

$$u = u_1 + u_2 = 0$$

$$v = v_1 + v_2 = \frac{g}{f}\left(\frac{\partial \zeta}{\partial x} - \frac{1}{\rho}\frac{\partial \rho}{\partial x}z\right) \qquad (6.24)$$

If there is no slip at the bottom, $v = 0$ at $z = -h$, so that

$$\frac{\partial \zeta}{\partial x} = -\frac{h}{\rho}\frac{\partial \rho}{\partial x}$$

Thus
$$v = -\frac{g}{\rho f}\frac{\partial \rho}{\partial x}(h + z) \ . \qquad (6.25)$$

The surface flow is in the negative $y$ direction, i.e. with the coast on its right-hand side (in the northern hemisphere), and the speed of the current decreases linearly from surface to bottom.

As a numerical example, let the density increase from 1020 to 1021 kg m$^{-3}$ over a distance of 40 km in the offshore direction, the depth of water be 50 m, the latitude 45°N and take $g$ as 9.80 m s$^{-2}$. Thus $\partial \rho/\partial x = 2.5 \times 10^{-5}$ kg m$^{-4}$, $\rho = 1.02 \times 10^3$ kg m$^{-3}$ and $f = 1.03 \times 10^{-4}$ s$^{-1}$. Then from equation (6.25), the surface current is given by:

$$v = -11.7 \times 10^{-2} \text{ m s}^{-1} \text{ at } z = 0 \ .$$

The surface current is, therefore, 11.7 cm s$^{-1}$ flowing with the coast on its right-hand side.

Differentiating (6.25) with respect to $z$, we see that

$$\frac{\partial v}{\partial z} = -\frac{g}{\rho f}\frac{\partial \rho}{\partial x} \qquad (6.26)$$

This is, in effect, the 'thermal wind' equation, so called because, in meteorology, it represents the variation with height of a wind due to a horizontal gradient of density associated with a horizontal gradient of temperature. The use of the thermal wind equation in oceanography is discussed by Pond and Pickard (1978, page 71).

The third boundary condition, equation (6.23), cannot be satisfied in this solution, since $u = 0$ for all values of $z$. The condition could be satisfied by allowing for a slope of the sea surface and a gradient of density parallel to the coast, i.e. finite values of $\partial \zeta/\partial y$ and $\partial \rho/\partial y$. In fact the failure to satisfy the condition would not be serious in practice, since the current required to balance the river flow, of order $R/h$, is usually two or three orders of magnitude smaller than the current associated directly with the density gradient in the $x$ direction.

### 6.4.3 Solution allowing for friction

To allow for internal friction the solution $W_3$ must be added to $W_1$ and $W_2$ so that

$$W = i \frac{g}{f} \left( \frac{\partial \zeta}{\partial x} - \frac{1}{\rho} \frac{\partial \rho}{\partial x} z \right) + A e^{\alpha z} + B e^{-\alpha z} \tag{6.27}$$

The boundary conditions have to be applied to the combined solution:

(i) At $z = 0$, $\quad \dfrac{\partial W}{\partial z} = 0$ $\hspace{4cm}$ (6.28)

(ii) At $z = -h$, either $\quad$ (a) $\quad W = 0$

$$\text{or} \quad \text{(b)} \quad N_z \frac{\partial W}{\partial z} = KW \tag{6.29}$$

(iii) $\displaystyle\int_{-h}^{0} u \, \mathrm{d}z = R$ as in equation (6.23) .

There are three equations to determine the three parameters $A$, $B$ and $\partial \zeta / \partial x$.

The analytical solutions for a given depth $h$ become quite complicated and will not be given here. The first treatment was given by Ekman in 1905 and his solutions were reproduced by Defant (1961, vol. 1,'pp. 482–485). A more detailed treatment was given by Nomitsu in 1933. A solution in a form suitable for application to a practical case was given by Heaps (1972). The problem was formulated as above, so that the equation for $W$ was given by (6.18) which, using equation (6.21), may be written in the form:

$$\frac{\partial^2 W}{\partial z^2} = \alpha^2 W + \frac{g}{N_z} \left( \frac{\partial \zeta}{\partial x} - \frac{1}{\rho} \frac{\partial \rho}{\partial x} z \right) \tag{6.30}$$

Since Heaps took the boundary condition (ii) (b), equation (6.30) was to be solved, satisfying equations (6.28) and (6.29).

A simple equation may be derived for the component of the bottom current parallel to the coast. Integrating equation (6.12) from the bottom to the surface, and using equation (6.22),

$$\rho f \int_{-h}^{0} u \, \mathrm{d}z = - \tau_{by} = - K \rho v_b$$

where $\tau_{by}$ is the component of the bottom stress and $v_b$ is the component of bottom current, each in the $y$ direction. It is assumed that there is no stress on the surface. Then by using equation (6.23) it is found that

$$v_b = - \frac{fR}{K} . \tag{6.31}$$

In the application discussed below it is found that $v_b$ is negligibly small, of the order of $0.01$ cm s$^{-1}$. Any significant density current at the sea bed is therefore directed normal to the coast.

Heaps applied his solution to compute the density currents in the Liverpool Bay area of the Irish Sea shown in Fig. 6.8. Although the coastline and the bottom contours are not straight in this area, they follow a fairly smooth curve and the $\sigma_t$ lines (the isopycnals) tend to run parallel to the coast. The density distribution obtained from observations on 27 to 29 May 1970 was used to calculate the currents at a series of points on the Line $A_1A_2$, in Fig. 6.8, approximately normal to the coast. The relevant parameters, in the above notation, had the following numerical values:

$$\frac{1}{\rho}\frac{\partial \rho}{\partial x} = 0.2 \times 10^{-3}/\text{naut. ml} = 0.108 \times 10^{-3}\,\text{km}^{-1}\ ,$$

$$f = 1.172 \times 10^{-4}\,\text{s}^{-1}\ , \qquad R = 2\,\text{m}^3\,\text{s}^{-1}\,\text{km}^{-1}\ ,$$

$$g = 9.80\,\text{m s}^{-2}\ , \qquad\qquad K = 0.2\,\text{cm s}^{-1}\ .$$

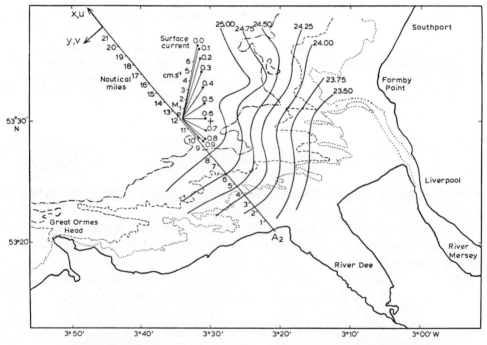

Fig. 6.8 – Density driven current in Liverpool Bay. The chart shows $\sigma_t$-lines for a period in May 1970. Calculated current vectors are drawn for 11 equidistant depths from surface to bottom at the position 12 nautical miles from the coast on line $A_1A_2$. Depth contours are: –.–.–. 10 fm (18 m), – – – 5 fm (9 m), ......3 fm (5.5 m). From Heaps (1972), by courtesy of the Royal Astronomical Society.

The combined effect of eddy viscosity in the water and bottom friction was represented by a parameter $b$, defined by

$$b = Kh/N_z \qquad (6.32)$$

where $h$ is the depth of water. The parameter $b$ was taken to be a constant along the section, although the depth varied. This is equivalent to taking $N_z$ as proportional to the product of the depth of water and a representative value $\bar{C}$ of the amplitude of the tidal current. Thus

$$N_z = k'h\bar{C}$$

where $k'$ is a constant. Since $K$ is given by

$$K = Ak\bar{C}$$

where $A$ is a factor of order one, as in Section 6.4.1, it is seen that

$$b = \frac{Ak}{k'}$$

As typical values, we may take $A = 1$, $k = 2.5 \times 10^{-3}$ and $k' = 2 \times 10^{-3}$ for homogeneous water. In that case $b = 1.25$. Solutions were given by Heaps for $b = 1, 2$ and $4$.

In Fig. 6.8 the current vectors are drawn for the case $b = 4$, at intervals of 0.1 h, for a point P, 12 nautical miles (22 km) from the coast where the mean depth was 32 m. It is seen that the surface current has an offshore component which is approximately equal to that parallel to the coast, so that the current vector is directed about 45° to the left of the alongshore direction. The current vector rotates to the right with increasing depth and the bottom current is directed towards the coast.

The offshore and alongshore components are shown plotted against depth in Fig. 6.9, for the same position and again with $b = 4$. From equation (6.31), with the numerical values given above, $v_b = 0.01$ cm s$^{-1}$ which is negligible compared with $u_b$ which, from Fig. 6.9, is about 3 cm s$^{-1}$.

A current meter mooring was maintained at a position close to P for the period March 1970 to February 1971. A comparison of the observed residual currents and the computed density currents indicated that satisfactory agreement could be obtained with a value of $b$ between 2 and 4. Bottom drifter experiments in the area also showed a general movement towards the shore, in agreement with the calculations.

## 6.4.4 Applications

In attempting to identify density-driven currents in records of current measurements the difficulty lies in separating the density component from residual currents due to tides, or to currents driven by wind or by surface gradients. In a gulf or a partially enclosed sea, the density-driven surface current, with the coast

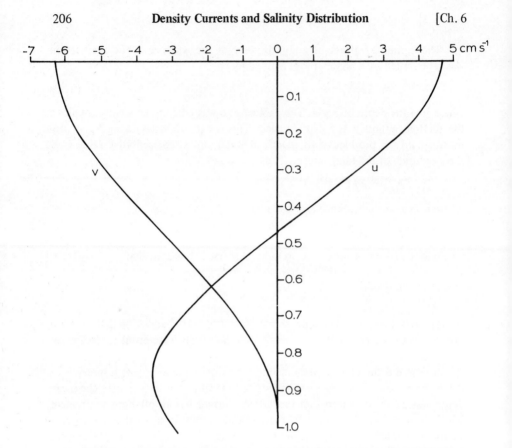

Fig. 6.9 – Vertical profiles of the current components $u$ and $v$ at the position shown in Fig. 6.8. The depth $h$ is 17.4 fm (31.8 m) and the parameter $b$ is taken as 4. From Heaps (1972), by courtesy of the Royal Astronomical Society.

on its right-hand side in the northern hemisphere, would be expected to produce a cyclonic, or anticlockwise, circulation. There is evidence in several areas of a residual circulation in this direction. In the Baltic Sea, with a large influx of fresh water around its coastal boundary, the density increases from the coast towards the centre and observations indicate the existence of a weak anticlockwise circulation with a velocity in the surface layer of a few cm s$^{-1}$, decreasing to about 1 cm s$^{-1}$ in the deeper water.

In the North Sea the coastal currents also form an anticlockwise circulation but this appears to be due, in part at least, to the wind stress effects. At the southern end of the Sea, along the coasts of Belgium, the Netherlands and West Germany, there is a sharp density gradient near the coast, associated with the outflow from the Rhine and other rivers. It seems likely that in this area the density-driven flow makes a significant contribution to the observed currents.

Conditions on the open continental shelf along the east coast of the USA are less clear-cut, since wind-driven currents and slope currents probably make a large contribution to the alongshore component of flow, especially in the surface layer, as discussed later. The observations agree, however, in indicating an on-shore component in the bottom current at almost all positions.

A systematic account of the dynamics of coastal circulations, including transient and longer term currents due to the wind as well as thermohaline effects, was given in a review article by Csanady (1981) and expanded into a book (Csanady, 1982). These accounts cover the effects of topography and bottom friction and discuss the application of theoretical ideas to conditions in several continental shelf areas and in the North American Great Lakes, which have a number of features in common with coastal areas.

## 6.5 MIXING OF WATERS ON THE CONTINENTAL SHELF

### 6.5.1 Flushing time

The initial mixing of river and coastal water produces a zone of low salinity water which gradually mixes with oceanic water further offshore and is eventually absorbed in it. If there is a long-term steady state, the average rate of loss of fresh water from the coastal zone must balance the river input. At any given time, however, there will be an accumulated volume of fresh water within the zone, its magnitude depending on the efficiency of the removal processes. The extent to which fresh water is retained in a given coastal zone is of interest not only in itself but because the fresh water acts as a tracer for other substances, such as nutrients or pollutants, which are brought in with the river water. The knowledge of retention times derived in this way may also be applied to the dispersion of substances discharged or dumped into the coastal zone in other ways.

The methods which have been used for estimating flushing times and rates of dispersion in estuaries may be applied, with certain modifications, to coastal regions. In the simplest method, using fresh water as a tracer, it is assumed that fresh water is being removed by flushing at the same rate as it is being added by river discharge. The flushing time $t$, is then given by

$$t_1 = \frac{F}{R} \tag{6.33}$$

where $R$ is the rate of influx of fresh water and $F$ is the total volume of fresh water accumulated in the region concerned. If $S$ denotes the salinity of a sample taken at any point within the region and $S_0$ is the salinity of the water further offshore which is available for mixing, the fresh water content at that point is given by

$$f = \frac{S_0 - S}{S_0} \tag{6.34}$$

To determine the total volume of fresh water $F$, the region is divided horizontally and vertically, into a suitable number of elements of volume $\delta V$ and the appropriate value of $f$ assigned to each element. The total fresh water content is then given by

$$F = \Sigma f \delta V \qquad (6.35)$$

where the summation is carried out over the total volume $V$.

This method of estimating the flushing time is quite general in that it does not involve any assumption about the processes by which the fresh water is removed.

In some cases, as in a gulf or a partially enclosed sea, it may be appropriate to treat the region as a simple basin with an inflow of river water and a two-layer exchange across the boundary section between the basin and the adjoining ocean, as in Fig. 6.10. There is an outflow of water of lower salinity $S_1$ above an inflow of water of salinity $S_2$, the corresponding rates of volume transport being $T_1$ and $T_2$. Assuming a steady state, the equations expressing the conservation of volume of water and mass of salt lead to the following equations for the rates of inflow and outflow across the section:

$$\text{Outflow:} \quad T_1 = \frac{S_2 R}{S_2 - S_1}$$

$$\text{Inflow:} \quad T_2 = \frac{S_1 R}{S_2 - S_1}$$

with $T_1 - T_2 = R$. In deriving these equations the effect of precipitation and evaporation over the basin itself has been neglected. If the effect is significant, the net volume of precipitation—evaporation must be added to river discharge to obtain the appropriate value of $R$.

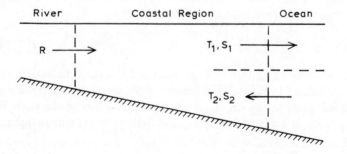

Fig. 6.10 – Two-layer exchange in a coastal region.

An alternative estimate of flushing time $t_2$ is then given by

$$t_2 = \frac{V}{T_1} = \frac{V(S_2 - S_1)}{S_2 R}.$$  (6.36)

The estimate $t_2$ is less general than $t$, in that it assumes a certain flushing process to be the only one of significance. On the other hand it requires salinity measurements across the bounding section only instead of throughout the region, as for $t_1$.

The same treatment can be used if the inflow and outflow are separated horizontally instead of vertically. At the mouth of a gulf in the northern hemisphere, for example, the outflow may be confined to the right-hand side of the section and the inflow to the left, looking towards the ocean. The same notation may be used, with $T_1, S_1$ referring to the outflow and $T_2, S_2$ to the inflow.

### 6.5.2 Mixing processes and effective horizontal diffusion

The above method treats the exchange between the coastal region and the ocean as being purely advective and does not take account of horizontal eddy diffusion. In general, both advective and diffusive processes contribute to the flux of material across a section. Consider a small element of area $\delta A$ in a plane perpendicular to the $x$ direction as in Fig. 6.11(a). Let $u$ be the component of velocity normal to the section and $c$ be the concentration, per unit volume, of any constituent of the sea water. As a special case, $c$ may be the fresh water content $f$. The rate of transport of the constituent through the area $\delta A$ is given by

$$\delta F_x = uc\delta A - K_x \frac{\partial c}{\partial x} \delta A$$  (6.37)

where $K_x$ is the coefficient of eddy diffusion in the $x$ direction. $\partial c/\partial x$ is the gradient of concentration and the negative sign occurs because it is assumed that eddy diffusion, like molecular diffusion, takes place from higher to lower concentrations. The total flux $F_x$ across a vertical section of area $A$ is found by integrating the above equation over the area. Thus

$$F_x = \int_A uc \, dA - AK_x \frac{\partial \bar{c}}{\partial x}$$  (6.38)

where

$$\bar{c} = \frac{1}{A} \int_A c \, dA$$

$\bar{c}$ is the average concentration over the cross-section.

In the advective term of equation (6.37), the values $u$ and $c$ of the velocity and concentration respectively at any point in the cross-section may be expressed as

$$u = \bar{u} + u', \qquad c = \bar{c} + c'$$

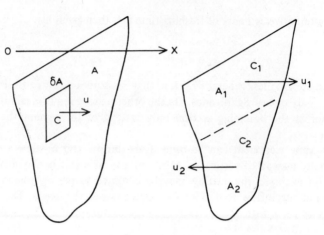

Fig. 6.11 – Flux of material across a vertical section: (a) general case, (b) two-layer flow.

where $\bar{u}, \bar{c}$ are the mean over the section and $u', c'$ are the deviations at a given point from the mean values. It follows that in equation (6.38),

$$\int_A uc \, \mathrm{d}A = A\bar{u}\bar{c} + \int_A u'c' \, \mathrm{d}A \ . \tag{6.39}$$

In a two-layer flow, as in Fig. 6.11(b) let $u'_1, c'_1$ be the deviations in the upper layer of area $A_1$ and $u'_2, c'_2$ those in the lower layer of area $A_2$. Then it follows that

$$\int_A uc \, \mathrm{d}A = (A_1 + A_2)\bar{u}\,\bar{c} + A_1 u'_1 c'_1 + A_2 u'_2 c'_2$$

where

$$\bar{u} = \frac{A_1 u_1 - A_2 u_2}{A_1 + A_2} \ , \quad \bar{c} = \frac{A_1 c_1 + A_2 c_2}{A_1 + A_2}$$

$$A_1 u'_1 = -A_2 u'_2 = \frac{A_1 A_2 (u_1 + u_2)}{A_1 + A_2}$$

$$c'_1 = \frac{A_2 (c_1 - c_2)}{A_1 + A_2} \ , \quad c'_2 = -\frac{A_1 (c_1 - c_2)}{A_1 + A_2} \ .$$

Writing $T_1 = A_1 u_1$, $T_2 = A_2 u_2$, $A = A_1 + A_2$, it follows, after some manipulation, that

$$\int_A uc \, dA = (T_1 - T_2)\bar{c} + T_1'(c_1 - c_2) \tag{6.40}$$

where          $T_1' = T_1 - A_1(T_1 - T_2)/A$

If the volume of water in the region is constant, then $T_1 - T_2 = R$. The flux of the constituent across the bounding section is then given by equations (6.38) and (6.40) as

$$F_x = R\bar{c} + \left(T_1 - \frac{A_1 R}{A}\right)(c_1 - c_2) - A K_x \frac{\partial \bar{c}}{\partial x} \tag{6.41}$$

### 6.5.3 Some examples

There are some bodies of water, such as the Bay of Fundy, which may be regarded as estuaries themselves although they receive the discharge from several smaller estuaries. A calculation by the first method described above, using equation (6.33), gave an average flushing time of 76 days for the Bay of Fundy (Ketchum and Keen, quoted by Officer, 1976). Another sea area of this type is Long Island Sound, which has a limited interchange with the waters of New York harbour at its western end and a free connection with the Atlantic Ocean through Block Island Sound at its eastern end. Investigations have shown that the exchange through Block Island Sound is of the two-layer type, with a lower layer inflow of 15,000 to 20,000 m$^3$ s$^{-1}$. The upper layer outflow exceeds this value by about 1,400 m$^3$ s$^{-1}$, of which about 1,100 enters from New York harbour at the eastern end and 300 m$^3$ s$^{-1}$ is from the discharge of rivers, including the Connecticut, into the Sound. The flushing time of Long Island Sound as whole, estimated from the rate of inflow, averages about three months (Riley, 1956).

An application of the fresh water accumulation method to a large area of the continental shelf off the eastern USA was made by Ketchum and Keen (1955). They considered the region from Cape Cod in the north to Chesapeake Bay in the south, extending from the coast to the 1000 fm (1830 m) line, as in Fig. 6.12. The sea area is approximately 9.6 × 10$^4$ km$^2$ and it receives the drainage from a land area of 30 × 10$^4$ km$^2$. The river discharge to it averages 4,750 m$^3$ s$^{-1}$, amounting to 150 km$^3$ in a year. The region was divided into six areas, A to F as in Fig. 6.12, the river flow to each area tabulated and the accumulated volume of fresh water in each calculated as described above from observations of salinity. The accumulated volume was found to be highest in the summer months (July, August, September) while the winter and spring values were similar. The salinity increased towards the south, although the mean flow was southwards and fresh water was being added to it from the coast. The increase in salinity was attributed to higher salinity water being mixed inwards from deep

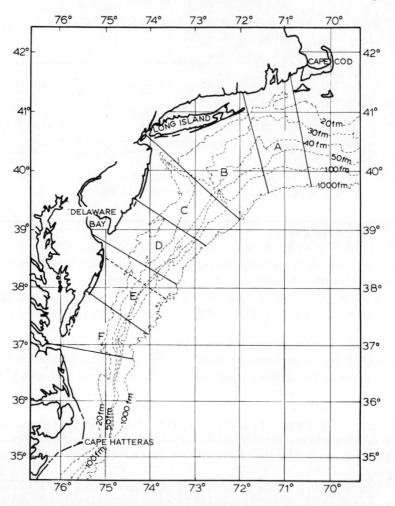

Fig. 6.12 – The eastern US continental shelf from Cape Cod to Chesapeake Bay, showing areas used in calculations of fresh water accumulation. From Ketchum and Keen (1955), by courtesy of Pergamon Press Ltd.

water while lower salinity water was mixed outwards. It was estimated that, averaged over a year, evaporation exceeded precipitation over the shelf and about 20% of the fresh water input was lost by excess evaporation while the rest was transported across the 1,000 fm contour by advection and eddy diffusion.

The flushing times for the whole shelf region were estimated for the spring, summer and winter seasons respectively and are shown in   Table 6.1 for two cases, according to whether the outer boundary is taken at the 100 fm or 1000 fm line. The fact that the flushing times are so large, in excess of a year in each case, indicates that a steady state is not achieved.

**Table 6.1** – Flushing times for USA continental shelf between Cape Cod and Chesapeake Bay (from Ketchum and Keen, 1955).

| Depth range fathoms | Flushing time in days April–June | July–Sept. | Oct.–March |
|---|---|---|---|
| 0–100  (183 m) | 472 | 612 | 479 |
| 0–1000 (1,830 m) | 603 | 752 | 589 |

The greater accumulation of fresh water in the summer, compared with the spring and winter months, corresponds to a lower salinity and hence a lower salt content in the summer. There is therefore, a flux of salt out of the region from spring to summer and a flux of salt inwards from summer to winter. If the average salinity of the volume $V$ of water changes by an amount $\Delta \bar{S}$ in time $\Delta t$ and $F_x$ is the rate of flux out of the region, then

$$V \Delta \bar{S} = - F_x \Delta t \tag{6.42}$$

Ketchum and Keen gave reasons for assuming that the transport of salt across the northern and southern boundaries was negligible compared with that across the ocean boundary. The transport across this boundary was assumed to be due entirely to horizontal eddy diffusion as data were not available to calculate the term involving the vertical variation of salinity. With these assumptions and using equation (6.38), the flux of salt out of the region is given by

$$F_x = R\bar{S} - AK_x \frac{\partial \bar{S}}{\partial x} \tag{6.43}$$

where $R$ is the river inflow across the coastal boundary and $\bar{S}$, $A$, $K_x$ and $\partial \bar{S}/\partial x$ refer to values at the ocean boundary. The values of $K_x$ corresponding to the spring/summer decrease of salinity and the summer/winter increase were calculated, taking the ocean boundary as being along the 30 fm (55 m), 40 fm (73 m) or 100 fm (183 m) contour, and are reproduced in Table 6.2.

**Table 6.2** – Coefficients of horizontal diffusion for USA continental shelf between Cape Cod and Chesapeake Bay (from Ketchum and Keen, 1955).

| Depth contour (fm) | (m) | Horizontal diffusion coefficient $(10^6 \text{ cm}^2 \text{ s}^{-1})$ spring–summer | summer–winter |
|---|---|---|---|
| 30 | 55 | 2.52 | 4.96 |
| 40 | 73 | 1.72 | 3.41 |
| 100 | 183 | 0.58 | 1.48 |

It is seen that the computed values of $K_x$ decrease in the offshore direction and were greater for the summer to winter than for the spring to summer change. The smaller values in the latter case may be associated with the higher degree of vertical stability at that time. If the term in equation (6.39) involving a vertical variation in velocity and salinity was not, in fact, negligible, it would increase the effective value of $K_x$ found by the calculation.

Estimates of the flushing rate for the Georgia Bight, off the coast of South Carolina, Georgia and north-east Florida, were made by Atkinson, Blanton and Haines (1978). The region considered contained about 1000 km$^3$ of water, extending from the 9 m (5 fm) to the 73 m (40 fm) line. The accumulated volume of freshwater varied seasonally between 5 and 12 km$^3$, in response to changing river discharge, but the flushing time remained almost constant at 2.7 months. Transport of fresh water out of the area might be due to alongshore currents or to offshore mixing with Gulf Stream water over the shelf edge. Because the coastal currents change in magnitude and direction fairly frequently, the authors considered that the constancy of the flushing rate indicated that the former process was unlikely to be important. They suggested that the offshore transport was achieved by the action of meanders of the Gulf Stream which, on a time scale of about 5 days, intruded on to the continental shelf and entrained filaments of the lower salinity water.

## 6.6 INTERACTION OF THE DENSITY DISTRIBUTION AND CURRENTS

### 6.6.1 Model of Stommel and Leetmaa
In Section 6.1.2 it was pointed out that the currents and the density distribution interact with one another and a physically realistic model should be able to simulate this interaction. The first attempt to formulate and solve such a model for a continental shelf region appears to be that of Stommel and Leetmaa (1972). The model was formulated so as to apply, in an idealised way, to wintertime conditions on the shelf off the east coast of North America. Winter-time was chosen because (i) the density is controlled primarily by salinity at that season and (ii) there is only a weak vertical stratification of density.

The shelf is taken to be of infinite length parallel to the coast, of semi-infinite width, extending from the deep ocean at $x = 0$ to infinity in the negative $x$ direction, and of uniform depth $H$, as in Fig. 6.13. A mean flux of water, $R$ per unit length of coastline, flows towards the sea as a result of river discharges. The density $\rho$ is related to salinity $S$ by the linear law

$$\rho = \rho_0 (1 + \beta s) \tag{6.44}$$

where $\beta$ is a constant. The model allows for the action of a wind stress on the surface, with components $\tau_{sx}$ and $\tau_{sy}$. It is assumed that the motion and the salinity distribution are independent of the $y$ coordinate. The coefficient of vertical eddy viscosity $N_z$ is taken as constant. The effect of surface slope is assumed to be negligible.

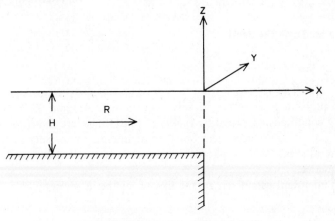

Fig. 6.13 – Model of a continental shelf.

In a steady state, the momentum equations in the $x$ and $y$ directions respectively are given by equations (6.16) and (6.17) of Section 6.4.1, but with $\partial \zeta / \partial x = 0$ and $\partial p / \partial x$ obtained from equation (6.44). Thus

$$fv = - \beta gz \frac{\partial s}{\partial x} - N_z \frac{\partial^2 u}{\partial z^2} \tag{6.45}$$

$$fu = N_z \frac{\partial^2 v}{\partial z^2} \tag{6.46}$$

The equation for the distribution of salinity, allowing for vertical eddy diffusion with a coefficient $K_z$ but assuming that the $x$ derivative of the diffusive term is negligible, is

$$u \frac{\partial s}{\partial x} + w \frac{\partial s}{\partial z} = K_z \frac{\partial^2 s}{\partial z^2} \tag{6.47}$$

The equation for continuity of volume of water applies, i.e.

$$\frac{\partial u}{\partial x} + \frac{\partial w}{\partial z} = 0 \ . \tag{6.48}$$

The boundary conditions to be applied are: at the surface, $z = 0$,

$$\tau_{sx} = \rho N_z \frac{\partial u}{\partial z} \ , \quad \tau_{sy} = \rho N_z \frac{\partial v}{\partial z} \ , \tag{6.49}$$

$$\frac{\partial s}{\partial z} = 0 \ ;$$

at the bottom, $z = -H$,

$$u = v = \frac{\partial s}{\partial z} = 0 \tag{6.50}$$

and integrated over the depth

$$\int_{-H}^{0} u \, dz = R \; . \tag{6.51}$$

The problem is therefore to solve equations (6.45) and (6.48) with the boundary conditions expressed by (6.49) to (6.51). The solution is complicated and will not be reproduced here but it is of interest to consider some of the general results and their application to conditions on the east coast shelf of North America.

Two important parameters are the Ekman number $E$, given by

$$E = \frac{N_z}{fH^2} \tag{6.52}$$

and a length scale $L$, characteristic of the horizontal gradient of salinity at the shelf edge, i.e.

$$\left(\frac{\partial s}{\partial x}\right)_{x=0} = \frac{s_0}{L} \tag{6.53}$$

where $s_0$ is the depth-mean salinity at $x = 0$. The solution for $L$ as a function of $E$, plotted on a log-log scale, is reproduced in Fig. 6.14. The scale of $L$ in centimetres corresponds to the following numerical values, chosen by Stommel and Leetmaa as being representative of the eastern USA continental shelf:

$$f = 0.7 \times 10^{-4} \, s^{-1} \; , \qquad H = 5 \times 10^3 \, cm \; ,$$

$$\beta g s_0 = 30 \, cm \, s^{-2} \; , \qquad R = 50 \, cm^2 \, s^{-1} \; , \qquad N_z = K_z \; .$$

The various curves in Fig. 6.14 correspond to different values of wind stress, as given by the values of $\tau_{sx}$ and $\tau_{sy}$ in dyne $cm^{-2}$ marked against them. (In Fig. 6.14, $\tau_x$ is written for $\tau_{sx}$ and $\tau_y$ for $\tau_{sy}$).

Let us look, first of all, at the curve marked $\tau_x = \tau_y = 0$, corresponding to zero wind stress and a purely density-driven circulation. It is seen that $L$ reaches a maximum, i.e. the horizontal salinity gradient is smallest, for a certain value of Ekman number $E$, given by $E = 3.5 \times 10^{-2}$ approximately. A smaller horizontal gradient $\partial s/\partial x$ corresponds to a higher salinity near the coast for a given value at the shelf edge and implies a higher rate of mixing in the onshore—offshore direction. Since no allowance is made explicitly for horizontal eddy-diffusion, the mixing is achieved by the vertical variation of velocity $u$ in conjunction with a vertical variation of salinity. There is an Ekman transport seaward in the upper layer and a transport towards the coast in the lower layer.

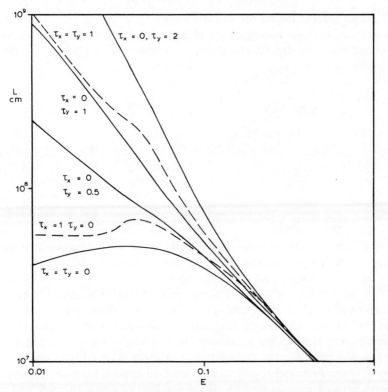

Fig. 6.14 – Salinity length scale $L$ as a function of Ekman number $E$. From Stommel and Leetmaa (1972), by courtesy of the authors and the National Academy of Sciences, USA.

At very low values of $E$ these transports are small and, although the vertical gradient of salinity is relatively large, the rate of horizontal mixing is small. At large values of $E$ the transports are large but vertical mixing is strong (since $K_z$ increases with $N_z$) and again the rate of horizontal mixing becomes small. There is an intermediate value of $E$. with corresponding values of $N_z$ and $K_z$, at which the product of Ekman transport and vertical difference of salinity is a maximum, providing optimum horizontal mixing.

The upper part of Fig. 6.14 corresponds to cases in which the horizontal mixing processes are dominated by the wind stress. It is seen that the $\tau_{sy}$ component has a greater influence than the $\tau_{sx}$ component, as one would expect since it is the wind stress parallel to the coast which produces an Ekman transport in the offshore direction. The Ekman transports are independent of the eddy viscosity $N_z$ in the purely wind-driven case but the vertical gradient of salinity is inversely proportional to $K_z$. Since it has been assumed that $N_z = K_z$, the horizontal mixing thus decreases with increasing values of $E$ and the lines in the upper part of Fig. 6.14 have a slope $-1$, i.e. $L$ is inversely proportional to $E$.

### 6.6.2 Application to the Middle Atlantic Bight

Stommel and Leetmaa compared the predictions of their model with observed conditions in the Middle Atlantic Bight on the east coast of USA. If the salinity changes by $\Delta s$ across a width $\Delta x$ of the shelf, $L$ is given by

$$L = \frac{s_0 \Delta x}{\Delta s}$$

From observations in the Middle Atlantic Bight for February and March, $\Delta s = 1.5$ $^o/_{oo}$ across a shelf width $\Delta x = 139$ km and hence $L = 3.2 \times 10^8$ cm. The wind stress may be represented approximately by $\tau_{sx} = \tau_{sy} = 1$ dyne cm$^{-2}$. The point corresponding to these values in Fig. 6.14 lies well away from the curve for a purely density-driven system and indicates that the shelf regime is essentially wind-driven. The corresponding value of the Ekman number $E$ is $2.6 \times 10^{-2}$. With the values of $f$ and $H$ assumed, this gives an eddy viscosity $N_z$ of 45 cm$^2$ s$^{-1}$. The Ekman layer depth, given as in Chapter 5 by $D = \pi(2N_z/f)^{1/2}$, is $D = 35$ m. The salinity difference between the upper and lower layers was estimated to be 0.14 $^o/_{oo}$.

The predicted value of the $v$ component of current is about 20 cm s$^{-1}$, directed parallel to the coast towards the north-east. This is primarily a wind-driven current, since the density distribution alone would produce a current with a $v$ component towards the south-west. In fact winter time current measurements show a mean flow to the south-west of about 5 cm s$^{-1}$. This discrepancy between observation and theory can be resolved if an alongshore gradient of sea level is taken into account. A rise in sea level of about 20 cm from Cape Hatteras to Nantucket Shoals would be sufficient to reverse the wind-driven flow and give a mean current to the south-west, as observed. With an alongshore slope of the sea surface, the onshore transport to compensate for the Ekman transport in the surface layer may be distributed throughout the depth, instead of being concentrated in a bottom Ekman layer.

On the basis of the model with an alongshore slope included, Stommel and Leetmaa deduced that conditions in the Middle Atlantic Bight could be satisfied with a value of $K_z = N_z = 30$ cm$^2$ s$^{-1}$. The transport of salt normal to the coast, resulting from the two-layer flow, was equivalent to diffusive transport with an effective coefficient of horizontal eddy diffusion $K_x = 2.3 \times 10^6$ cm$^2$ s$^{-1}$.

It appears from this and other studies that, on the continental shelf scale, the currents and mixing processes off the east coast of USA are dominated by wind-driven events and that density-driven currents play a relatively minor role. In smaller scale regions adjacent to the coast, however, density-driven currents may predominate. From a study of currents in Massachusetts Bay, for example, Butman (1976) concluded that the density distribution associated with the spring river run off, particularly from the Merrimack River, dominated the currents, which varied on a time scale of 5–10 days.

# 7

# Temperature distribution and the seasonal thermocline

## 7.1 HEAT BUDGET OF OCEANIC AND COASTAL AREAS

The distribution of temperature in any region of sea or ocean is determined by the fluxes of heat through the sea surface and exchanges of heat, by advection or eddy diffusion, with the water of adjacent regions. The main source of heat flux through the sea surface is solar radiation, received either directly or by reflection and scattering from the clouds and the atmosphere. Against this there is a loss of heat by longer wavelength back radiation from the sea surface to the atmosphere and space. Another process causing loss of heat is evaporation, since the latent heat required to vaporise the water is abstracted from the surface layer. The opposite process is condensation, producing a heating of the surface, but this is usually of only slight significance. Exchange of sensible heat with the atmosphere takes place by eddy conduction and may represent either a gain or loss to the water, depending on whether the air is warmer than the sea or vice versa.

Advective changes in the heat content of a region are produced by currents of warmer or cooler water flowing into or out of it. In a coastal region this includes the inflow of rivers. Vertical movements of water, such as upwelling or sinking, also lead to changes in the heat content of the surface layer. Diffusive fluxes of heat occur where there are horizontal or vertical gradients of temperature. In the vertical, such fluxes take place by the action of small scale turbulent mixing or, if the surface layer is cooled sufficiently, by convective overturning. In the horizontal, diffusive exchanges of heat may be brought about by eddying motions or shear flows on a wide range of scales. As in the case of salt exchanges, diffusive fluxes of heat are often represented by terms involving the product of an eddy diffusion coefficient: $K_x$, $K_y$ or $K_z$, with the corresponding temperature gradient. The exchange of heat between the water and the sea bed will cause a small change in the heat content of the water, but this is usually negligible compared with other terms in the heat budget. The heating produced by the dissipation of the kinetic energy of currents by bottom friction is also negligible in this respect.

The net gain of heat by a vertical column of water of unit horizontal cross-sectional area, per unit time, may be denoted by $Q_T$ and represented by the equation

$$Q_T = Q_s - Q_b - Q_c - Q_e - Q_v \tag{7.1}$$

where  $Q_s$  is the heat absorbed from incoming solar radiation,
  $Q_b$  is the heat lost by effective back radiation,
  $Q_c$  is the heat lost by conduction from the sea surface,
  $Q_e$  is the heat lost by evaporation from the sea surface,
  $Q_v$  is the net transfer of heat out of the column by currents and mixing processes.

In this equation the terms $Q_c$, $Q_e$ and $Q_v$ may be negative if heat is being gained by conduction, by condensation or by net transfer into the column respectively. The terms in the equation are represented in Fig. 7.1.

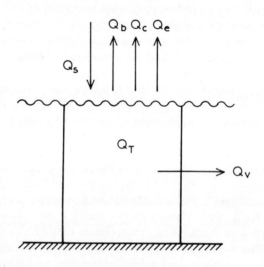

Fig. 7.1 – Terms in the heat budget of a water column.

The term in equation (7.1) which varies most from one region to another is $Q_v$, expressing the effects of advection and eddy diffusion. The other four terms on the right-hand side of (7.1) all represent fluxes of heat through the sea surface and may be denoted collectively by $Q$. Thus

$$Q = Q_s - Q_b - Q_c - Q_e \tag{7.2}$$

and (7.1) may be written

$$Q_T = Q - Q_v \, . \tag{7.3}$$

The specification of the various terms on the right-hand side of equation (7.2) is discussed in detail in textbooks such as those of Pickard and Emery (1982), McLellan (1965) or Kraus (1972) and only a brief description will be given here. The intensity of solar radiation incident on the sea surface may be obtained directly from measurements on board ship or at nearby coastal stations. In the absence of such measurements, a reasonable estimate may be made from tables giving the radiation from a cloudless sky, as a function of latitude and time of year, with a correction for the cloud cover as given by meteorological observations. To obtain $Q_s$, the solar radiation absorbed in the sea, the incident radiation must be corrected by a factor which allows for reflection from the surface.

The intensity of solar radiation was usually expressed, until recently, in units of langleys per unit time. A langley (ly) is defined as one gram calorie per square centimetre. In SI units, the use of which is now recommended, radiation flux is measured in watts per square metre ($W\ m^{-2}$), a watt being equivalent to one joule per second or, in heat units, 0.239 gram calorie per second. 1 $W\ m^{-2}$ is equivalent to $2.39 \times 10^{-5}\ cal\ cm^{-2}\ s^{-1}$ or $2.056\ ly\ day^{-1}$.

Average values of the solar radiation reaching the sea surface, allowing for atmospheric absorption, mean cloud amount, scattering and other factors were given by Budyko and quoted by Pickard and Emery (1982). The annual average value over the oceans ranges from about 90 $W\ m^{-2}$ in the Arctic and Antarctic regions to about 230 $W\ m^{-2}$ between 25°N and 20°S. The seasonal variations are small in the tropics but much larger in higher latitudes. In the summer hemisphere, the values averaged over the month of June in the northern hemisphere, or December in the southern, reach 240 to 300 $W\ m^{-2}$ at 80° latitude, decrease to a minimum of 130 to 150 $W\ m^{-2}$ at 55° latitude, increase to a maximum of 260 to 280 $W\ m^{-2}$ at 30° to 25° latitude and then decrease somewhat towards the equator. The high values in the polar regions are due to the long summer days and the low content of water vapour in the atmosphere. In the winter hemisphere, at the same time, the values decrease from the equator to about 15 $W\ m^{-2}$ at 60° latitude and to zero poleward of 70° latitude. If the above values in $W\ m^{-2}$ are doubled in magnitude they give the approximate values in langleys per day.

The effective back radiation from the sea surface, $Q_b$, is the outward radiation from the surface minus the downward radiation from the atmosphere. In cloudless conditions, $Q_b$ depends on the sea surface temperature and the humidity of the atmosphere, but it does not vary greatly with latitude and season. The overall range is from 115 to 70 $W\ m^{-2}$, the higher rates occurring at low temperatures and low humidity. In the presence of cloud $Q_b$ is reduced because the downward radiation is increased. Complete cloud cover may reduce $Q_b$ to as low as 0.2 of its value for a clear sky. The value of $Q_b$ may be measured directly by radiometer but such measurements are less commonly made than those of solar radiation. In their absence, $Q_b$ may be estimated from a formula which takes into account the sea surface temperature, humidity and cloud cover.

The conduction and evaporation terms, $Q_c$ and $Q_e$ respectively, are seldom measured directly but are calculated from equations which involve the difference between sea surface temperature and the air temperature at a standard height above the surface, in the case of $Q_c$, or the difference between the saturated vapour pressure at the sea surface and the actual water vapour pressure at the standard height, in the case of $Q_e$, and the wind speed $W$ in both cases. Usually a linear dependence of both $Q_c$ and $Q_e$ on $W$ is assumed. In many cases $Q_e$ is greater than $Q_c$ and in some areas it is the largest of the heat loss terms. The average value of $Q_e$ for the oceans is 80 W m$^{-2}$ but it ranges from zero to about 200 W m$^{-2}$, the highest values occurring at mid-latitudes of the western North Atlantic or North Pacific.

Averaging the value of $Q$, as given by equation (7.2), over a year, there is a net gain of heat by the oceans from the equator to latitude 30°N or 30°S and a net loss from these latitudes polewards. In equatorial regions there is a net gain of heat throughout the year but in the higher latitudes there is a net gain (positive $Q$) in the summer months and a net loss (negative $Q$) in the winter.

The terms contributing to the net flux of heat through the sea surface, $Q$, do not differ greatly between oceanic and coastal waters. There are differences in their magnitudes arising from local variations in factors such as cloud cover, wind speed, air and sea surface temperatures. These are taken into account if the appropriate factors are used in estimating the terms. Where coastal waters often differ significantly from the deeper waters further offshore is in their response to the heat flux and its seasonal variation.

## 7.2 TEMPERATURE RESPONSE TO HEAT BUDGET VARIATIONS

### 7.2.1 Oceanic response

If unit volume of water absorbs a quantity $\delta q$ of heat, then its temperature will increase by an amount $\delta T$ given by

$$\delta T = \frac{\delta q}{\rho c}$$

where $\rho$ is the density and $c$ is the specific heat at constant pressure. If the gain of heat $\delta q$ takes place in a time $\delta t$, it follows that the rate of increase of temperature is given by

$$\frac{\partial T}{\partial t} = \frac{1}{\rho c} \frac{\partial q}{\partial t} \tag{7.4}$$

In equation (7.1) the rate of gain of heat by a vertical column of water of unit horizontal area was denoted by $Q_T$, so that, if the height of the column is $h$, we have

$$\frac{\partial q}{\partial t} = \frac{Q_T}{h} \tag{7.5}$$

Then the rise in the average temperature of the column may be calculated from (7.4).

Neglecting, for the moment, the advective and diffusive term $Q_v$, $Q_T = Q$, the net flux of heat through the sea surface. The solar radiation $Q_s$ is absorbed gradually as it penetrates downwards from the surface, at a rate which depends on the turbidity of the water. According to figures given by Pickard (1979), in the clearest oceanic water 55% of the total radiation is absorbed in the first metre while in very turbid coastal water 82% is absorbed in the first metre. In the first 10 m, 78% is absorbed in the clearest oceanic water and practically 100% in turbid coastal water. The back radiation $Q_b$ takes place from a surface layer less than 1 cm in thickness and the loss by conduction and evaporation also takes place from a very thin layer. The overall result is that the net flux of heat $Q$ is absorbed initially in a surface layer only a few metres in thickness. If $Q$ is positive, therefore, a thin surface layer tends to become warmer and less dense than the water below. The effect of wind stress and wave action, however, is to generate enough turbulent energy to mix the heat input downwards through a well mixed surface layer, extending to a depth which may reach several tens of metres. Below this depth the rate of generation of turbulence is not adequate to continue to mix the heat downwards at the same rate and a thermocline, a layer of steep temperature gradient, is formed at the base of the mixed layer. The increased stability in the thermocline reduces further the turbulent intensity, thus providing positive feedback to the process of thermocline formation.

In equatorial regions, where $Q$ is positive throughout the year, the temperature structure just described persists as a permanent feature. There is a warm surface mixed layer, at the base of which is the thermocline in which the temperature gradient is of the order of 10°C in 10 m. The transport of heat to greater depths is inhibited by the thermocline and takes place only very slowly.

In temperate and polar latitudes the net heat flux $Q$ is positive during the summer months, for a period which becomes shorter with increasing latitude, and is negative during the winter. The process described above operates during the summer and a surface mixed layer above a seasonal thermocline is developed. When $Q$ becomes negative in the autumn, however, a thin surface layer is cooled and becomes denser than the water below. Vertical convection currents are set up so that the cooling extends to a greater depth. As the loss of heat from the surface continues, the convective overturning extends to increasing depths until the thermocline has been completely eroded. In some regions the mixed layer of uniform temperature extends throughout the whole water column. Further cooling at the surface can then lead to the sinking of surface water and the formation of a deep or bottom water mass.

### 7.2.2 Coastal waters response: vertically mixed regions

In the open ocean the formation of a seasonal thermocline in the summer months is of almost universal occurrence in temperate and higher latitudes. Over the continental shelf, however, turbulence generated by the action of bottom friction on the tidal currents may provide a sufficient level of kinetic energy, at the base of the wind-mixed layer, to maintain vertical mixing throughout the depth of the water column. Whether or not a thermocline develops in a particular area may be expected to depend on the strength of the tidal currents and the depth of water. Variations in these parameters may lead to one area of a shelf region becoming stratified while an adjacent area remains mixed. The transition between the two may be marked by a strong horizontal gradient of temperature, forming a front. A criterion for the formation of a seasonal thermocline will be derived later, in Section 7.3.

Firstly, we will consider the case where the water column remains vertically well mixed throughout the year. If $\Delta T$ denotes the increase in temperature of a column of water of depth $H$ produced by a net gain of heat $Q_T$, as in equation (7.1), acting for a time $\delta t$, then

$$\Delta T = \frac{Q_T \delta t}{\rho c H} \tag{7.6}$$

Thus, if $Q_T$ is given, the increase in temperature of the column may be calculated. It is seen that for a given heat input the increase in temperature will be greater the shallower the water. This effect is commonly observed, with charts of isotherms for the summer months showing an increase of temperature towards the coast.

There is a limit to the rise of temperature which can occur in shallow water and this is set in two ways. In the first place, the loss of heat from the surface increases with the surface temperature. The losses by evaporation $Q_e$ and conduction $Q_c$ increase with sea surface temperature, in general, while the back radiation $Q_b$ changes only slightly. Since the solar radiation $Q_s$ is probably similar to that further offshore, the net result is a reduction in $Q_T$. Secondly, the decrease of temperature seawards will lead to an offshore transport of heat by horizontal eddy diffusion, given by

$$Q_v = -\rho c K_x \frac{\partial T}{\partial x} \tag{7.7}$$

where the $x$-axis is directed offshore and $K_x$ is the coefficient of eddy diffusion in that direction. The value of $K_x$ will depend on the conditions in a particular location and is likely to be of order $10^5$ to $10^6$ cm$^2$ s$^{-1}$.

In the winter season the net heat input term $Q_T$ will be negative, producing a decrease in the temperature of a water column. In accordance with equation (7.6), the fall in temperature will be greater in shallower water and the isotherms will indicate a fall of temperature towards the coast. This will lead to a horizontal diffusive flux of heat shorewards from the deeper water, tending to reduce the difference in temperature. The overall result is that the annual range of temperature will be greatest near the coast and decrease towards the deeper water offshore. The time of maximum and minimum will tend to become later in the offshore direction, the highest temperature, in the northern hemisphere, probably occurring in early August near the shore but in late August or September in the deeper water.

In Fig. 7.2(a) and (b), the mean surface temperature of the Irish Sea is shown for the months of February and August respectively. In winter, as represented by the chart for February, the water column is vertically well mixed throughout the whole area. The decrease in temperature from the deep channel towards the shallower water near the coasts, particularly on the east side of the Sea, is clearly seen. In August the greater part of the area is again well mixed, although a seasonal thermocline develops in areas to the south-west and to the east of the Isle of Man. At this season there is a general increase of temperature from the deep channel towards the coasts.

## 7.3 OCCURRENCE OF A SEASONAL THERMOCLINE

### 7.3.1 Seasonal variation of conditions

Where a thermocline develops, the seasonal variation of temperature in the surface layer follows a different course from that in the layer below the thermocline. The following example, taken from a paper by Pingree (1975), is for a station E.1 in the western end of the English Channel, south of Plymouth, for which the mean seasonal variation could be determined from many years' observations. Fig. 7.3 shows the annual variation of the net gain of heat $Q$ through the sea surface, where $Q$ is given by equation (7.2) and is expressed in the figure as calories per square centimetre per month. $Q$ is negative in winter and becomes positive in mid-March, reaching a maximum in June in phase with the maximum incoming solar radiation, and remaining positive until mid-September.

The response of the water column at station E.1 is shown in Fig. 7.4. The water is well mixed in winter and the temperature reaches its minimum in March. At this time the heat flux $Q$ becomes positive and the temperature of the water column starts to rise. Very soon, however, a thermocline forms and the downward flux of heat through it is restricted. The surface temperature continues to rise at an increasing rate while the temperature in the mixed layer below the thermocline rise more slowly. In fact from April until the end of the heating season in September the temperature rises at an almost uniform rate, suggesting that tidal mixing is only able to transmit heat downwards through a thermocline at a fixed rate, regardless of the heat flux in the upper layer. The surface temperature reaches its maximum in August but the temperature in the lower layer continues to rise, even after mid-September when $Q$ becomes negative. At this stage the surface layer is losing heat both upwards from the surface and downwards to the lower layer. The temperature of the lower layer continues

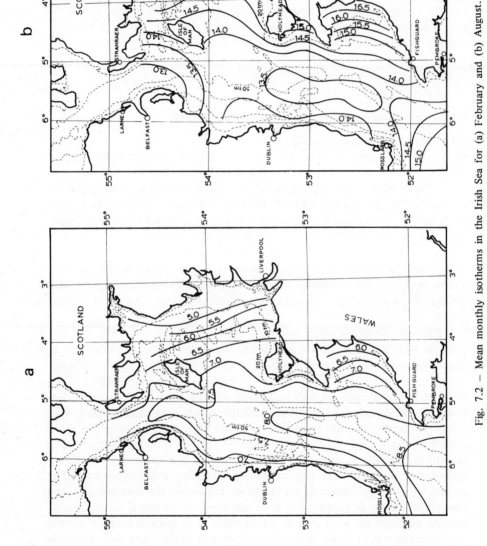

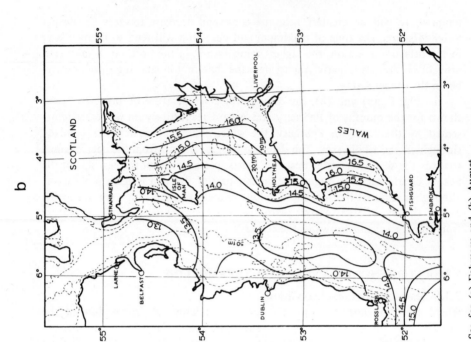

Fig. 7.2 – Mean monthly isotherms in the Irish Sea for (a) February and (b) August.

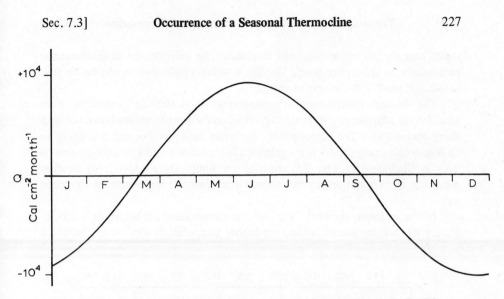

Fig. 7.3 – Seasonal variation of heat input through the sea surface in the English Channel. From Pingree (1975), by courtesy of the Cambridge University Press.

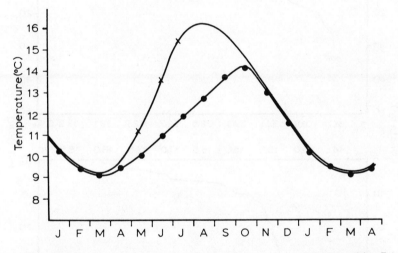

Fig. 7.4 – Seasonal variation of surface and bottom temperature at position E.1 in the English Channel: ——— surface temperature, —•—•— bottom temperature. From Pingree (1975), by courtesy of the Cambridge University Press.

to rise, by gaining heat from above, until the temperature of the two layers is equal and the thermocline disappears. The whole column then becomes well mixed by convective overturning.

Figure 7.4 is based on over 60 years' data and advective effects have probably been averaged out. In a particular year the advection of warmer or colder water past the station would tend to obscure the uniform rise of temperature, particularly in the lower layer. Varying weather conditions from year to year would also modify the course of events.

The vertical distribution of temperature in a stratified region is often idealised by representing it as two layers of uniform temperature separated by a sharp thermocline. The actual profile measured on a given occasion is likely to be less simple, owing to local irregularities in the mixing and advective processes. This is illustrated by Fig. 7.5, showing the temperature and salinity profiles measured at two stations in the eastern Irish Sea, 10 km apart, on the same day.

In the example shown in Fig. 7.5 the temperature stratification is accompanied by salinity stratification, the higher temperature upper layer having a

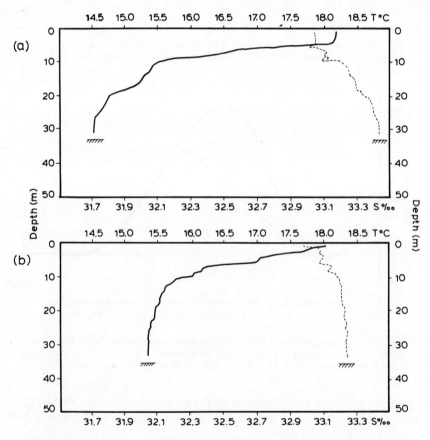

Fig. 7.5 (a) and (b) − Temperature and salinity profiles at two stations, 10 km apart, in the eastern Irish Sea, on 3 August, 1975: ──────── temperature, − − − − salinity.

lower salinity. This combination of temperature and salinity layering occurs in some areas but not in others. Salinity stratification may arise from a flux of fresh water through the surface, precipitation causing a reduction in salinity and in density and corresponding to a positive downward heat flux $Q$. Evaporation acts in the opposite sense, causing an increase in salinity and in density, as would a negative heat flux, $Q$. Evaporation thus acts to increase the density in two ways: by increasing the salinity of the surface layer and by cooling it through the abstraction of latent heat.

A process which is usually more important in tending to produce salinity stratification, however, is the advection of low salinity water seawards from a coastal zone directly affected by river inflow. This aspect was mentioned in Chapter 6, where the tendency of a river discharge to spread over the coastal water as a plume and the generation of density-driven currents by horizontal salinity gradients were considered. The advective processes are more difficult to deal with quantitatively than those of fluxes through the sea surface but their importance must be borne in mind. The occurrence of density stratification in a particular area, at a particular season, may be due primarily to either heat flux or low salinity water inflow or to a complex interaction of the two.

### 7.3.2 Some effects of the thermocline

The thermocline is essentially a layer within which the vertical flux of heat is restricted because of the reduction in turbulent mixing. This reduction will have a similar effect on the vertical transport of other properties such as salinity, the nutrient salts, including nitrate, phosphate and silicate, and dissolved oxygen. In early summer the growth of phytoplankton in the surface layer uses up the nutrients present there and slows down as they become depleted. Their concentration is still high in the lower layer but their transport upwards through the thermocline is limited. The further growth of phytoplankton may thus be severely restricted until the autumn overturn of the thermocline allows an upward transport of nutrients into the surface layer to take place.

The suppression of mixing between the upper and lower layers means that a discharge of effluent into the surface layer, for example, will be largely trapped there, with only a very slow mixing downwards. Whereas in vertically mixed water the whole depth is available for the dispersion of the effluent, in stratified water the effective depth for this purpose is only that of the surface layer. Conversely, if the effluent is discharged into the lower layer and its buoyancy is not sufficient to enable it to break through the thermocline, it will tend to be trapped in the lower layer. The occurrence of a storm, however, may produce sufficient turbulent mixing in the thermocline to lead to a temporary breakdown in the effective separation between the layers.

Quantitatively the effect of stratification in the thermocline is to reduce the value of the coefficient of vertical eddy diffusion $K_z$ by a factor of the order of 10 or even 100. At station E.1 in the English Channel, mentioned above, Pingree and Pennycuick (1975) calculated the value of $K_z$ as a function of depth and time from the heat balance equation and found minimum values of about 1 cm$^2$ s$^{-1}$ at a depth of 10–20 m during the period July to September. They used the values of $K_z$ derived in this way to calculate the vertical transport of salt and phosphate in the water column.

### 7.3.3 Criterion for the formation of a thermocline

The development of a thermocline in the late spring or early summer depends on whether there is enough turbulent kinetic energy present throughout the depth of a water column to mix heat downwards at the rate at which it is being received from above. Solar radiation is absorbed in the surface layer at a rate which depends on the wavelength of the radiation and the transparency of the water. In typical coastal sea water, as mentioned in Section 7.2.1, most of the heat energy of sunlight is absorbed within the first few metres. We shall not be concerned here with the detailed distribution of temperature within the surface layer but will assume that all the solar heat energy is absorbed within a shallow layer of thickness $h$ as in Fig. 7.6. The back radiation takes place from a thin surface layer of the order of a few millimetres in thickness, as does the exchange of sensible and latent heat between the sea and the atmosphere. It is assumed further that the net influx of heat is mixed throughout the layer of thickness $h$ by wind and wave action. The point to be considered in deriving a criterion is whether the heat content of this layer can be mixed throughout the total depth $H$ of the water column. The following derivation follows closely that of Simpson and Hunter (1974) and Fearnhead (1975).

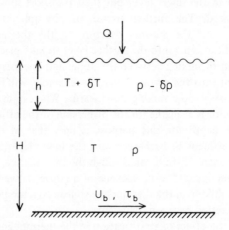

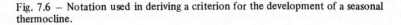

Fig. 7.6 – Notation used in deriving a criterion for the development of a seasonal thermocline.

Let $Q$ be the net heat flux per unit area of surface per unit time. The mass of water in a volume of unit horizontal area and thickness $h$ is $\rho h$, so that the absorption of a quantity of heat $Q\delta t$ in time $\delta t$ will produce a rise in temperature $\delta T$ given by

$$\delta T = \frac{Q\delta t}{\rho c h} \tag{7.8}$$

where $c$ is the specific heat at constant pressure.

This increase in temperature will give rise to an increase in volume, which may be regarded as an increase $\delta h$ in the thickness of the layer since unit horizontal area is being considered. Thus

$$\delta h = \alpha h\,\delta T \tag{7.9}$$

where $\alpha$ is the coefficient of thermal expansion of the water. This corresponds to a decrease in density $\delta\rho$ given by

$$\delta\rho = \rho\,\frac{\delta h}{h}$$

which from (7.8) and (7.9) gives

$$\delta\rho = \frac{\alpha Q\,\delta t}{ch}\ . \tag{7.10}$$

Now if the surface layer, of thickness $h$ and density $\rho - \delta\rho$, is completely mixed with the lower layer, of thickness $H - h$ and density $\rho$, it may be shown that there is an increase of gravitational potential energy given by

$$\delta V = \frac{1}{2}g\delta\rho\,h(H-h)\ .$$

Thus, using equation (7.10) the rate of increase of potential energy is

$$\frac{\mathrm{d}V}{\mathrm{d}t} = \frac{1}{2}\frac{g\alpha Q(H-h)}{c}\ . \tag{7.11}$$

The rate of loss of energy from the tidal currents by bottom friction is given by

$$\frac{\mathrm{d}E}{\mathrm{d}t} = \tau_b U_b$$

where $\tau_b$ is the bottom friction per unit area and $U_b$ is the instantaneous value of the bottom current. If the bottom friction is given by a quadratic law

$$\tau_b = k\rho\,|U_b|\,U_b$$

where $k$ is a friction coefficient, then

$$\frac{dE}{dt} = k\rho \, |U_b^3|$$

For a harmonic constituent of the tidal current, given by

$$U_b = U_0 \cos \sigma t$$

then, by averaging over a tidal period, it follows that the mean rate of loss of energy from the tidal current is given by

$$\frac{\overline{dE}}{dt} = \frac{4k}{3\pi} \rho U_0^3 \, . \tag{7.12}$$

It is assumed that the energy lost from the tidal current is all converted initially into turbulent kinetic energy and that a fraction $\epsilon$ of this energy is available for increasing the potential energy of the water column. Then the condition for complete mixing to be possible is

$$\frac{dV}{dt} \leqslant \epsilon \frac{\overline{dE}}{dt} \, . \tag{7.13}$$

From (7.11) and (7.12),

$$\frac{(H-h)Q}{U_0^3} \leqslant \frac{8}{3\pi} \frac{\epsilon \, k\rho c}{g\alpha} \, . \tag{7.14}$$

To a first approximation, the quantities $k$, $\rho$, $c$, $g$ and $\alpha$ may be regarded as constant. If $\epsilon$ is assumed to be constant to a first approximation also, the right-hand side of (7.14) is approximately constant. In deriving their criterion, Simpson and Hunter (1974) assumed further that $h \ll H$ and that $Q$ could be regarded as roughly constant when comparing different areas in similar latitudes during the same months. Since data on tidal currents at the surface are more readily available than those on bottom currents, $U_0$ in equation (7.12) was replaced by $U_s$, the amplitude of the tidal constituent at the surface, with an appropriate change in the value of $k$.

The criterion for complete vertical mixing may then be expressed in terms of a parameter $P$ such that

$$P \equiv \frac{H}{U_s^3} \leqslant P_{crit} \tag{7.15}$$

where

$$P_{crit} = \frac{8}{3\pi} \frac{\epsilon k'\rho c}{g\alpha Q} \tag{7.16}$$

and the bottom stress $\tau_b$ is related to the surface tidal current by a coefficient $k'$.

Applying the criterion (7.15) to the Irish Sea, where they had observed well-defined fronts between well-mixed and stratified areas, Simpson and Hunter found empirically that $P_{crit} = 70$ approximately, where $H$ is in metres and $U_s$ in metres per second.

The criterion was given in a slightly different form by Fearnhead (1975), who expressed the change of potential energy $dV/dt$ in terms of buoyancy flux $B$, allowing for a flux of fresh water through the surface by precipitation or evaporation as well as the heat flux $Q$. $B$ is given by

$$B = g \left( \frac{\alpha Q}{\rho c} + \beta Sf \right) \qquad (7.17)$$

where there is a net flux $f$ of fresh water downward through the surface, $S$ is the salinity of the surface layer and $\beta$ is the coefficient of haline contraction. When a quantity $f\delta t$ of fresh water is added to a layer of thickness $h$, the salinity decreases by $\delta S = fS\delta t/h$ and the density $\delta \rho$ by $\beta \rho \delta S$. This change is to be added to the value of $\delta \rho$ given by equation (7.10). The equation (7.11) for the rate of increase of potential energy becomes

$$\frac{dV}{dt} = \frac{1}{2} \rho B (H - h) \ . \qquad (7.18)$$

The criterion for complete vertical mixing, retaining the finite thickness $h$ of the wind-mixed layer, is

$$P' \equiv \frac{H - h}{U_s^3} \leqslant P'_{crit} \qquad (7.19)$$

where $\qquad P'_{crit} = \frac{8}{3\pi} \frac{\epsilon k'}{B} \ . \qquad (7.20)$

By comparing the calculated values of $P'$ with data on the occurrence of summer stratification in a number of coastal areas around the British Isles, Fearnhead found that $P'_{crit}$ was approximately 100 when $h$ was taken as 10 m. A variation of $h$ between 10 and 30 m did not appear to be critical in applying the criterion.

The form of the criterion, using the parameter $P$ or $P'$, assumes that the buoyancy flux $B$, or the heat flux $Q$ where this is predominant, does not vary significantly over the geographical region considered. If this assumption is relaxed, the buoyancy flux $B$ may be retained in the parameter and the condition for vertical mixing expressed as

$$\frac{BH}{U_s^3} \leqslant \frac{8}{3\pi} \epsilon k' \qquad (7.21)$$

assuming that $h$ is small compared with $H$.

The parameter on the left-hand side of (7.21) is a dimensionless number and was given in this form by Garrett *et al.* (1978).

### 7.3.4 Examples of seasonal stratification and fronts

The transition from a vertically well-mixed region to one in which stratification occurs is often marked by a transition zone, in which there is a sharp horizontal gradient of temperature and hence of density. In some cases the thermocline is accompanied by salinity stratification and the front is also marked by an intensified horizontal gradient of salinity. Dynamically the thermal or thermohaline fronts formed in this way are similar to the fronts mentioned in Chapter 6, arising from the spreading of low salinity water from the coast over denser water on the continental shelf.

The horizontal transition in surface temperature is often sufficiently marked to be clearly visible in infra-red photographs from satellites and this technique has been widely used in recent years to determine the position of fronts and their movements. Following the work of Simpson and Hunter (1974) and Fearnhead (1975), the position of fronts in the waters around the British Isles has been established from satellite photographs, confirmed by surveys from ships.

The degree of stratification in the water column at a given place and time may be expressed rather crudely by $\Delta T$, the overall difference in temperature between surface and bottom, or by $\Delta\rho$, the corresponding difference in density which includes the effect of salinity stratification as well, if present. The difference $\Delta T$ or $\Delta\rho$ does not take any account of the way in which the variation with depth occurs and a better measure of the stratification is the potential energy anomaly $\phi$, given by

$$\phi = \frac{1}{H}\int_{-H}^{0} (\bar{\rho} - \rho)\, gz \, dz \tag{7.22}$$

where $\bar{\rho}$, given by

$$\bar{\rho} = \frac{1}{H}\int_{-H}^{0} \rho \, dz$$

is the mean density of the water column.

The parameter $\phi$ is the deficit of potential energy due to stratification, averaged over the depth, compared with the potential energy of a completely mixed column. Figure 7.7, taken from Simpson *et al.* (1977), shows the values of $\log_{10}\phi$ for the month of August, calculated from the available temperature and salinity data, for waters to the west and south of Great Britain. The positions of known fronts A to E are marked on the figure, which is to be compared with Fig. 7.8, showing the values of $\log_{10}P$, where $P = H/U_s^3$, for the same area.

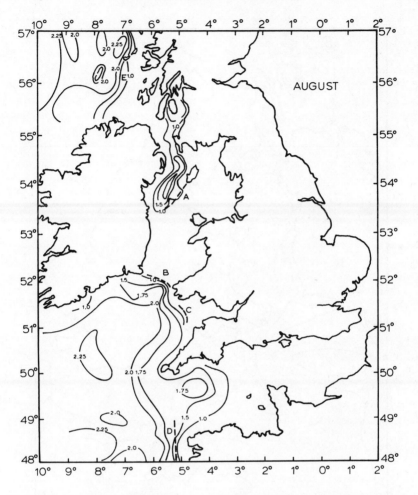

Fig. 7.7 – Values of $\log_{10}\phi$, where $\phi$ is the deficit of potential energy, for the Irish Sea and English Channel. A to E are the positions of fronts. From Simpson *et al.* (1977), by courtesy of Pergamon Press.

The value of $\phi$ varies from about 200 J m$^{-3}$ (joules per cubic metre) in regions of high stratification in the northwest and southwest of the area down to virtually zero in large areas of the English Channel and Irish Sea which were well mixed. The frontal regions occur where the value of $\phi$ drops from about 10 J m$^{-3}$ to almost zero. It is seen from Fig. 7.8, that these are also regions where $H/U_s^3$ is slightly less than 100 m$^{-2}$ s$^3$, in approximate agreement with the result quoted above that the critical value of $H/U_s^3$ is about 70.

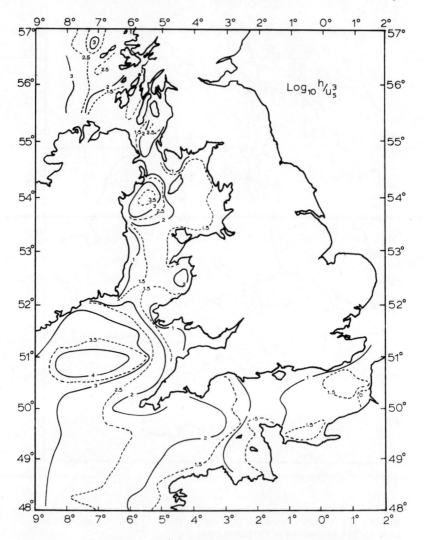

Fig. 7.8 – Values of $\log_{10}(H/U_s^3)$ for the Irish Sea and English Channel. From Simpson *et al.* (1977), by courtesy of Pergamon Press.

Having established a relationship between the potential energy anomaly $\phi$, the occurrence of fronts between stratified and well mixed regions and the parameter $H/U_s^3$, one may use the distribution of $H/U_s^3$, with the values of $U_s$ computed from a tidal model of the area, to predict the occurrence of fronts where they have not already been observed. This approach was adopted by Pingree and Griffiths (1978), using a model covering the shelf around the British Isles, including the North Sea as well as the areas shown in Figs. 7.7 and 7.8.

An example of an infra-red image of waters to the west and south of Great Britain is given in Fig. 7.9, taken from the TIROS–N satellite in May 1980. In the sea areas, the darker shades represent warmer surface temperatures. The vertically well-mixed areas have lower surface temperatures and show up as lighter shades. The positions of the Islay, western Irish Sea and Celtic Sea fronts are indicated on the figure and other fronts, less well defined, can be seen at the western end of the English Channel.

Fig. 7.9 – Infra-red image of the shelf area around the British Isles, taken from the TIROS–N satellite on 16 May 1980. Frontal zones between stratified and well-mixed areas are indicated as follows: A, Islay front; B, western Irish Sea front; C, Celtic Sea front. From Simpson (1981) by courtesy of the Royal Society.

A similar treatment was applied to the transition between stratified and well mixed regions in the Bay of Fundy and Gulf of Maine by Garrett *et al.* (1978), who found that the critical value of $H/U_s^3 = 80$ approximately was applicable to that area. They considered the effect of the proposed tidal power barriers across the Bay of Fundy, pointing out that the reservoir areas inside the barriers, now well mixed, would probably become stratified, an effect which would be accentuated by the inflow of fresh water. Outside the barriers the well-mixed areas might be slightly expanded, possibly merging with the existing mixed areas over Georges Bank and Nantucket Shoals.

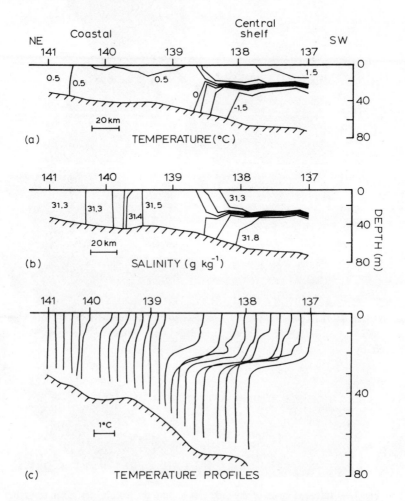

Fig. 7.10 – Sections across a front in the Bristol Bay area of the Bering Sea, June 1976: (a) temperature, (b) salinity, (c) temperature profiles. From Schumacher *et al.* (1979), by courtesy of the American Meteorological Society.

The occurrence of areas of summer stratification in the Greater Cook Strait region, between the North and South Islands of New Zealand, was found by Bowman *et al.* (1980) to correspond to a similar critical parameter. The current amplitudes were calculated using a numerical model of the $M_2$ tides.

The development of density stratification due to the addition of fresh water to the surface layer, rather than to a heat flux, was described by Schumacher *et al.* (1979) in the, Bristol Bay area of the Bering Sea. Owing to the melting of the ice-cover in spring, fresh water is added to the surface layer and, where tidal mixing is insufficient, a low salinity surface layer is formed, separated by a pycnocline from the denser water below. A front is formed, following fairly closely the 50 m depth contour, separating the well mixed coastal waters from the stratified region. The temperature and salinity distributions in the region of the front are illustrated in Fig. 7.10. The critical value of the parameter $\log_{10}$ $H/U_s^3$ was found to be about 3.5, compared with about 2 in waters around the British Isles. The considerably higher value may be largely attributed to the lower value of $\alpha$, the coefficient of thermal expansion, which is about $36 \times 10^{-6}$ $°C^{-1}$ at the temperature and salinity of the Bering Sea water compared with about $167 \times 10^{-6} \, °C^{-1}$ in water around the British Isles in summer.

The Islay front, west of Scotland, indicated as E in Fig. 7.7 and as A in Fig. 7.9, is an example of a stratified region in which both temperature and salinity differences contribute to its structure. The low salinity water in the upper layer is attributed, in this case, not to fresh water influx through the surface but to horizontal flow offshore of the coastal zone of water which is diluted by river inflows. A detailed description of conditions in this frontal region was given by Simpson *et al.* (1979).

## 7.4 DEVELOPMENT OF STRATIFIED CONDITIONS

### 7.4.1 Efficiency of tidal mixing

It is seen from equation (7.16) that the critical value of $H/U_s^3$ should be proportional to an efficiency factor $\epsilon$, representing the fraction of tidal energy dissipated by bottom friction which is available for vertical mixing. If the value of $P_{crit}$, in (7.15), is determined empirically from observations, as described above, it is possible to estimate the value of $\epsilon$, since the other factors occurring in equation (7.16) may be given their numerical values. Thus

$$\epsilon = \frac{3\pi\alpha g Q}{8k'\rho c} P_{crit} .$$  (7.23)

Taking $P_{crit} = 70$, $Q$ as 40 cal m$^{-2}$ s$^{-1}$, $k' = 2 \times 10^{-3}$ and the appropriate values of $\alpha, g, \rho$ and $c$, Simpson *et al.* (1977) found that $\epsilon = 2.8 \times 10^{-3}$.

It seems surprising at first sight that so small a fraction of the tidal energy dissipated should be available for mixing. A high proportion of the turbulent kinetic energy is generated in a boundary layer near the bottom, however, and much of it is dissipated there also. More than 90% of the turbulent energy is typically generated in the bottom 10% of the water column. Only a small fraction of this energy is advected or diffused upwards to add to the turbulent energy generated locally at higher levels. It is more relevant to compare the potential energy required for mixing with the rate of generation of turbulent kinetic energy in a thin layer near the base of the wind-mixed layer. When this is done it is found that the efficiency is increased to a value of the order of $5 \times 10^{-2}$ rather than $2.8 \times 10^{-3}$. This fraction is still small but it is approaching the magnitude of the critical flux Richardson number $Rf$, the parameter which has been used to characterise mixing in a shear flow. $Rf$ represents the ratio of the rate of increase of potential energy to the rate of production of turbulent energy. It is essentially less than 1 and there is some evidence, particularly from the atmospheric boundary layer, that it does not exceed about 0.2. Looked at in this way, tidal mixing is not such an inefficient process as it appears at first sight.

### 7.4.2 Models of changing stratification

There is a tendency for the potential energy anomaly $\phi$ of a water column, defined by equation (7.22), to be increased by a downward heat flux through the surface and reduced by vertical mixing, arising from tidal friction at the bottom and wind stress acting on the surface. These processes may be represented by the equation

$$\frac{d\phi}{dt} = \frac{\alpha g Q}{2c} - \frac{4}{3\pi} \epsilon k\rho \frac{U_b^3}{H} - \delta \gamma k_a \rho_a \frac{\overline{W^3}}{H} \qquad (7.24)$$

given by Simpson et al. (1978). In this equation the last term on the right-hand side represents the effect of wind mixing. $W$ is the wind speed near the surface, the bar denoting an average over the period considered, $\rho_a$ is the density of the air, $k_a$ is the drag coefficient relating the surface stress to the square of the wind speed, $\gamma$ is the ratio of the speed of the wind-induced surface current to the wind speed and $\delta$ is a factor representing the efficiency of the wind mixing process, corresponding to $\epsilon$ for tidal mixing. The symbols used in the other terms of the equation are as already defined. No allowance is made for advective processes.

Equation (7.24) may be integrated forward in time, starting at the onset of stratification, to give $\phi$, representing the degree of stratification, as a function of time at a given place. The quantities $Q$, $U_b$ and $W$ need to be known as functions of time from observations or from a suitable model and the efficiencies $\epsilon$ and $\delta$ are taken as constant. The calculation may be repeated for other locations in the vicinity, using the appropriate values of $U_b$ and $H$. The other parameters are likely to change only slowly with position. In this way the development of a front and its movement with time in the course of the season may be predicted. Predictions made in this way were found to be in general agreement with the stratification as shown by the observed values of $\phi$ but there were some significant differences. In particular the position of the front, as indicated by a given value of $\phi$, did not vary as much with the springs-neaps cycle as calculated from the changing values of $U_b{}^3$. The discrepancy can be much reduced by treating the efficiency coefficients $\epsilon$ and $\delta$ as variable instead of constant.

In the variable efficiency model, the efficiency of mixing is assumed to be reduced as the stratification increases. $\epsilon$ and $\delta$ are given by

$$\frac{\epsilon}{\epsilon_0} = \frac{\delta}{\delta_0} = \left(\frac{C}{C+\phi}\right)^{1/2} \tag{7.25}$$

where $\epsilon_0$ and $\delta_0$ are the efficiencies at neutral stability and $C$ is a constant. $\epsilon_0$ and $\delta_0$ were taken as $3.7 \times 10^{-3}$ and $2.3 \times 10^{-2}$ respectively. The ratio $\epsilon/\epsilon_0$ was allowed to decrease with increasing $\phi$ until it reached 0.25 and was then held constant if $\phi$ increased further. The introduction of positive feedback into the development of stratification in this way is physically realistic, as discussed in Section 7.2.1.

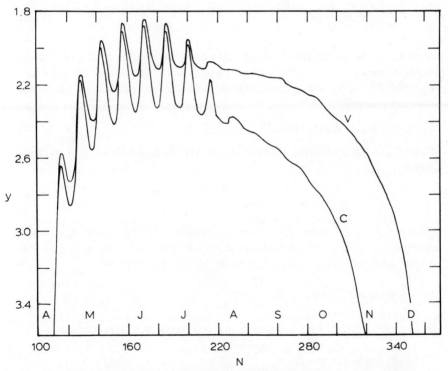

Fig. 7.11 – Comparison of the prediction of frontal movement from constant (C) and variable (V) efficiency models. Results are displayed as the value of $y = \log H/U_b^3$ for marginal stratification ($\phi = 1$ J m$^{-3}$) plotted against day number $N$. From Simpson (1981) by courtesy of the Royal Society.

In Fig. 7.11 taken from Simpson (1981), the value of the parameter $y = \log H/U_b^3$ for marginal stratification, represented by $\phi = 1$ J m$^{-3}$, is plotted against time, as calculated by the two models. The variable efficiency formulation is an improvement on the constant efficiency model in several respects. The fortnightly springs—neaps variation is reduced to an extent closer to that observed. The sharpness of the front is increased, consistent with the observation that contours of $\phi$ are usually somewhat closer together than those of $H/U^3$. In addition, the incorporation of feedback accelerates the development of stratification in spring and leads to a period of nearly constant frontal position from early June to late August, which is also in accordance with observations.

### 7.4.3 Model of vertical mixing
In the models described above, the overall state of a water column is considered but no attempt is made to simulate the actual distribution of temperature with depth. A model to do this was described by James (1977), making use of the one-dimensional diffusion equation for temperature:

$$\frac{\partial T}{\partial t} = \frac{\partial}{\partial z}\left(K_z \frac{\partial T}{\partial z}\right) \qquad (7.26)$$

where $K_z$ is the coefficient of vertical eddy diffusion of heat. The $z$-axis is taken vertically upwards and advection or mixing in the horizontal direction are neglected. The reduction in vertical mixing with increasing stability is taken into account by setting

$$K_z = K_0(1 + \sigma Ri)^{-p} \qquad (7.27)$$

where $K_0$ is the coefficient for neutral stability, $Ri$ is the Richardson number, given by

$$Ri = g\alpha \frac{\partial T}{\partial z}\bigg/\left(\frac{\partial U}{\partial z}\right)^2 \qquad (7.28)$$

and $\sigma$ and $p$ are constants, determined empirically. The best agreement with the observed series of events was obtained by taking $\sigma = 0.3$ and $p = 1.5$. The solution of equation (7.26) is subject to the boundary conditions:

at the surface, $z = 0$: $\qquad K_z \frac{\partial T}{\partial z} = \frac{Q}{\rho c}$

where $Q$ is the flux of heat downwards through the surface, as previously;

at the bottom, $z = -H$: $K_z \frac{\partial T}{\partial z} = 0$ .

The temperature gradient $\partial T/\partial z$ is determined in the course of the calculation. The heat input $Q$ and the wind speed are obtained from meteorological data. The term $(\partial U/\partial z)^2$ in equation (7.28) is evaluated by assuming that the velocity profile is formed by the superposition of two logarithmic profiles, one due to the wind stress on the surface and the other due to the tidal current. The eddy diffusivity $K_0$, corresponding to $Ri = 0$, is expressed as the sum of two parts, i.e.

$$K_0 = K_{0w} + K_{0T}$$

where $K_{0w}$ is proportional to the wind speed and $K_{0T}$ is proportional to the amplitude of the tidal current and to the depth of water. When a thermocline forms at a certain depth $z = z_0$, it is assumed that wind mixing cannot penetrate below that depth or tidal mixing above it. If $\partial T/\partial z$ becomes negative, indicating instability, instantaneous mixing over a certain range of depth is assumed to occur, thus restoring stability.

By integrating equation (7.26) numerically from given initial conditions, it is possible to compute the development of the temperature profile with time. The method was applied to stations in the St. George's Channel area of the Irish Sea, where a transition between well-mixed and stratified conditions occurs in summer. Figure. 7.12 shows the temperature profiles at 28-day intervals from mid-March onwards at a station where a summer thermocline is formed. The development of the thermocline from April to August is seen, followed by a

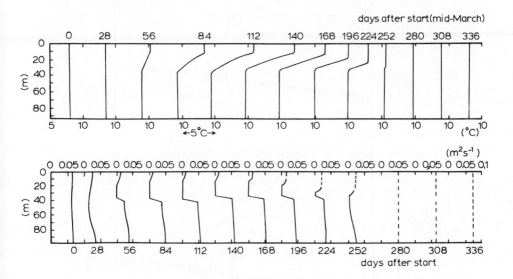

Fig. 7.12 – Development of a seasonal thermocline, computed from a one-dimensional model: above, temperature profiles at 28-day intervals; below, profiles of the coefficient of eddy diffusion at the same intervals. With permission from I. D.James. *Estuar. Coastal. Mar. Sci.*, **7**, 197–202. Copyright Academic Press Inc. (London) Ltd.

deepening and gradual breakdown until October–November. The profile of the eddy diffusion coefficient $K_z$ is also shown in Fig. 7.12. This relatively simple model thus simulates quite well the formation of a seasonal thermocline as the heat input $Q$ increases to a maximum, followed by a deepening as Q decreases and an eventual overturning of the water column when $Q$ becomes negative in the late autumn.

## 7.5 SOME PROPERTIES OF THERMOHALINE FRONTS

### 7.5.1 General character

The structure of a thermal front, between a stratified and a well mixed region is illustrated diagrammatically in Fig. 7.13(a). The isotherms, which are horizontal and crowded together in the thermocline, diverge on entering the mixed region,

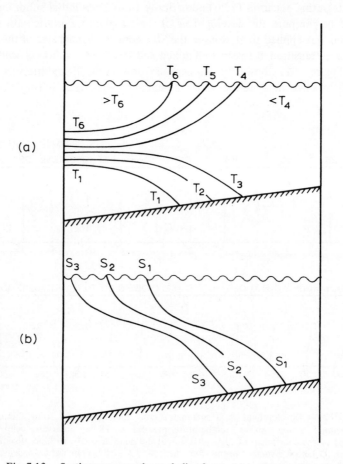

Fig. 7.13 – Sections across a thermohaline front: (a) isotherms, (b) isohalines.

the higher ones sloping upwards to the surface and the lower ones going downwards to the bottom. At the surface the frontal region is marked by a transition area where the isotherms are fairly close together, between areas of nearly uniform temperature, colder on the well-mixed and warmer on the stratified side of the front. If the salinity is nearly uniform, the isopycnals will take the same form as the isotherms, fanning out in the vertical on approaching the front from the stratified side.

The structure is somewhat more complicated if the salinity is also stratified, with a lower salinity in the upper layer. If the lower salinity were due entirely to excess precipitation at the sea surface, the isohalines would follow the same course as the isotherms, and the salinity in the well mixed region would be intermediate between the salinities in the upper and lower layers of the stratified region. It is more likely, however, that the lower salinity in the upper layer will be due to a flow seawards of water from a coastal zone of low salinity. In this case the salinity in the well-mixed region will be similar to that in the upper layer of the stratified region and the isohalines will take the form shown in Fig. 7.13(b). At the surface the salinity front occurs further seaward than the temperature front, but a sloping salinity front occurs at mid-depth below the surface temperature front.

The Islay Front, mentioned above in Section 7.3.4, is an example of a thermohaline front in which the density distribution is dominated by the salinity. Vertical sections of temperature, salinity and density across this front are shown in Fig. 7.14. In this case the surface signature of the front is a fairly weak temperature transition and a slight indication of a salinity maximum just to the seaward of it.

It has already been pointed out that infra-red photographs from satellites play an important role in locating fronts by the temperature transition at the surface. It is clear, however, that fronts have varying temperature and salinity structures at depth and in some cases there may be a pronounced subsurface front which has little to identify it at the surface.

### 7.5.2 Water movements near fronts

It was shown in Chapter 6 that a horizontal gradient of density gives rise to a density-driven current which, in the absence of friction, is in geostrophic balance and flows parallel to the isopycnals. In a region where the isopycnals are closer together, the velocity of the current would be increased. Thus one would expect the current near a front to have a geostrophic component, flowing parallel to the isopycnals. Because of its intensification where the horizontal density gradient is greatest, this current would tend to take on the character of a jet flow. At the same time, since currents in relatively shallow water are affected by friction, one would expect a component of flow perpendicular to the isopycnals, with a current flowing from lower to higher density in the upper layer and in the opposite direction below it.

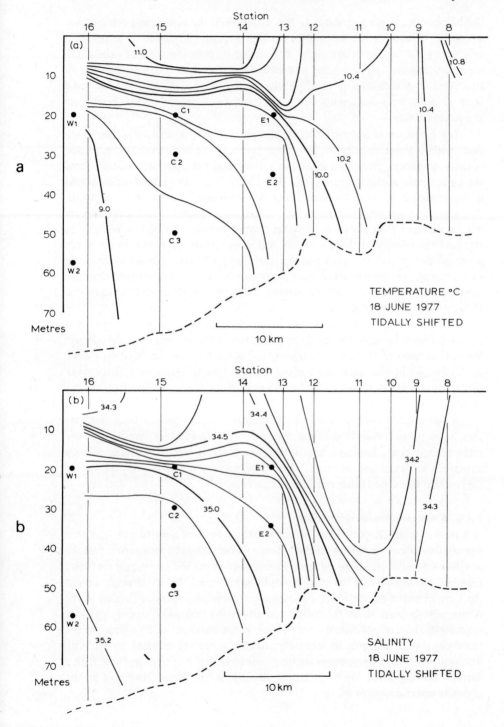

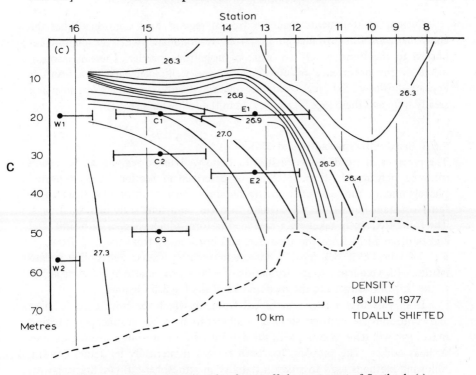

Fig. 7.14 – Sections across the Islay front, off the west coast of Scotland: (a) temperature, (b) salinity, (c) density. With permission from J. H. Simpson *et al.*, *Estuar. Coastal Mar. Sci.*, **9**, 713–726. Copyright Academic Press Inc. (London) Ltd.

These expectations were confirmed quantitatively by James (1978), using a numerical model in which the density distribution in a vertical section across the front was assumed and the corresponding horizontal and vertical components of flow calculated. The model included a vertical eddy viscosity, varying with the Richardson number of the flow in a somewhat similar way to the eddy diffusivity in the James (1977) model, described in Section 7.4.3, and also horizontal eddy viscosity and bottom friction. Taking a density distribution corresponding to the front in St. George's Channel at the end of August, the calculated flow along the front reached a maximum at the surface of 12 cm s$^{-1}$, with the well-mixed water on the right. The maximum velocity normal to the front, towards the stratified region in the surface layer, was about 4 cm s$^{-1}$. Upwelling occurred on the well-mixed side of the front and a horizontal convergence at the surface on the stratified side of it, taking the front to be at the position of maximum density gradient. The model was two-dimensional, in a vertical plane normal to the front, in that conditions were assumed to be uniform in a direction parallel to the front, and a steady state was assumed.

Current measurements made in frontal regions have confirmed that the component of flow parallel to the front is dominant, with the component normal to the front usually an order of magnitude smaller. There is also evidence of the occurrence of upwelling on the well-mixed side of a front. It appears, however, that real fronts are seldom strictly two-dimensional or in a steady state and these aspects are treated in the following section.

### 7.5.3 Instabilities, meanders and eddies

The presence of fronts between stratified and well-mixed regions can be seen in infra-red photographs from satellites, as described in Section 7.3.4. Repeated photographs of the same area usually show the mean position of a front to be fairly constant but significant changes to occur on a time scale of several days. The front frequently takes on a meandering form which changes with time, and eddies often form from the meanders and break away from the man front. In Fig. 7.9, the Celtic Sea front follows a meandering course and similar irregularities, with a tendency to the formation of eddies, can be seen at the approaches to the Bristol Channel and the western end of the English Channel.

It appears that a two-dimensional front, in which the front itself is linear and conditions are uniform along it, is inherently unstable. A small perturbation in its form will tend to grow, with the development of three-dimensional features such as eddies. The problem has been treated numerically by James (1981), following methods used to study instability in atmospheric flows. Starting with a two-dimensional sloping front between water masses of different densities, he was able to follow the development of a small wave-like perturbation into a meander of large amplitude and then to the formation of eddies, as in the satellite photographs. The generation of eddies indicates one mechanism by which properties characteristic of the water on one side of a front may be transferred across it to the other side.

### 7.5.4 Biological activity at fronts

One of the main reasons for the interest taken in fronts in shelf seas is the increased biological productivity which is often associated with them. On the north-west European continental shelf, for example, the spring bloom of diatoms occurs at the same time as the seasonal thermocline is being developed. The diatom production is made possible by the combination of favourable light conditions with an adequate supply of inorganic nutrients at that season. Similar conditions occur again in the autumn when the thermocline is being eroded. In summer, however, the growth of phytoplankton is limited by the depletion of nutrients in the surface layer, which is practically isolated from the lower layer by the low level of turbulent mixing in the thermocline. High concentrations of phytoplankton are confined to the boundary region between the warm, but nutrient depleted, surface layer and the cooler, tidally stirred, water below. At greater depths, although the nutrient concentrations are high, growth is restricted by the lower light intensity. The high concentrations of phytoplankton, as shown by measurements of chlorophyll $a$, are found at the surface in the frontal zone and also below the surface in the thermocline layer.

Since phytoplankton provide the source of food for the zooplankton, both the animal and plant populations of coastal waters are strongly influenced by the formation of the seasonal thermocline and associated fronts. A number of observations on the biological aspects of frontal systems of the north-west European continental shelf have been summarised and discussed by Holligan (1981). Similar work has been done in other areas such as Chesapeake Bay, the Nova Scotian Shelf and the Bering Sea. Most of the observations support the hypothesis, put forward by Pingree *et al.* (1975), that the sustained growth of phytoplankton in frontal regions requires the favourable combination of three factors: (1) adequate illumination, (2) a sufficient degree of vertical stability to retain the plants in the photic layer, (3) a continuing flux of nutrients into the layer. There would appear to be an optimum level of turbulent mixing, since too much mixing would cause the plants to diffuse out of the layer of growth while too little would restrict unduly the supply of nutrients.

### 7.5.5 Mixing across fronts

The mixing of water masses across fronts is an important consideration, since it controls the exchange of coastal water, including any pollutants which it contains, with water on the outer shelf and its eventual disposal in deep water. A number of possible mechanisms have been identified including:

(1) mean flows associated with the frontal structure, such as an offshore surface flow across the front and an onshore flow below it;

(2) baroclinic instability of the front, as mentioned in Section 7.5.3, leading to the formation of eddies which could entrain water on one side of the front and transport it to the other side;

(3) shear effects, in which gradients of the horizontal velocity interact with vertical mixing to produce an increased rate of horizontal mixing;

(4) interleaving of the two water masses, producing intrusions, across the boundaries of which steep gradients occur, so that small-scale mixing processes can operate efficiently.

These mechanisms and others have been studied theoretically and estimates made of the cross-frontal transport which each might produce. It is not possible to say at present, however, which mixing processes are likely to be dominant in a given frontal situation. In the absence of fronts cross-shelf mixing takes place by other mechanisms, of which horizontal eddies present in the tidal currents are probably one of the most important. A wind-driven circulation may also develop horizontal eddies and contribute to the mixing processes.

# 8

# Exchange processes and mixing

---

## 8.1 NATURE OF EXCHANGE PROCESSES

Reference was made in Chapter 6 to the processes acting on the continental shelf by which the river water flowing in from the coast was mixed with the oceanic water from beyond the edge of the shelf. On the long-term average, the salinity of water on the shelf is maintained at a lower value than that of the ocean, while the inflowing river water is gradually removed from the shelf region by mixing with the oceanic water. One process by which this can take place is a two-layer flow at the edge of the shelf, the upper layer water of lower salinity flowing towards the ocean while higher salinity water flows inwards in the lower layer to replace it. This is an 'advective' process in that it involves the bodily movement of two water masses, each carrying its own salt content with it. It is implicit in this process that, on the continental shelf itself, a certain amount of mixing will take place between the low salinity inflow from the coast and the high salinity influx of oceanic water, although it is not necessary to specify the details of the mixing.

An alternative process which can be visualised is that of a horizontal eddy over the shelf edge. As water in the eddy moves over the shelf it may entrain some of the adjacent low salinity shelf water while shedding some of the high salinity ocean water in exchange.When the modified water moves out into the ocean it may shed some of the modified, reduced salinity, water and entrain a new fraction of ocean water before flowing back on to the shelf. The eddy acts as a kind of rotary pump, transferring low salinity water from the shelf to the ocean and high salinity water in the opposite direction. The eddy may be regarded as an advective feature, transferring water bodily, but it is again understood that some sort of mixing or entrainment takes place between the eddy and water adjacent to it.

If a sufficiently dense array of observations is made, the properties of any eddy, such as that described above, and its exchange effects can be measured. Over a large area of shelf there may be a number of eddies, of different sizes and intensities of flow, so that it may not be practicable or desirable to consider their effects individually. In that case a statistical treatment may be applied to estimate the average rate of transport of river water across a length of the shelf. The most general treatment is to regard the exchange process as one of horizontal eddy diffusion, assuming that the flux of any constituent of concentration c is proportional to the concentration gradient in the cross-shelf direction, i.e.

$$F = - K_x \frac{\partial c}{\partial x}$$

where $K_x$ is the coefficient of eddy diffusion in the $x$ direction, taken to be in the offshore direction. If the properties of the eddies can be specified, in a statistical sense, it may be possible to estimate the value of $K_x$ from these properties. If not, one may have to estimate $K_x$ empirically from observations of the distribution of the constituent and its rate of input to the system.

Some eddies may be associated with the topography of the region and change little with time. Others may be generated by the wind and develop and decay on a time scale of several days. Eddies associated with tidal currents may also be present, changing their character during a tidal period. The average rate of exchange over a period of several weeks or months will thus involve an average with respect to time. The definition of an effective eddy coefficient of diffusion must therefore specify a certain time interval as well as the area of cross-section, parallel to the coastline or shelf edge, to which it applies.

The above discussion has been in terms of the exchange of river water and ocean water, as shown by the distribution of salinity. Fresh water content or salinity is often used as a tracer to indicate how other substances, such as nutrient salts or pollutants, would be dispersed by the processes acting in the area. An alternative approach is to consider the dispersion of a tracer introduced artificially, either as an instantaneous release at a fixed point or as a continuous discharge at a point. Experiments of this type may be used to indicate the probable effects of an effluent discharged in a similar way or, less directly, the general mixing characteristics of the area.

Most mixing processes in the sea involve both an advective and a diffusive element. If the velocity varies with position, as in an eddy or a shear flow, a finite patch of water, marked in some way, will become distorted in shape and size and possibly drawn out into filaments. A certain amount of dispersion may be said to have taken place, without any diffusion. Normally there will be diffusive processes acting at the same time, tending to reduce initial diffferences in concentration of the marker substance. These processes will be more effective if the patch is distorted in such a way that the area across which diffusion takes place is increased and the average concentration gradients are enhanced.

The distinction between the two types of processes is that advective changes are reversible, in the sense that if the velocities were completely reversed the distorted patch would be restored to its original size and shape. Diffusive processes always act so as to reduce concentration differences and increase the area affected by the marker substance, so that they are irreversible. In the hypothetical case of the velocity field being reversed, the centre of the patch might return to its original position but the marked water would cover a larger area and the concentration within the patch would be reduced.

It is clear that in any region of sea there are water movements taking place on a wide range of scales, from the molecular to a scale comparable with the dimensions of the region itself. Molecular movements must obviously be treated statistically and their effects are taken into account as molecular viscosity and diffusion. The smaller scale turbulent movements and their effects must also be dealt with statistically, possibly up to scales of centimetres or metres vertically and tens or hundreds of metres, or even kilometres, horizontally. The separation of the movements into mean flow and turbulence is somewhat arbitrary and may be made at different scales, depending on the purpose in view and the amount of detailed information available.

## 8.2 TREATMENT OF TURBULENT DIFFUSION

There are two alternative approaches to the process of turbulent diffusion. The first is Lagrangian and is based on the movement of individual particles of fluid, supposing them to be marked in some way. A particle, released at a given point, is assumed to execute random movements, due to collisions with fluid molecules or turbulent stresses due to surrounding fluid elements. The simplest case is that of a 'random walk', made up of a succession of steps, each step being in a random direction, independent of the previous steps. As a result of such movements the particle will gradually move further away, on the whole, from its release point. If two particles are released at the same time at the same point, but then move independently, the separation between them will gradually increase with time. We may proceed to the case of a large number of particles, released in a small volume surrounding the given point but moving independently under the action of random impulses from the fluid surrounding them. The result is an expanding cloud of diffusing particles.

The behaviour of particles acted on by molecular collisions only is the Brownian movement, the statistical theory of which was given by Einstein in 1905. The theory was extended to turbulent diffusion in 1922 by Taylor. Instead of a series of discrete steps, Taylor considered a particle to change its velocity continuously but still in a random way. Considering a given time, the particle would have a certain velocity and a short time later it would still have a velocity similar in magnitude and direction. As the time interval increased, however, the velocity would have a larger random element so that the correlation of the velocity with its original value would gradually decrease. After a certain interval the velocity would be independent of its initial value.

In a particular experiment, such as the release of a number of particles from a small volume around a given point, the subsequent development of the diffusing cloud of particles would itself be subject to random fluctuations. Repeating the experiment would give a rather different set of developing distributions. If a large number of releases were made and their results averaged, the 'ensemble average' development of the cloud with time would be expected to be a smoothly changing process. The theory of diffusion by continuous movements leads to predictions of the ensemble average conditions.

The second approach, which is Eulerian in character, treats the water and the diffusing substance as continuous media and considers the concentration of the diffusing substance per unit volume of water. A conservation equation is derived, expressing the rate of change of concentration in a certain volume in terms of the flux of material through its bounding faces. The flux across a face is assumed to be proportional to the concentration gradient perpendicular to the face, as in the case of molecular diffusion. In the case of turbulent diffusion, however, the corresponding diffusion coefficients differ, in general, in different coordinate directions and their magnitudes may vary from one position to another in the region concerned. A fuller discussion of the various aspects of turbulent diffusion is given in the book by Csanady (1973).

## 8.3 THE ADVECTION-DIFFUSION EQUATION

Taking the continuous medium approach, let $c$ be the concentration of the material of interest per unit volume and let the velocity at a point $x, y, z$ have the components $u, v, w$. Referring to Fig. 8.1, the flux of material per unit time across unit area perpendicular to the $x$-axis, resulting from transport with the water and from molecular diffusion is given by

$$F_x = uc - \kappa \frac{\partial c}{\partial x} \tag{8.1}$$

where $\kappa$ is the coefficient of molecular diffusion.

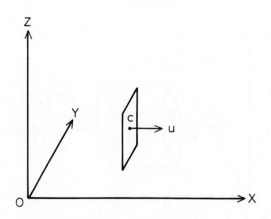

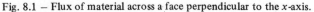

Fig. 8.1 — Flux of material across a face perpendicular to the $x$-axis.

Now in turbulent flow the concentration $c$ as well as the velocity components $u, v, w$ are subject to random fluctuations. Let $\bar{c}$ denote the mean value of concentration, averaged over a certain volume and a certain time interval, and let $c'$ be the deviation of the instantaneous value of concentration from the mean. Similarly let $\bar{u}$ denote the mean value of $u$ and $u'$ the deviation from the mean, with corresponding definitions of $\bar{u}, \bar{w}$ and $v', w'$. Thus at any instant:

$$c = \bar{c} + c', \quad u = \bar{u} + u' \text{ etc.}$$

Then the mean value of a product such as $uc$ is given by

$$\begin{aligned} \overline{uc} &= \overline{(\bar{u}+u')(\bar{c}+c')} \\ &= \overline{\bar{u}\bar{c}} + \overline{\bar{u}\,c'} + \overline{u'\bar{c}} + \overline{u'c'} \\ &= \overline{\bar{u}\bar{c}} + \overline{u'c'} \end{aligned}$$

since $\overline{u'} = \overline{c'} = 0$ by definition. In general, however, $\overline{u'c'}$ is not zero, a finite value of $\overline{u'c'}$ implying a correlation between the fluctuations of $u$ and $c$. If, for example, the mean concentration increases in the positive $x$ direction, a water particle with a higher than average $u$ is likely to have a lower than average concentration. In other words, a positive $u'$ is likely to be associated with a negative $c'$ and $\overline{u'c'}$ would be negative. An argument of this type leads to the introduction of a coefficient of eddy diffusion $K_x$, such that

$$\overline{u'c'} = - K_x \frac{\partial \bar{c}}{\partial x} . \tag{8.2}$$

Thus $K_x$ is analogous to the coefficient of molecular diffusion $\kappa$ but is usually several orders of magnitude larger. Eddy coefficients $K_y$ and $K_z$ may be defined similarly for turbulent diffusion in the $y$ and $z$ directions.

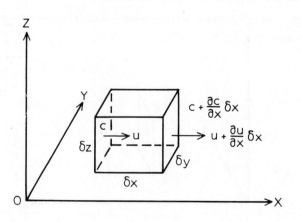

Fig. 8.2 – Fluxes of material across the faces of a small cuboid.

By considering the concentration $c$ within a small cuboid of sides $\delta x$, $\delta y$ and $\delta z$, as in Fig. (8.2), and the fluxes of material through its faces, the following equation may be derived for the conservation of material within the cuboid:

$$\frac{\partial c}{\partial t} + u \frac{\partial c}{\partial x} + v \frac{\partial c}{\partial y} + w \frac{\partial c}{\partial z} = \kappa \nabla^2 c \tag{8.3}$$

where $\nabla^2$ denotes the operator

$$\frac{\partial^2}{\partial x^2} + \frac{\partial^2}{\partial y^2} + \frac{\partial^2}{\partial z^2}$$

and $\kappa$ is the coefficient of molecular diffusion, as before.

By writing $c = \bar{c} + c'$, $u = \bar{u} + u'$ etc. in this equation and then taking mean values, it is found that

$$\frac{\partial \bar{c}}{\partial t} + \bar{u} \frac{\partial \bar{c}}{\partial x} + \bar{v} \frac{\partial \bar{c}}{\partial y} + \bar{w} \frac{\partial \bar{c}}{\partial z} + \frac{\partial}{\partial x} \overline{(u'c')} + \frac{\partial}{\partial y} \overline{(v'c')} + \frac{\partial}{\partial z} \overline{(w'c')}$$

$$= \kappa \nabla^2 c \ . \tag{8.4}$$

Introducing the coefficients of eddy diffusion, this becomes

$$\frac{\partial \bar{c}}{\partial t} + \bar{u} \frac{\partial \bar{c}}{\partial x} + \bar{v} \frac{\partial \bar{c}}{\partial y} + \bar{w} \frac{\partial \bar{c}}{\partial z} = \frac{\partial}{\partial x} \left( K_x \frac{\partial \bar{c}}{\partial x} \right) + \frac{\partial}{\partial y} \left( K_y \frac{\partial \bar{c}}{\partial y} \right)$$

$$+ \frac{\partial}{\partial z} \left( K_z \frac{\partial \bar{c}}{\partial z} \right) + \kappa \nabla^2 c \ . \tag{8.5}$$

In deriving these equations it has been assumed that no material has been produced or destroyed within the small volume itself. For a non-conservative property, such as oxygen content, a nutrient salt such as nitrate, bacteria or a radioactive constituent, this is not the case and a source or sink term, $Q(x, y, z, t)$, must be added to the right hand side of equation (8.4) or (8.5). In many cases the molecular diffusion term may be neglected.

The advection–diffusion equation in the form (8.5), with a source or decay term added when necessary, is the basis of all methods of calculating dispersion in the sea by using the Eulerian approach. In many cases some of the advective of diffusive terms are negligible and the problem can be reduced to two dimensions or even one dimension. The main difficulty is in assigning appropriate values to the eddy coefficients $K_x$, $K_y$ and $K_z$.

## 8.4 ONE-DIMENSIONAL DIFFUSION

### 8.4.1 Diffusion equation approach

The relation between the Eulerian and Lagrangian approaches to turbulent diffusion can be illustrated by considering a plane source of material normal to

the $x$-axis, so that diffusion takes place in the $x$ direction only. Assuming that
the fluid has no mean velocity and that molecular diffusion can be neglected,
equation (8.5) reduces to

$$\frac{\partial c}{\partial t} = \frac{\partial}{\partial x}\left(K_x\frac{\partial c}{\partial x}\right) \tag{8.6}$$

where the bar over $c$ has been omitted for simplicity as we shall be dealing with
the mean concentration throughout the rest of this chapter.

If the diffusion coefficient $K_x$ is independent of position, so that $K_x = K$,
a constant, equation (8.6) becomes

$$\frac{\partial c}{\partial t} = K\frac{\partial^2 c}{\partial x^2} \; . \tag{8.7}$$

This has the solution

$$c(x, t) = \frac{A}{t^{1/2}}\exp\left(-\frac{x^2}{4Kt}\right) \tag{8.8}$$

where $A$ is a constant. The total amount of diffusing material, per unit area
normal to the $x$-axis, is given by

$$Q = \int_{-\infty}^{\infty} c \, dx = 2A\,(\pi K)^{1/2} \; .$$

Thus equation (8.8) may be written

$$c(x, t) = \frac{Q}{2\,(\pi Kt)^{1/2}}\exp\left(-\frac{x^2}{4Kt}\right) \; . \tag{8.9}$$

The curve of concentration $c$ as a function of $x$ for a given time $t$ is seen
from (8.8) or (8.9) to be a Gaussian or normal distribution. The second moment
of the distribution may be calculated, giving

$$\int_{-\infty}^{\infty} cx^2 \, dx = 2QKt \; .$$

Dividing the second moment by the total amount of material $Q$ gives a quantity
which may be regarded as the mean square distance to which the particles have
diffused:

$$\sigma_x^2 = 2Kt \; . \tag{8.10}$$

Thus equation (8.9) may be written in the alternative form

$$c(x, t) = \frac{Q}{(2\pi)^{1/2}\sigma_x}\exp\left(-\frac{x^2}{2\sigma_x^2}\right) \; . \tag{8.11}$$

In turbulent diffusion, the coefficient $K_x$ is not, in general, independent of $x$, but it may be shown that equation (8.11) is still valid. The variance of the distribution, $\sigma_x^2$, is not, in the general case, given by (8.10) but is a different function of time.

It may be shown, however, that the rate of change of the variations of the distribution with time is given by

$$\frac{d\sigma_x^2}{dt} = 2 K_x \tag{8.12}$$

in the general case, This may be verified from (8.10) for the special case of $K_x = K$.

In the kinetic theory of gases, in which it is assumed that the molecules are so far apart that they move independently of one another between collisions, it is shown that the coefficient of molecular diffusion $\kappa$ is given by

$$\kappa = u_m \, l_m \tag{8.13}$$

where $u_m$ is the mean speed of a molecule (independent of direction) and $l_m$ is its mean free path. A similar equation may be assumed to apply in a liquid if $u_m$ is interpreted as a characteristic mean velocity of the molecules and $l_m$ as a mixing length indicating the average distance over which an initial velocity will persist before being lost by interactions with other molecules.

### 8.4.2 Random walk approach

The corresponding random walk problem is that in which movements take place in the positive or negative $x$ direction only. If $l$ is the length of each step, then at the completion of a given step, the next step is either $+l$ or $-l$, determined purely at random. If a large number of particles are released at time $t = 0$ from a plane surface normal to the $x$-axis at $x = 0$, and they each move independently by random walks in the way just described, then the number of particles found between distance $x$ and $x + dx$ at time $t$ may be interpreted as the concentration of material between $x$ and $x + dx$. The calculation by the random walk approach shows that the distribution is exactly the same as that given by equation (8.9) if $K$ is taken as

$$K = \frac{1}{2} nl^2 \tag{8.14}$$

where $n$ is the number of steps, or displacements, per unit time and $l$ is the step length. If we write

$$u_n = \frac{1}{2} nl$$

then          $$K = u_n l \tag{8.15}$$

analogous to equation (8.13) for the molecular diffusivity $D$. $u_n$ may be interpreted as a kind of 'diffusion velocity'.

In the theory of diffusion by continuous movements, the extent to which the velocity of a particle persists with time is represented by an auto-correlation function $R(\tau)$. If $u(t)$ is the velocity at time $t$ and $u(t + \tau)$ the velocity at time $t + \tau$, then

$$R(\tau) = \frac{\overline{u(t)u(t + \tau)}}{\overline{u^2}} \qquad (8.16)$$

where the over-bars indicate ensemble averages over a large number of particles. It is assumed that the mean properties of the turbulence do not change with time, so that $R(\tau)$ is independent of the initial time $t$. It is also assumed that as $\tau \to \infty$, $R(\tau) \to 0$ or, in other words, that after a sufficiently long time the velocity of the particle is completely independent of its initial value.

Applying the theory to the case of dispersion in the $x$ direction only, the displacement $x(t)$ of an individual diffusing particle may be found. Taking an ensemble average over the movements of a large number of particles, the variance $\sigma_x^2$ may be defined by

$$\sigma_x^2(t) = \overline{x^2(t)} \ .$$

Then it may be shown that

$$\frac{d\sigma_x^2}{dt} = 2\,\overline{u^2} \int_0^t R(\tau)\, d\tau \qquad (8.17)$$

where $R(\tau)$ is given by equation (8.16) and $\overline{u^2}$ is the mean square velocity of the diffusing particles.

### 8.4.3 Comparison of the methods

Comparing equation (8.17) with equation (8.12) for diffusion in a continuous medium, it is seen that the two are equivalent if

$$K_x = \overline{u^2} \int_0^t R(\tau)\, d\tau \ . \qquad (8.18)$$

The effective diffusion coefficient $K_x$ is thus a function of the time $t$ during which diffusion has been taking place, since the integral is a function of $t$. However, $R(\tau)$ is a decreasing function of $\tau$ and $R(\tau) \to 0$ as $\tau \to \infty$, so that for large values of $t$ the integral will approach a constant value. Let

$$\int_0^\infty R(\tau)\, d\tau = t_L \ , \qquad (8.19)$$

then for large values of diffusion time $t$,

$$K_x \rightarrow \overline{u^2}\, t_{\mathrm{L}} \,. \tag{8.20}$$

$t_{\mathrm{L}}$ may be interpreted as a 'persistence time' for the turbulent velocity of the particle and $(\overline{u^2})^{1/2}\, t_{\mathrm{L}}$ as the average distance travelled by a particle in that time. The expression for $K_x$ for diffusion times long compared with the persistence times is then analogous to equation (8.13) for molecular diffusion in that it is the product of a characteristic velocity and a characteristic length.

The above discussion has been in terms of diffusion in the $x$ direction only but it may readily be generalised to apply to diffusion in two or three dimensions.

In the sea the irregular movements present, which may be described loosely as 'eddies', without implying that they have any particular structure, cover a very wide range of scales. The smaller eddies, of centimetres to metres in scale, may be approximately isotropic in their properties but with increasing scale the eddies become anisotropic, with the horizontal components of motion being of larger scale than the vertical components. In some cases the larger eddies may be horizontally isotropic but in other cases their properties may vary with direction. In the presence of a current, for example, diffusion often takes place more rapidly parallel to the current direction than across it.

When a small volume of water, marked by dye or in some other way, is released at a point in the sea, the turbulence present will cause it to diffuse both vertically and horizontally at first. After a certain interval of time it is likely that further diffusion in the vertical will be limited by the presence of the surface and bottom boundaries or by a pycnocline in which vertical mixing is severely inhibited. Subsequent diffusion will take place horizontally and, as mentioned above, may or may not be isotropic in two dimensions.

A special case of two-dimensional dispersion is that of floating substances which are constrained by their low density to remain at the sea surface. They undergo horizontal dispersion only, at all scales, by the action of currents and horizontal diffusion.

## 8.5 PARTICULAR CASES OF DISPERSION

### 8.5.1 Radial spreading of a patch

The term 'dispersion' will be used to describe the spreading of a patch of substance or group of particles by the combined action of advection and diffusion. As stated earlier, a diffusive process always acts so as to smooth out concentration gradients and enlarge a patch while advective processes may either assist or limit dispersion. In this section some cases of dispersion by eddy diffusion only are considered. Turbulent motions on a range of scales may be present but it is assumed that their diffusive effects are all represented by the appropriate coefficient of eddy diffusion.

The simplest case to consider is that of radially symmetric spreading, so that the concentration $c$ of the diffusing substance is a function of radial distance $r$ from the source. The substance is assumed to be released at time $t = 0$ as a point source, or vertical line source, at $r = 0$. It is assumed that vertical spreading is limited by the depth of water or the presence of a pycnocline so that the dispersion is two-dimensional, in the horizontal. Let a coefficient $K_r$ of eddy diffusion in the radial direction be defined. In general $K_r$ may be a function of $r$.

Referring to Fig. 8.3, the flux of material across the arc AB, per unit depth, in time $\delta t$ is given by

$$- K_r \frac{\partial c}{\partial r} r \, \delta\theta \, \delta t \; .$$

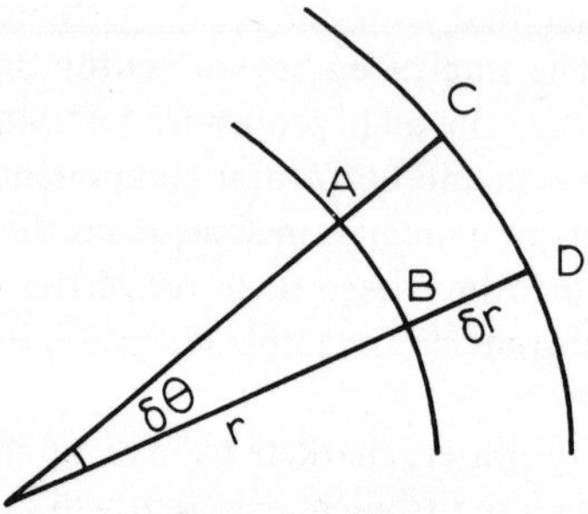

Fig. 8.3 – Radial spreading of a diffusing substance.

Similarly, across CD the flux is

$$- \left[ K_r \frac{\partial c}{\partial r} + \frac{\partial}{\partial r} \left( K_r \frac{\partial c}{\partial r} \right) \delta r \right] (r + \delta r) \, \delta\theta \, \delta t \; .$$

The difference between these two fluxes gives the increase of material within a volume of horizontal area ABCD and unit depth in time $\delta t$. Relating this to the change of concentration within the volume, and neglecting a term in $(\delta r)^2 \, \delta\theta$, leads to the equation:

$$\frac{\partial c}{\partial t} = \frac{1}{r} \frac{\partial}{\partial r} \left( K_r \, r \, \frac{\partial c}{\partial r} \right) . \tag{8.21}$$

The solution of equation (8.21) depends on the form taken for the diffusion coefficient $K_r$.

(i) $K_r$ independent of $r$

If $K_r$ is independent of $r$, i.e. $K_r = K = $ constant, then

$$c(r, t) = \frac{c_0}{4\pi K t} \exp\left( -\frac{r^2}{4K t} \right) \tag{8.22}$$

where $c_0$ is a constant. Putting $\sigma_r^2 = 2Kt$, this may be written

$$c(r, t) = \frac{c_0}{2\pi\sigma_r^2}\exp\left(-\frac{r^2}{2\sigma_r^2}\right).$$ (8.23)

At the initial time $t = 0$, the concentration is all at $r = 0$. At any subseqent time $t$ the concentration as a function of $r$ follows a Gaussian distribution with a standard deviation $\sigma_r = (2Kt)^{1/2}$.

The concentration at the centre of the patch, $c(0, t)$, is seen to be proportional to $t^{-1}$. Equations (8.22) and (8.23) are analogous to (8.8) and (8.11) which were derived for the case of one-dimensional diffusion.

(ii) $K_r$ proportional to $r$.

If a wide spectrum of eddies is present then, as the patch expands, one may expect larger eddies to take part in its dispersion and the value of $K_r$ to increase. Sverdrup in 1946 suggested taking a diffusion coefficient which increased linearly with the scale of the distribution, i.e. $K_r \propto r$. The idea of a 'diffusion velocity' $P$ for this case was introduced by Joseph and Sendner (1958). $P$ was assumed to be independent of $r$ but the scale of the diffusing process to increase linearly with $r$. This is equivalent to taking $K_r = Pr$. Then equation (8.21) becomes

$$\frac{\partial c}{\partial t} = \frac{1}{r}\frac{\partial}{\partial r}\left(Pr^2\frac{\partial c}{\partial r}\right).$$ (8.24)

The solution is

$$c(r, t) = \frac{c_0}{2\pi P^2 t^2}\exp\left(-\frac{r}{Pt}\right).$$ (8.25)

Thus the distribution with respect to $r$ follows an exponential instead of a Gaussian curve and the concentration at the centre decreases with time as $t^{-2}$, instead of as $t^{-1}$. The standard deviation of the distribution is given by $\sigma_r = Pt$.

Joseph and Sendner applied their theory to a number of naturally occurring distributions in the seas and ocean, on scales ranging from $r = 10$ km to $r = 1,500$ km. They concluded that dispersion in all cases followed the theory reasonably well, the deduced values of $P$ being $P = 1.0 \pm 0.5$ cm s$^{-1}$.

(iii) $K_r$ proportional to $r^{4/3}$

It was first suggested by L. F. Richardson in 1926, in relation to the atmosphere, that the effective coefficient of eddy diffusion should increase with the scale of the process being studied. He proposed, on empirical grounds, a coefficient proportional to $r^{4/3}$, where $r$ is the scale concerned. Later a similar relationship was derived from the theory of locally isotropic turbulence as applying to the inertial sub-range of eddies, those which receive their energy from larger eddies and pass it on to smaller ones. A number of workers starting with Stommel (1949) have suggested that the same law should apply to horizontal diffusion in the sea. In this case $K_r$ is taken as

$$K_r = C \epsilon^{1/3} r^{4/3}$$

where $\epsilon$ is the rate of transfer of energy per unit mass through the spectrum and $C$ is a constant. Inserting this expression for $K_r$ in equation (8.21) leads to the solution

$$c(r, t) = \frac{c_0}{6\pi\gamma^3 t^3} \exp\left(-\frac{r^{2/3}}{\gamma t}\right) \tag{8.26}$$

where $\gamma = 4/9\, C\epsilon^{1/3}$. At the centre of the patch the concentration $c(0, t) \propto t^{-3}$, while the standard deviation $\sigma_r \propto t^{3/2}$.

The main results of the three solutions are summarised in Table 8.1.

**Table 8.1** – Radial dispersion of a patch.

| Case | Coefficient of eddy diffusion $K_r$ | Concentration at centre $c(0, t)$ | Standard deviation $\sigma_r$ |
|------|:---:|:---:|:---:|
| (i)   | constant         | $\propto t^{-1}$ | $\propto t^{1/2}$ |
| (ii)  | $\propto r$      | $\propto t^{-2}$ | $\propto t$ |
| (iii) | $\propto r^{4/3}$ | $\propto t^{-3}$ | $\propto t^{3/2}$ |

(iv) *Comparison with observations*

If a tracer experiment has been carried out, the values of the measured concentration at a given time may be plotted on a chart and contours of equal concentration drawn. The actual contours will probably be irregular, as indicated in Fig. 8.4, rather than showing radial symmetry. The particular release may be regarded as one realisation of an ensemble of distributions and so subject to random fluctuations. On the assumption that the ensemble mean of the distributions would be radially symmetrical, each contour $c$ is assigned an effective radius $r_e$, such that

$$\pi r_e^2 = A$$

where $A$ is the actual area within the contour $c$.

The amount of tracer, per unit depth, between contours with radii $r_e$ and $r_e + dr_e$ is $2\pi c r_e\, dr_e$. It follows that the variance $\sigma_r^2$ of the distribution is given by

$$\sigma_r^2 = \int_0^\infty c r_e^3\, dr_e \Big/ \int_0^\infty c r_e\, dr_e \; .$$

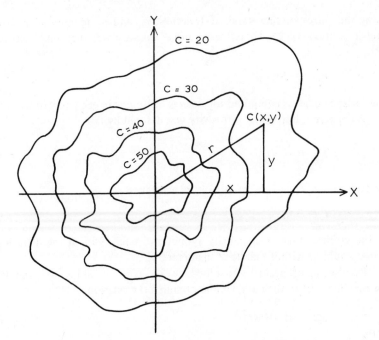

Fig. 8.4 — Irregular spreading of a patch of diffusing substance.

The rate of increase of $\sigma_r$ with time may be compared with the various model solutions discussed above.

The effective coefficient of eddy diffusion as a function of time is given by

$$K_r = \frac{1}{2} \frac{d\sigma_r^2}{dt}$$

analogous to equation (8.12) for the one-dimensional case.

Many instantaneous release experiments have been carried out in coastal waters during the last 25 years. Off the east coast of USA experiments have been done off New Jersey, Long Island, Bahama Bank and the Cape Kennedy area. Experiments in the North Sea included a particularly large-scale one in August—September 1965 when 2,000 kg of rhodamine B dye were released and the resulting patch tracked by a number of ships over a period of 3 weeks. A review of data from a number of such experiments was given by Okubo (1971), who selected 20 sets of data, obtained during the period 1961–67, which satisfied certain criteria. The main points were that the conditions of release approximated as nearly as possible to that of an instantaneous point source and that the patch stayed a sufficient distance from vertical boundaries for diffusion to be regarded as taking place in an unbounded horizontal plane. The concentration data were analysed with respect to horizontal axes $Ox$ and $Oy$, as in Fig. 8.4, giving the corresponding standard deviations $\sigma_x$ and $\sigma_y$ (computed as described later in Section 8.5.2). The effective radial variance was then taken as $\sigma_{rc}$ given by

$$\sigma_{rc}^2 = 2\sigma_x\sigma_y \ .$$

The variance $\sigma_{rc}^2$ was computed for a series of times $t$ in each experiment.

An apparent horizontal diffusivity was defined by

$$K_a = \frac{\sigma_{rc}^2}{4t} \tag{8.17}$$

for each time $t$. The 'scale' of diffusion $l$ was taken as

$$l = 3\sigma_{rc} \tag{8.28}$$

on the grounds that, in a radially symmetric patch, 95% of the diffusing substance would be within a circle of diameter $3\sigma_{rc}$.

By plotting $\sigma_{rc}^2$ against $t$ on a log-log scale, as shown in Fig. 8.5, and deriving the best linear fit to the data, Okubo obtained the relation

$$\sigma_{rc}^2 = 0.0108 t^{2.34} \tag{8.29}$$

where $\sigma_{rc}$ is in centimetres and $t$ in seconds. In a similar way, by plotting the apparent diffusivity $K_a$ against scale $l$, as in Fig. 8.6, Okubo found the relation

$$K_a = 0.0103 l^{1.15} \tag{8.30}$$

where $l$ is in cm and $K_a$ in $cm^2 \, s^{-1}$.

It is quite remarkable that data from widely distant areas and on such a large range of scales — diffusion time $t$ from about 1 hour to 1 month and length scale from 100 m to 100 km — can be represented by the same pair of equations. Figures 8.5 and 8.6 and equations (8.29) and (8.30) are a useful order of magnitude guide to the rate of dispersion to be expected in a given area. For a closer approximation one would have to take into account the particular features of the area, such as tidal and other currents, topography and any special temperature or salinity structure.

It may be noted that the exponent of $l$ in equation (8.30), i.e. 1.15, lies between the value 1, appropriate to the Joseph and Sendner theory, and 1.33 as in the locally isotropic turbulence theory. Similarly the exponent of $t$ in equation (8.29), i.e. 2.34, lies between the values 2 and 3 corresponding to the two theories respectively. It is not possible to deduce that the data support one theory rather than the other. In fact if the diffusion velocity $P$ in the one case or the energy parameter $\epsilon$ in the other were allowed to vary with scale, instead of being constant over the whole range, either theory could be made to fit the data.

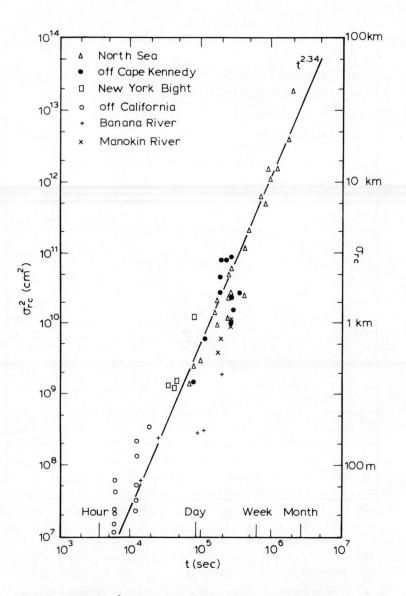

Fig. 8.5 – Variance $\sigma_{rc}^2$ of a dye distribution plotted against diffusion time $t$ for data from various areas. (Based on Okubo, 1971.)

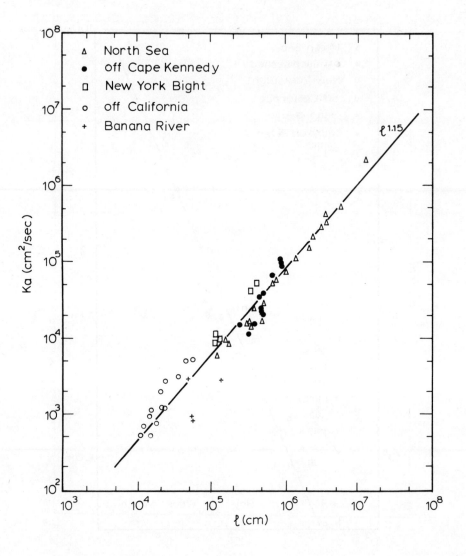

Fig. 8.6 – Apparent diffusivity $K_a$ plotted against scale of diffusion $l$ for data from various areas. (Based on Okubo, 1971.)

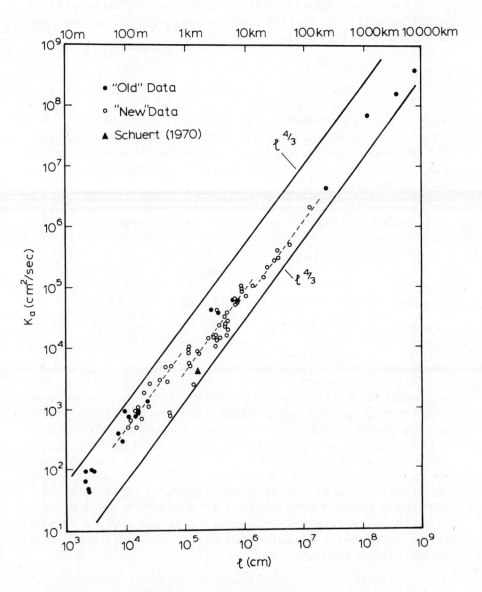

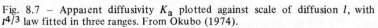

Fig. 8.7 – Apparent diffusivity $K_a$ plotted against scale of diffusion $l$, with $l^{4/3}$ law fitted in three ranges. From Okubo (1974).

In a subsequent paper Okubo (1974) showed that the data would fit the predictions based on the theory of locally isotropic turbulence if split into three ranges, as shown in Fig. 8.7. Thus:

$$\sigma_r^2 = C_1 \epsilon t^3$$
$$K_a = C_2 \epsilon^{1/3} l^{4/3}$$

where $C_1$ and $C_2$ are constants, while the energy transfer parameter $\epsilon$ has a constant value within each range but changes from one range to the other. The first break occurs at a length scale of about 1 km or a time scale of half a day to a day. The values of $C_1\epsilon$ deduced for the two ranges separated by this break are shown in Table 8.2.

**Table 8.2** – Turbulent energy parameter and horizontal diffusion.

| Time scale $t$ | Length scale $l$ | $C_1 \epsilon$ $cm^2 s^{-3}$ | $\epsilon$ $cm^2 s^{-3}$ |
|---|---|---|---|
| 1 hr – ½ day | 100 m – 1 km | $2.5 \times 10^{-5}$ | $2.5 \times 10^{-3}$ |
| > ½ day | > 1 km | $5.4 \times 10^{-6}$ | $5.4 \times 10^{-4}$ |

According to the theory of locally isotropic turbulence, energy is put into large eddies and is then transferred to smaller and smaller eddies. Within an inertial subrange, in which energy transfer is purely by internal processes, the rate of energy transfer from one scale to a smaller one is constant and equal to $\epsilon$, the rate at which it is being put into the largest eddies. However, if more energy is put into the turbulence at an intermediate scale, the larger eddies will not be affected but the smaller eddies will gain energy at an increased value of $\epsilon$. Okubo suggested that the much larger energy transfer at scales less than about half a day in time or 1 km in length was due to an input of turbulent energy from tidal motions. Other evidence indicates that the value of $C_1$ is of the order of 0.01, so that the energy transfer parameter $\epsilon$ would have the values shown in the last column of Table 8.2.

### 8.5.2 Anisotropic horizontal dispersion

In many dye release experiments it has been observed that the shape of the expanding patch becomes roughly elliptical rather than circular, the major axis of the ellipse often being aligned with the direction of the current. In this case it is more reasonable to take a coordinate system with the $x$-axis parallel to the current direction and the $y$-axis across the current. The concentration may be expressed as a function $c(x, y)$ of the $x$ and $y$ coordinates and variances computed for the two directions

$$\sigma_x^2 = \frac{1}{Q} \int_{-\infty}^{\infty} \int_{-\infty}^{\infty} c(x, y) x^2 \, dx \, dy$$

$$\sigma_y^2 = \frac{1}{Q} \int_{-\infty}^{\infty} \int_{-\infty}^{\infty} c(x, y) y^2 \, dx \, dy$$

where         $$Q = \int_{-\infty}^{\infty} \int_{-\infty}^{\infty} c(x, y) \, dx \, dy \ .$$

Coefficients of eddy diffusion $K_x$ and $K_y$ in the $x$ and $y$ directions respectively may be defined by

$$K_x = \frac{1}{2} \frac{d\sigma_x^2}{dt} , \qquad K_y = \frac{1}{2} \frac{d\sigma_y^2}{dt} .$$

The distribution of the concentration at a time $t$ may be represented by the two-dimensional analogue of equation (8.11), i.e.

$$c(x, y, t) = \frac{Q}{2\pi \sigma_x \sigma_y} \exp \left( -\frac{x^2}{2\sigma_x^2} - \frac{y^2}{2\sigma_y^2} \right) . \tag{8.31}$$

A number of diffusion experiments in coastal and estuarine waters around the British Isles were described by Talbot and Talbot (1974). The results differed considerably from one area to another and it was difficult to draw general conclusions. In many cases, however, the diffusing patches were elongated to a considerable extent and the effective value of $K_x$ was greater than that of $K_y$ by an order of magnitude or more. It was often found that, in the early stages of an experiment, the diffusion coefficients appeared to increase with the size of the patch but that, at longer times, the coefficients tended towards a constant value. This suggests that as the patch expanded, larger eddies took part in its dispersion but that after several days the patch was large compared with the scale of the largest eddies contributing to its dispersion. At what scale this stage is reached would be expected to depend on the local topographic and tidal current conditions. It might also vary with the weather conditions, since strong winds might set up larger scale currents and eddies which could increase the dispersion.

### 8.5.3 Spreading plume from a continuous source
The case of continuous release of marked material into a uniform flow is relevant to the discharge of sewage from an outfall into a current. The effluent will

be carried downstream with the current while undergoing diffusion in a transverse direction, so that a plume of gradually increasing width is formed. The problem will be simplified by assuming that the discharge is in the form of a vertical line source, so that vertical diffusion need not be considered, and that the effect of diffusion in the direction of the current may be neglected in comparison with advection. Diffusion is then regarded as taking place in one direction, transverse to the current.

Let axes be taken as in Fig. 8.8, with the origin at the point of release, the $x$-axis downstream in the direction of the current, assumed to have a uniform velocity $U$, and the $y$-axis across the current. Assuming the plume to be in a steady state, the advection-diffusion equation reduces to

$$ U \frac{\partial c}{\partial x} = \frac{\partial}{\partial y} \left( K_y \frac{\partial c}{\partial y} \right) . \tag{8.32} $$

The solution $c(x, y)$ depends on the form chosen for the transverse eddy diffusion coefficient $K_y$.

Instead of using $x$ as an independent variable, the time which has elapsed since water particles, in a transverse section at distance $x$, left the source may be used. Denoting this time by $t$, it is seen that $t = x/U$ where $U$ is uniform. If U varies with time, as in a tidal current, $t$ is given by

$$ t = \int_0^x \frac{dx'}{U} . \tag{8.33} $$

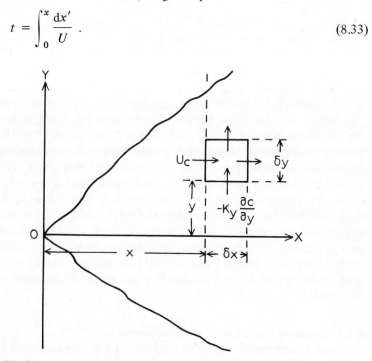

Fig. 8.8 – Lateral dispersion in a plume from a continuous source.

From a diffusion experiment, the standard deviation $\sigma_y$ of the distribution may be determined as a function of downstream distance $x$ and hence of $t$. Assuming the transverse distribution of the concentration $c$ to be Gaussian, the eddy diffusion coefficient $K_y$ is given by

$$K_y = \frac{1}{2}\frac{d\sigma_y^2}{dt} \tag{8.34}$$

where $t$ is the diffusion time, as defined above. If the curve of $\sigma_y$ as a function of $t$ for a given release can be represented by a power law:

$$\sigma_y^2 = at^m \tag{8.35}$$

where $a$ and $m$ are constants, the eddy diffusion coefficient, using equation (8.34), is given by

$$K_y = \frac{1}{2}mat^{m-1} . \tag{8.36}$$

It also follows from (8.35) and (8.36) that

$$K_y = b\sigma_y^n \tag{8.37}$$

where $n = 2\,(m-1)/m$ and $b$ is a constant. If $\sigma_y$ is regarded as a measure of the scale of the distribution, then (8.37) represents the dependence of $K_y$ on scale.

Table 8.3 shows the dependence of the standard deviation $\sigma_y$, the concentration at the axis of the plume $c(x,\,0)$ and the diffusion coefficient $K_y$ for values of $m = 1, 2$ and $3$, which correspond to the cases of constant $K_y$, a constant diffusion velocity and the inertial subrange respectively.

A number of investigators have found that, as in the case of radial spreading of a patch, the rate of lateral spreading of a plume corresponds to a diffusion coefficient $K_y$ which increases with scale, in this case the width of the plume. From a series of dye release experiments in areas of the Irish Sea, Bowden, Krauel and Lewis (1974) found that the data could be fitted to equation (8.35)

**Table 8.3** — Lateral spreading of a plume in a uniform current $U$.

| Value of $m$ | Standard deviation $\sigma_y$ | Concentration at axis $c(x,\,0)$ | Coefficient $K_y$ | Comments |
|---|---|---|---|---|
| 1 | $\propto x^{1/2}$ | $\propto x^{-1/2}$ | constant | — |
| 2 | $\propto x$ | $\propto x^{-1}$ | $\propto \sigma_y$ | constant diffusion velocity |
| 3 | $\propto x^{3/2}$ | $\propto x^{-3/2}$ | $\propto \sigma_y^{4/3}$ | inertial subrange |

with $m = 1.5$ or $m = 2$ without loss of significance but a considerable loss of significance occurred if curves with $m = 1$ or $m = 3$ were fitted. The implication of $m > 1$ is that diffusion took place at a faster rate than that corresponding to a constant $K_y$, i.e. to diffusion by eddies of scale small compared with the width of the plume. On the other hand, since $m < 3$, diffusion was slower than that corresponding to an inertial subrange in turbulence which was locally isotropic in the horizontal plane.

The case $m = 2$ corresponds to a constant diffusion velocity $B$, by analogy with the diffusion velocity $P$ in the radial diffusion case, since if $m = 2$, equation (8.35) may be written

$$\sigma_y = Bt$$

where $a = B^2$. Equation (8.36) becomes

$$K_y = B^2 t$$

and (8.37) becomes

$$K_y = B\sigma_y \ .$$

In the experiments by Bowden *et al.* (1974), the values derived for $B$ ranged from 0.4 to 1.6 cm s$^{-1}$ with a median of 1.0 cm s$^{-1}$. The value of $B$ tended to be greater in areas with stronger currents.

It has been assumed above that the current flows in a straight line and that the plume is symmetrical about the $x$-axis. In practice, the plume at a particular time will probably have a form somewhat like that shown in Fig. 8.9, with its axis meandering about the downstream direction. This is the effect of large-scale eddies which cause a displacement and distortion of the plume as a whole.

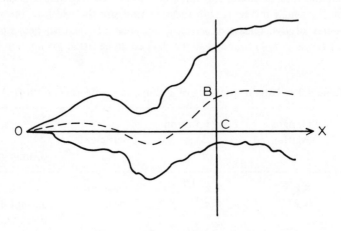

Fig. 8.9 – Diagram of a meandering plume.

Figure 8.10 shows a plot of concentration $c$ against distance $y$ on a single crossing of the plume. The centre of mass of the distribution, corresponding to the point $B$ in Fig. 8.9, is displaced a distance $y_0$ from the origin O in Fig. 8.10, which corresponds to the point C in Fig. 8.9. Most experiments have dealt with 'relative diffusion', i.e. the dispersion of marked particles about the centre of the plume in a given section, as at $B$. If a large number of crossings of the plume are

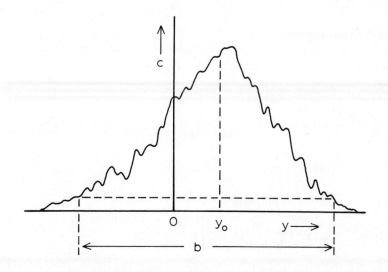

Fig. 8.10 – Concentration $c$ plotted against lateral distance $y$ for one traverse of a diffusing plume.

made, at the same downstream distance $x$, while the plume is meandering, then the position of $B$ will vary relative to the $x$-axis. The average dispersion about the point C on the $x$-axis will be considerably greater than the average of the relative dispersions about the varying plume axis $B$. In fact the 'absolute dispersion' $\sigma_{ya}$ about the fixed $x$-axis is related to the 'relative dispersion' $\sigma_{yr}$ and the standard deviation $\sigma_{ym}$ of the varying centre of the plume by

$$\sigma_{ya}^2 = \sigma_{yr}^2 + \sigma_{ym}^2 .$$

The mean concentration measured at the point C on the axis will be correspondingly lower than the mean of the concentrations measured at the instantaneous centre of the plume. In fact if $C_{pa}$ and $C_{pr}$ are the corresponding peak concentrations.

$$\frac{C_{pa}}{C_{pr}} = \frac{\sigma_{yr}}{\sigma_{ya}} .$$

The plume produced by the dispersion of an effluent from a sewage outfall, for example, will be of finite width initially and cannot be treated as a point source. A number of solutions for cases of this type were derived by Brooks (1960), for a constant diffusion coefficient and for coefficients increasing with the width of the plume. In the more general case, when both the rate of release and the velocity field may vary with time, a more tractable method is to treat the formation of the plume as the superposition of a number of overlapping patches.

### 8.5.4 Vertical dispersion

The dispersion of a contaminant in the vertical direction only, in the absence of a mean vertical velocity, is represented by the equation

$$\frac{\partial c}{\partial t} = \frac{\partial}{\partial z}\left(K_z \frac{\partial c}{\partial z}\right) . \tag{8.38}$$

For the simplest case of a constant diffusion coefficient $K_z$, this becomes

$$\frac{\partial c}{\partial t} = K_z \frac{\partial^2 c}{\partial z^2} . \tag{8.39}$$

For a point source at depth $z_0$ at time $t = 0$, the solution is

$$c(z, t) = \frac{Q}{2(\pi K_z t)^{1/2}} \exp\left[-\frac{(z - z_0)^2}{4K_z t}\right] \tag{8.40}$$

where $Q$ is the total amount of diffusing material. The standard deviation in the vertical, $\sigma_z$, is given by

$$\sigma_z^2 = 2 K_z t . \tag{8.41}$$

If the release takes place at mid-depth in a channel of depth $H$, the distribution may be regarded as extending effectively over the whole depth when $\sigma_z = H/2$. If this occurs at time $t_z$, it follows that

$$t_z = \frac{H^2}{8K_z}$$

Thus $t_z$ may be taken as the time scale of vertical diffusion. A bounding surface may be regarded as a reflecting or absorbing barrier, depending on whether the diffusing substance is reflected back into the water or is removed by absorption. In practice intermediate cases are also possible. In the reflecting case, after a time of order $t_z$ further dispersion in the vertical is no longer possible and subsequent dispersion may be treated as two-dimensional.

In neutrally stable conditions in a fairly strong tidal current, $K_z$ may be of order 100 cm$^2$ s$^{-1}$, so that for a depth $H = 20$ m, $t_z$ would be 5000 s or about 83 minutes. In weaker currents and stably stratified conditions $K_z$ might be only of the order of 5 cm$^2$ s$^{-1}$ and $t_z$ would be of order $10^5$ s or about 28 hours.

### 8.5.5 Effects of stability

The effect of a stable density gradient in reducing the rate of vertical mixing has been mentioned earlier in several places. It arises because vertical mixing involves an increase in potential energy which has to be derived from the turbulent kinetic energy in the water. Such energy is usually generated by shearing action in the mean flow. This consideration has led to the use of the Richardson number $Ri$ as a parameter to express the effect of stability on vertical mixing. The Richardson number is defined by

$$Ri = -\frac{g}{\rho}\frac{\partial \rho}{\partial z}\left(\frac{\partial U}{\partial z}\right)^{-2} \tag{8.42}$$

where $\rho$ is the density and $U$ is the resultant horizontal velocity. The negative sign is introduced so that $Ri$ is positive in stable stratification, when $\partial \rho/\partial z$ is negative with $z$ measured positively upwards. Strictly speaking, the potential density $\rho_\theta$ should be used in equation (8.42) rather than the *in situ* density.

The coefficients of eddy viscosity $N_z$ and eddy diffusion $K_z$ are both reduced with increasing $Ri$, but $K_z$ is reduced to a greater extent, so that the ratio $K_z/N_z$ is reduced. An alternative parameter is the flux Richardson number $Rf$, which is related to $Ri$ by

$$Rf = \frac{K_z}{N_z}Ri \ . \tag{8.43}$$

$Rf$ is the ratio of the vertical flux of buoyancy to the vertical flux of momentum and can be expressed in terms of these fluxes, if it is practicable to measure them.

A number of empirical equations have been proposed to express the dependence of $N_z$ and $K_z$ on $Ri$. In developing a theory of the formation of a thermocline, Munk and Anderson (1948) introduced the following equations:

$$\begin{aligned} N_z &= A_0(1 + 10Ri)^{-1/2} \\ K_z &= A_0(1 + 3.33Ri)^{-3/2} \end{aligned} \tag{8.44}$$

where $N_z = K_z = A_0$ in conditions of neutral stability ($Ri = 0$). Various other equations of the general form:

$$\begin{aligned} N_z &= N_0(1 + aRi)^{-\alpha} \\ K_z &= K_0(1 + bRi)^{-\beta} \end{aligned} \tag{8.45}$$

where $a$, $b$, $\alpha$ and $\beta$ are positive constants to be determined empirically, have been suggested by various workers. Each form of equation was found to be satisfactory in the area and conditions for which it was derived but there are no standard forms which have been generally accepted. A number of proposed functions were examined by Officer (1976), who considered that the following simple equations were a reasonably good fit to the observational data:

$$N_z = A_0 (1 + Ri)^{-1}$$
$$K_z = A_0 (1 + Ri)^{-2}$$

(8.46)

Table 8.4 shows the reduction in the coefficients of eddy viscosity and diffusion with increasing Richardson number as given by the Munk and Anderson equations (8.44) and the Officer equations (8.46) respectively. These figures should be taken as a guide to the extent of reduction in vertical mixing, rather than as exact predictions, because of the variation in conditions from one region to another.

**Table 8.4** – Effect of stability on mixing coefficients.

| Richardson number $Ri$ | Munk and Anderson equations (8.44) | | Officer equations (8.46) | |
|---|---|---|---|---|
| | $N_z/A_0$ | $K_z/A_0$ | $N_z/A_0$ | $K_z/A_0$ |
| 0 | 1 | 1 | 1 | 1 |
| 0.1 | 0.71 | 0.65 | 0.91 | 0.83 |
| 0.2 | 0.58 | 0.47 | 0.83 | 0.69 |
| 0.5 | 0.41 | 0.23 | 0.67 | 0.44 |
| 1 | 0.30 | 0.11 | 0.50 | 0.25 |
| 2 | 0.22 | 0.05 | 0.33 | 0.11 |
| 5 | 0.14 | 0.015 | 0.17 | 0.028 |
| 10 | 0.10 | 0.005 | 0.09 | 0.008 |

$Ri$ as defined by equation (8.42) is sometimes called the 'local Richardson number', since it is derived from the gradients of density and velocity at a particular depth. It is implied that the generation of turbulent energy and its use in vertical mixing occur at the same place and time, which may not be true. It is sometimes more helpful to use a 'bulk Richardson number', defined in terms of larger-scale features of the flow. In a shear flow, for example, extending to a depth $H$ with a total change of $\Delta\rho$ in density and of $\Delta U$ in velocity over that depth, a bulk Richardson number $(Ri)_B$ may be defined by

$$(Ri)_B = \frac{gH\Delta\rho}{\rho(\Delta U)^2} .$$

(8.47)

In very highly stratified conditions, such as a sharp thermocline, it is no longer appropriate to regard vertical exchanges of momentum, heat and matter as taking place by eddy diffusion. It may be better to treat the thermocline as a surface of discontinuity across which exchanges take place by entrainment only. Officer (1976) suggested that this would apply for values of $Ri > 10$.

Stability affects vertical mixing but would not be expected to have any direct effect on the lateral mixing of water masses. It may have indirect effects, however, where interleaving layers of water occur, as in some frontal regions. If vertical mixing is small, such a layer may penetrate a considerable distance into another water mass before its properties are changed appreciably. In this way the horizontal exchange of properties may be enhanced by vertical stability.

## 8.6 DISPERSION IN SHEAR FLOW

### 8.6.1 Effective longitudinal diffusion

Vertical diffusion in a shearing current can produce longitudinal dispersion, as illustrated by the simple example shown in Fig. 8.11. A channel of depth $H$ is considered in which the longitudinal velocity decreases linearly from $2\bar{U}$ at the surface to zero at the bottom, as in Fig. 8.11(a), where $\bar{U}$ is the depth-mean velocity. After a certain time the vertical column AB of material in Fig. 8.11(b) will become distorted into the slanting column AC of Fig. 8.11(c). If vertical diffusion has been taking place, the material in the column will also have been dispersed vertically and, if the time interval was sufficiently long, the material would be distributed throughout the whole volume ABCD. Thus the vertical column AB will have undergone horizontal dispersion in the direction of the current. For sufficiently long diffusion times, an effective coefficient of longitudinal dispersion $K_{xe}$ may be defined and in the above simple case it may be shown to be given by

$$K_{xe} = \frac{\bar{U}^2 H^2}{30 K_z} \qquad (8.48)$$

where $K_z$ is the coefficient of vertical eddy diffusion, assumed to be uniform throughout the depth (Saffman, 1962).

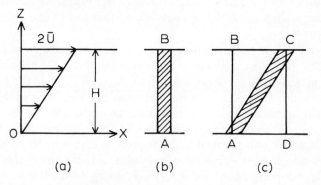

Fig. 8.11 – Simple representation of longitudinal dispersion in a shear flow.

As a numerical example of (8.48), if $\bar{U} = 50$ cm s$^{-1}$, $H = 20$ m, $K_z = 100$ cm$^2$ s$^{-1}$, then $K_{xe} = 3.3 \times 10^6$ cm$^2$ s$^{-1}$.

In general, the velocity gradient need not be linear as in Fig. 8.11 and the coefficient of vertical diffusion $K_z$ may vary with depth. A derivation applicable to various velocity profiles was given by Bowden (1965), who also showed that an alternating flow, such as a tidal current, could produce an effective longitudinal dispersion, under certain conditions. The shear in the current may arise in various ways, as in a tidal current, a wind-driven current or in density-driven flow. With typical values of the relevant parameters, it may be shown that, in vertically well-mixed water, the order of magnitude of $K_{xe}$ is given by

$$K_{xe} \sim \bar{U}H$$

where $\bar{U}$ is the depth-mean current. It was shown earlier, as in equation (8.20), that the coefficient of horizontal diffusion $K_x$ has the order of magnitude

$$K_x \sim u'l$$

where $u'$ is the r.m.s. turbulent velocity and $l$ is a mixing length. Since $u'$ is likely to be an order of magnitude smaller then $\bar{U}$ while $l$ is probably of the same order as $H$, it is seen that the effective longitudinal dispersion coefficient $K_{xe}$ due to shear is likely to be an order of magnitude greater than the coefficient $K_x$ due directly to the turbulent fluctuations of velocity.

It is characteristic of the shear effect that when the dispersion is bounded in the vertical direction the effective longitudinal diffusivity $K_{xe}$ is *inversely* proportional to the vertical diffusivity $K_z$. Thus a stable stratification which tends to reduce $K_z$ will tend to increase the effective horizontal dispersion. As $K_z$ decreases, however, it follows from the argument in Section 8.5.4 that the time needed for a pollutant released at a given depth to become mixed throughout the depth $H$ may become quite large. The solution for the shear effect when vertical diffusion does not extend to the surface and bottom boundaries shows that the effective $K_{xe}$ is then *directly* proportional to $K_z$ (Saffman, 1962). Further treatment of the shear effect, in steady and oscillatory currents and in both the unbounded and bounded cases, can be found in Okubo (1967) and in Csanady (1973).

In a rectilinear current, whether steady or alternating, the above considerations indicate that the coefficient of dispersion parallel to the direction of the current is increased by the shear effect from $K_x$ to $K_{xe}$, while the coefficient $K_y$, corresponding to dispersion in the transverse direction, remains that due to the turbulent fluctuations alone. This provides an explanation for the observed feature of many dye diffusion experiments that dispersion parallel to the mean current direction is often several times as great as transverse to it. Where the current direction changes with depth or with time, as in the case of tidal currents following an elliptical pattern, the shear effect acting on the transverse component of velocity would also increase the value of the coefficient $K_y$ to an effective value $K_{ye}$. It is likely, however, that the rate of dispersion parallel to the minor axis of the ellipse would be less than that parallel to the major axis.

In a region of strong tidal currents and vertical mixing, such as the southern North Sea, one may expect horizontal dispersion, at least up to scales of several kilometres, to be dominated by shear effect in the tidal currents. Where the tidal currents are weak, shear in the wind-driven or density-driven currents may be more significant. At larger scales, of the order of 10 to 100 km, it is likely that horizontal eddies will play a more important part than shear effects.

### 8.6.2 General case of shear flow

A shear-diffusion model of a more general kind was introduced by Carter and Okubo (1965), based on the idea of a spectrum of turbulence which could be separated into two parts. The first part included eddies of scales large compared with the dimensions of the diffusing patch being considered while the second covered the eddies of much smaller scale. The large-scale eddies were represented by a non-uniform field of mean flow, as far as the patch was concerned, while the effect of the small-scale eddies was represented by coefficients of eddy diffusion. In the simplest case, the mean flow was assumed to be in the $x$-direction, so that $V = W = 0$, but $U$ was taken as varying linearly in the $y$ and $z$ directions. Thus

$$U = U_0(t) + \beta y + \gamma z$$

where $U_0(t)$ is a function of time while $\beta$ and $\gamma$ are constants. This expression for $U$ was substituted in the advection-diffusion equation (8.5), and the coefficients $K_x$, $K_y$ and $K_z$ taken as constants. Solutions for an instantaneous source corresponding to this model were derived by Carter and Okubo and were applied to the analysis of some of the dye-release experiments in the Cape Kennedy area, referred to earlier, where the conditions were appropriate. Satisfactory agreement was found with the observed development of the dye distributions.

Other fields of mean flow, more complex than a linear shear, may be treated in a similar way. In fact flows involving convergence, divergence, stretching or shearing deformation and vorticity may be represented, together with the appropriate diffusive processes. In some cases analytical solutions may be derived for the distributions arising from given initial and boundary conditions but in other cases it may be more convenient to consider the behaviour of moments of the distribution. An alternative procedure is to take the Lagrangian approach and to calculate the trajectories of each of a number of particles comprising a group, starting from given initial positions. This is particularly useful in dealing with the horizontal dispersion of floating particles, constrained to remain at the sea surface. In the absence of diffusion, the computations will give the changes in size and shape of the group due to the non-uniform mean flow alone. By introducing random movements as well, the additional effects of turbulent diffusion may be simulated.

# 9

# Interaction between coastal and oceanic circulation

## 9.1 NATURE OF THE INTERACTION

In earlier chapters there have been a number of references to the interaction between phenomena in the deep ocean and in coastal waters. The tides and tidal currents are generated almost entirely in the oceans and are propagated into coastal waters as gravity waves. The surface waves experienced in coastal waters are generated to a large extent by local winds but in many areas waves generated in the ocean and travelling towards the coast as swell make an important contribution. Currents driven by the wind and the elevations associated with them, on the other hand, appear to be generated largely on the continental shelf and it is often difficult to distinguish any component attributable to input from the ocean.

In this chapter we are concerned mainly with the interaction between the major ocean currents and the circulation in coastal waters. In many cases the ocean currents do not appear to extend across the adjacent shelf areas and there is little obvious connection between the oceanic and coastal circulations. An example is the Florida Current, considered in more detail in Section 9.2. After passing through the Strait of Florida and turning northwards it flows along the continental slope and seems to have little effect on water on the narrow shelf between it and the east coast of Florida. North of Cape Hatteras, where the Florida Current turns away from the slope and becomes known as the Gulf Stream, the long-term flow on the shelf is towards the south-west, forming a counter-current.

The formation of a coastal counter-current on the inshore side of an ocean current appears to be a common occurrence. In some cases the counter-current is of topographic origin, as when an eddy is formed in an embayment on the coastline. In other cases the cause is less obvious but the counter-current appears to be linked dynamically with the ocean current and is often associated with the development of a transverse circulation. This can result in oceanic water being brought on to the shelf, facilitating the exchange of coastal and oceanic water.

The coastal upwelling which occurs in regions affected by the eastern boundary currents, such as the California Current and the Peru Current in the Pacific and the Canary and Benguela Currents in the Atlantic, is a particular example of interaction. The immediate cause of the upwelling often appears to be the local wind but the water which rises into the surface layer has been brought from the ocean by the offshore currents. In some cases the occurrence of upwelling appears to be due to an event some distance away, the effect of which has been propagated as a wave to the coastal location in question.

## 9.2 GULF STREAM AND THE EASTERN USA CONTINENTAL SHELF

Reference was made in Section 6.5.3 to the intrusion of Gulf Stream meanders on to the continental shelf in the Georgia Bight and their possible role in promoting flushing of low salinity water out of the area (Atkinson *et al.*, 1978). Blanton (1971) had presented evidence of a vigorous movement of shelf water into the Florida Current and the intrusion of Gulf Stream water along the bottom of the North Carolina shelf off Onslow Bay. A section taken on 22 July 1968 showed Gulf Stream water covering the entire shelf whereas a month earlier only a slight intrusion at the shelf break had been apparent. It is interesting to consider what evidence there is of interactions between the Florida Current and Gulf Stream and the coastal circulation at other positions along the continental shelf. A chart of the shelf region is given in Fig. 9.1.

The currents along the continental shelf, from the Gulf of Maine to the south of Florida, were described by Bumpus (1973) making use of observations over many years. Charts were presented showing the monthly mean flow for each calendar month. In general there was a surface flow to the south, of the order of 5 to 10 cm s$^{-1}$, along the coast from the Gulf of Maine through the Middle Atlantic Bight to Cape Hatteras. In the months from May to November this flow extended southwards as far as Florida but in other months the flow along that part of the coast was northwards from Florida to Cape Hatteras. The current near the bottom, along the whole of the coast and throughout the year, was mainly to the south but usually with a component towards the shore. In the southern part of the region the Florida Current does not, on average, extend on to the shelf and appears to have little influence on the coastal current.

Off Cape Hatteras the Florida Current diverges from the coast, becoming the Gulf Stream and leaving a zone of slower moving water, of gradually increasing width, between it and the continental slope. The shelf region extending from Cape Hatteras northwards to Cape Cod has been defined as the Middle Atlantic Bight. A detailed review of the circulation in this region has been given by Beardsley and Boicourt (1981). As shown by Bumpus, the annual mean flow is to the south-west, parallel to the coast, throughout the depth along the whole of this stretch of the shelf. Although this flow is opposite in direction to that of the Gulf Stream, flowing some distance offshore from the continental slope, all the evidence suggests that the shelf current is connected dynamically with the Gulf Stream and is driven by large-scale features of the circulation in the western North Atlantic as a whole.

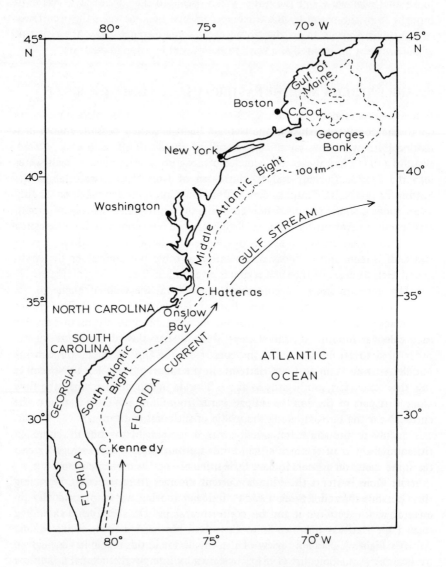

Fig. 9.1 — East coast of the USA and the continental shelf, showing features mentioned in the text. The edge of the shelf is marked by the 100 fathom (183 m) contour. The arrows show the general course of the Florida Current and the Gulf Stream.

The immediate driving force for the shelf current appears to be an along-shore pressure gradient corresponding to a surface slope of the order of $10^{-7}$, the sea level rising from south-west to north-east. Such a gradient has long been suspected but has proved difficult to establish. In section 6.6.2 it was pointed out that a gradient in this direction was found necessary by Stommel and Leetmaa (1972) to reconcile the mean flow in the Middle Atlantic Bight with their theoretical treatment of density and wind driven flow on a continental shelf. The cause of the alongshore gradient has been discussed by a number of dynamical oceanographers and it seems to be agreed that the general circulation in the western North Atlantic can impose a suitable pressure gradient at the continental slope and that this is transmitted almost unchanged across the shelf, so driving the coastal current.

Turning to the transient currents on shorter time scales than the annual mean, currents on the synoptic time scale of 2 to 10 days are closely correlated with wind forcing (Beardsley and Boicourt, 1981). The coastal region from North Carolina to New England is an area of intense cyclogenesis in winter, arising from the juxtaposition of cool continental air over the eastern United States and warm moist maritime air offshore. Cyclones also form in summer but are generally much weaker and less frequent. The atmospheric disturbances drive strong transient current fields which tend to move along the shelf in phase with the forcing. The currents reach a magnitude of 20 to 40 cm $s^{-1}$, i.e. several times greater than the long-term mean. These currents are coherent across the width of the shelf and for distances of the order of 200 km along the shelf.

The monthly mean currents are also largely due to direct wind-forcing although on this time scale other processes, such as run-off and forced motions originating beyond the shelf and propagating on to it, may play some part.

The observations at various positions on the shelf of synoptic scale currents, taken in conjunction with the corresponding changes of coastal sea level, can be interpreted in terms of continental shelf waves. These waves, which are considered further in Section 9.3, are generated by atmospheric pressure and wind stress and travel along the shelf, trapped by the sloping bottom.

Infra-red mapping from satellites has shown the occurrence in the Middle Atlantic Bight area of thermal structures and fronts on a wide range of scales. In some cases these include tongues of cooler shelf water extending into the warmer slope water and anticyclonic Gulf Stream eddies in the slope water. It is possible that Gulf Stream eddies and similar relatively long period features may have some influence on the shelf currents, but this remains to be determined.

The two main results of studies in the Middle Atlantic Bight, i.e. that the long-term flow along the shelf is largely determined by the oceanic circulation while synoptic scale transient currents are due mainly to wind forcing on the shelf, are probably applicable to a number of other shelf areas throughout the world, where sufficiently detailed observations have not yet been made.

## 9.3 CONTINENTAL SHELF WAVES

### 9.3.1 Nature of the waves

In Chapter 2 it was explained that a perturbation of the sea surface generated at one place could be propagated to distant areas by wave motion, involving inter-related oscillations of elevations and currents. The tides in coastal waters are produced mainly by wave motion generated in the deep oceans and propagating on to the continental shelf. The waves are primarily gravitational in that gravity provides the restoring force which acts on a displaced element of water. They are also influenced by the Coriolis force arising from the rotation of the earth. A particular type of wave, the Kelvin wave, is associated with the presence of a lateral boundary, the wave propagating with the coast on its right-hand side in the northern hemisphere and on the left in the southern hemisphere. The Coriolis effect gives rise, in this case, to an exponential decrease in the amplitude of the wave with distance from the coast. The lateral scale of the wave, as represented by the distance at which the amplitude falls to $e^{-1}$ of its coastal value, is large in deep water but is reduced to the order of 400 km on the continental shelf. In the simplest case the coast may be assumed to be vertical and the sea bed to be a horizontal plane of uniform depth. The Kelvin wave may be regarded as 'trapped' against the coastline, the trapping mechanism arising from the Coriolis effect.

Trapping of waves against a coast can also be produced by refraction if the velocity of propagation increases with increasing depth in the offshore direction. Consider conditions parallel to a straight coast, as in Fig. 9.2. It is assumed that there is a vertical wall at the coast, at which the waves are reflected, and that the bottom then slopes downwards in the offshore direction. The velocity of gravity waves in shallow water increases with depth, so that in water of varying depth the waves are refracted, as described in Section 3.6.2. For a wave train approaching the coast obliquely, the rays will be refracted so that they approach a normal to the coast. Similarly, in the reflected waves, a ray will be refracted away from the normal, as in Fig. 9.2. In suitable conditions, depending on the wavelength, the slope of the bottom and the angle of reflection, the ray may become parallel to the coast and then turn back towards it to be reflected again. In such conditions multiple reflections along the coast will occur and wave energy will be trapped in a coastal strip. When gravity waves are trapped in this way they are known as 'edge waves'. This example illustrates how trapping of waves can occur although the mechanism is not the same for all types of waves.

In addition to the gravity waves described above, which include the surface waves of Chapter 3 as well as the tidal waves of Chapter 2, other types of wave motion are possible on the rotating earth. Their motion is governed by the conservation of potential vorticity. For a column of water extending from the surface to the bottom at depth $H$, the potential vorticity is defined as $(\zeta + f)/H$,

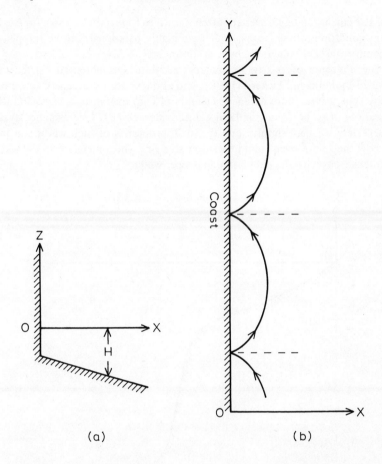

Fig. 9.2 – Trapping of gravity waves on a sloping shelf: (a) profile of sea wall and sloping bed; (b) plan view, showing multiple reflection at the shore.

where $\zeta$ is the relative vorticity about a vertical axis given by

$$\zeta = \frac{\partial v}{\partial x} - \frac{\partial u}{\partial y}$$

and $f$ is the Coriolis parameter, given by $f = 2\omega \sin \phi$ where $\omega$ is the angular velocity of rotation of the earth and $\phi$ is the latitude. If the column of water moves so that either $f$ or $H$ is changed, the conservation of potential vorticity requires a change in $\zeta$, the vorticity relative to the earth. In the deep oceans the variation of $f$ with latitude is usually the important factor and the waves which are generated are the Rossby waves or planetary waves. In the continental slope and shelf regions, the variation in depth is more important than the variation in

$f$ and the corresponding waves are often known as topographic Rossby waves. In certain conditions these waves, which are highly rotational, can be trapped on the continental shelf and are known as continental shelf waves.

The concepts of relative, planetary, absolute and potential vorticity are described by Pond and Pickard (1978), who also give an introductory account of Rossby type waves. More detailed accounts of continental shelf waves and their applications may be found in LeBlond and Mysack (1977, 1978) and Mysack (1980). Here we shall simply state the main properties of such waves and indicate how they have been found useful in studying phenomena in coastal waters and interactions with the circulation in deeper water.

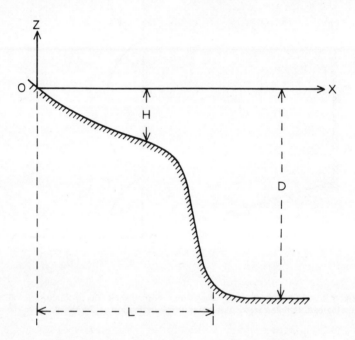

Fig. 9.3 – Typical shelf and slope profile on which continental shelf waves may be produced.

A typical depth profile over which trapped shelf waves may occur is shown in Fig. 9.3, where the $x$-axis is taken perpendicular to he coast, the $y$-axis along it and the $z$-axis vertically upwards. The depth of water $H$ may be expressed as $H(x)$, a monotonically increasing function of $x$. The width of the shelf and slope combined is denoted by $L$ while $D$ is the deep-sea depth, beyond the slope. The main properties of continental shelf waves may be summarised as follows:

(1) Their periods are longer than the inertial period, i.e. their angular frequencies are less than the Coriolis frequency $f$.

(2) Their phase velocity is such that the wave crests travel with the coast on the right in the northern hemisphere and on the left in the southern hemisphere.

(3) In some circumstances, however, the group velocity is opposite in direction to the phase velocity, so that energy is then propagated in the opposite direction along the coast.

(4) Compared with gravity waves, the phase velocity is relatively slow, of the order of $1 \text{ m s}^{-1}$.

(5) The elevations are relatively low, of order 10 cm, but the velocity components can be of order $20 \text{ cm s}^{-1}$.

(6) The waves are quasi-geostrophic, in that the balance in the momentum equation is approximately geostrophic.

In the simplified discussion above, it has been assumed that the water is of uniform density so that the wave motions are barotropic. If the water is stratified, other types of topographic Rossby waves can occur, just as internal gravity waves can occur in these conditions. In many cases the water over the continental shelf and slope is stratified so that a series of baroclinic as well as barotropic shelf waves may be generated. A further complexity arises if the waves are superposed on steady currents. These various aspects are considered in the review paper by Mysack (1980).

### 9.3.2 Applications of continental shelf waves

The main generating process for continental shelf waves has been found to be wind-forcing. Typical cyclonic or anticyclonic wind systems, having a time scale of 2 to 10 days and a space scale large compared with the shelf width, are able to generate shelf waves with periods of several days. The direct action of atmospheric pressure variations probably plays some part but the main driving force appears to be the wind stress.

The presence of continental shelf waves was determined initially by the analysis of records of sea level at a number of positions along a coast. They were first found in this way off the east coast of Australia, later off the west Australian coast, the west and east coasts of USA, the west coast of Scotland and other areas. In later investigations they were also found in observations of currents. Having established the occurrence of shelf waves, observations of sea level at the coast may be used to calculate the distribution of currents on the shelf. If the mechanism of generation of such waves by wind-forcing can be confirmed, the theory of shelf waves provides a method of computing both sea level changes and transient currents on the shelf from information on the wind systems.

It appears that interactions may occur between continental shelf waves and a mean flow along the slope and that these may lead to instabilities and a transfer of energy between the two types of motion. It has been suggested that unstable shelf waves may contribute to meanders in the Florida Current and Gulf

Stream. Meso-scale eddies impinging on the shelf may also interact with shelf waves and possibly transfer energy to them. Off the east coast of Japan variations in the Kuroshio, probably induced by atmospheric systems, cause abnormally high sea level disturbances at the coast which appear to propagate as shelf waves.

Three-dimensional models of coastal upwelling, in which variations parallel to the direction of the coast as well as in a plane perpendicular to it are taken into account, have shown the possible importance of continental shelf waves as well as internal Kelvin waves in transmitting disturbances along the shelf. Movements of the isotherms at one location may be influenced in this way by wind stress at earlier times in other areas, as mentioned in Section 5.4.4. If the shelf waves can interact with currents further offshore, as suggested above, they may play a significant part in linking upwelling events with the large-scale ocean circulation. This may be the case with the El Niño phenomena, which appear to be related to changes in currents and hydrographic conditions over the whole width of the Pacific Ocean (Section 5.3.4).

## 9.4 OTHER EXAMPLES

The influence of water from the River Amazon on the salinity of the offshore coastal waters and the Guiana Current has been cited already in Section 6.2.2. Current observations at a number of stations on the adjoining shelf have been described recently by Gibbs (1982). The outflowing water from the river mouth flows across the shelf initially, then turns north-westwards parallel to the coast, forming part of a broad shelf current driven by the prevailing south-easterly trade winds. This merges over the outer shelf and slope with the Guiana Current, a branch of the South Equatorial Current, flowing in the same direction. The river plume, wind-driven shelf current and adjacent ocean current appear to blend naturally in this case, without any indication of a counter-current, at least during the period covered by the observations. The salinity of water in the Guiana Current is significantly reduced from the Equator as far as $10°N$.

On the eastern side of the North Atlantic, the long-term circulation in the North-west European shelf seas appears to be largely determined by the North Atlantic Drift, the rather weak and diffuse extension of the Gulf Stream which reaches this region. There is a northward flow along the shelf to the west of Ireland, joined off the west of Scotland by a branch which has flowed through the Celtic Sea and Irish Sea. Another branch flows eastwards through the English Channel into the southern North Sea. Since the prevailing winds over the region are south-westerly, however, the driving force for these flows may be provided largely by the residual wind stress. On the monthly or synoptic time scales these flows, which do not exceed 1 or 2 cm s$^{-1}$, are obscured by the much larger wind-driven currents. In this respect the conditions in this region resemble those on the eastern continental shelf of the USA.

Water of Atlantic origin enters the North Sea in three streams. In addition to the flow through the English Channel, there is a flow around the north of Scotland and a more pronounced inflow along the western slope of the Norwegian Trench. This branch also supplies water for the deep inflow through the Skagerrak into the Baltic Sea. The Norwegian Coastal Current forms an outflow along the eastern slope of the Trench, carrying the surface outflow from the Baltic with the addition of coastal water from the Norwegian fjords (Mork, 1981). Exchanges between the inflowing and outflowing currents appear to take place through a cross-circulation and eddying motions. In the rest of the North Sea, which is relatively shallow, density-driven currents may play some part in determining the long-term circulation, as mentioned in Section 6.4.4, but on the evidence at present available it is not possible to assess the relative significance of density-driven currents, wind-driven currents and the influence of the Atlantic inflow. On shorter time scales the wind-driven effects appear to be dominant.

# Bibliography

Allen, J. S. 1973. Upwelling and coastal jets in a continuously stratified ocean. *J. Phys. Oceanogr.,* **3**, 245–257.

Atkinson, L. P., Blanton, J. O. and Haines, E. B. 1978. Shelf flushing rates based on the distribution of salinity and freshwater in the Georgia Bight. *Estuar. Coastal Mar. Sci.,* **7**, 465–472.

Backhaus, J. 1979. First results of a three-dimensional model on the dynamics in the German Bight. In *Marine forecasting,* ed. J. C. J. Nihoul, pp. 333–349. Elsevier, Amsterdam.

Bang, N. D. 1973. Characteristics of an intense ocean frontal system in the upwelling regime west of Cape Town. *Tellus,* **25**, 256–265.

Banks, J. E. 1974. A mathematical model of a river–shallow sea system used to investigate tide, surge and their interactions in the Thames–Southern North Sea region. *Phil. Trans. R. Soc. Lond.,* **A275**, 567–609.

Barber, N. F. and Ursell, F. 1948. The generation and propagation of ocean waves and swell. *Phil. Trans. R. Soc. Lond.,* **A240**, 527–560.

Barton, E. D., Huyer, A. and Smith, R. L. 1977. Temporal variation observed in the hydrographic regime near Cabo Corveiro in the N.W. African upwelling region, February–April 1974. *Deep-Sea Res.,* **24**, 7–23.

Beardsley, R. C. and Boicourt, W. C. 1981. On estuarine and coastal shelf circulation in the Middle Atlantic Bight. In *Evolution of physical oceanography,* ed. B. A. Warren and C. Wunsch, pp. 198–233. MIT Press, Cambridge, Massachusetts.

Beardsley, R. C. and Hart, J. 1978. A simple theoretical model for the flow of an estuary on to a continental shelf. *J. Geophys. Res.,* **83**, 873–883.

Bendat, J. S. and Piersol, A. G. 1971. *Random data: analysis and measurement procedures.* Wiley–Interscience, New York.

Blanton, J. O. 1971. Exchange of Gulf Stream water with North Carolina shelf water in Onslow Bay during stratified conditions. *Deep-Sea Res.,* **18**, 167–178.

Boje, R. and Tomczak, M. 1978. *Upwelling ecosystems.* Springer-Verlag, Berlin.

Bowden, K. F. 1953. Note on wind drift in a channel in the presence of tidal currents. *Proc. R. Soc. Lond.*, **A219**, 426–446.

Bowden, K. F. 1965. Horizontal mixing in the sea due to a shearing current. *J. Fluid Mech.*, **21**, 83–95.

Bowden, K. F., Krauel, D. P. and Lewis, R. E. 1974. Some features of turbulent diffusion from a continuous source at sea. *Advances in Geophysics*, **18A**, 315–329.

Bowman, M. J. 1978. Spreading and mixing of the Hudson River effluent into the New York Bight. In *Hydrodynamics of estuaries and fjords*. ed. J. C. J. Nihoul, pp. 373–384. Elsevier, Amsterdam.

Bowman, M. J. and Iverson, R. L. 1978. Estuarine and plume fronts. In *Oceanic fronts in coastal processes*, ed. M. J. Bowman and W. E. Esaias, pp. 87–104. Springer-Verlag, Berlin.

Bowman, M. J., Kibblewhite, A. C. and Ash, D. E. 1980. $M_2$ tidal effects in Greater Cook Strait, New Zealand. *J. Geophys. Res.*, **85**, (C5), 2728–2742.

Bretschneider, C. L. 1970. Forecasting relations for wave generation. *Look Lab./Hawaii*, **1**, (3), 31–34.

Bretschneider, C. L. 1973. Prediction of waves and currents. *Look Lab./Hawaii*, **3**, (1), 1–17.

Brink, K. H., Allen, J. S. and Smith, R. L. 1978. A study of low-frequency fluctuations near the Peru coast. *J. Phys. Oceanogr.*, **8**, 1025–1041.

Brooks, N. H. 1960. Diffusion of sewage effluent in an ocean current. In *Waste disposal in the marine environment*, ed. E. A. Pearson, pp. 246–267. Pergamon Press, Oxford.

Bumpus, D. F. 1973. A description of the circulation on the continental shelf of the east coast of the United States. *Progress in Oceanogr.*, **6**, 111–159.

Burling, R. W. 1959. The spectrum of waves at short fetches. *Dtsch. Hydrogr. Z.*, **12**, 45–64, 96–117.

Butman, B. 1976. Hydrography and low frequency currents associated with the spring run-off in Massachusetts Bay. *Mem. Soc. Roy. Sci. Liège*, 6$^e$ ser., **10**, 247–275.

Carter, D. J. T. 1982. Prediction of wave height and period for a constant wind velocity using the JONSWAP results. *Ocean Engng.*, **9**, 17–33.

Carter, D. J. T. and Challenor, P. G. 1981. Estimating return values for wave heights. Institute of Oceanographic Sciences, Report No. 116, N.E.R.C. (unpublished manuscript).

Carter, H. H. and Okubo, A. 1965. A study of the physical processes of movement and dispersion in the Cape Kennedy area. Chesapeake Bay Institute, Johns Hopkins Univ., Report Ref. 65–2.

Cartwright. D. E. 1958. On estimating the mean energy of sea waves from the highest waves in a record. *Proc. Roy. Soc.*, **A247**, 22–48.

Cartwright, D. E. 1962. Waves: Analysis and statistics. In *The Sea*, ed. M. N. Hill, Vol. **1**, pp. 567–589, Interscience, London.

Cartwright, D. E. 1963. The use of directional spectra in studying the output of a wave recorder on a moving ship. In *Ocean wave spectra*, pp. 203–218. Prentice-Hall, Englewood Cliffs, N. J.

Cartwright, D. E. and Smith, N. D. 1964. Buoy techniques for obtaining directional spectra. *Trans. 1964 Buoy Technology Symposium*, pp. 112–121. Marine Technology Society, Washington, D.C.

Cartwright, D. E., Edden, Anne C., Spencer, R. and Vassie, J. M. 1980. The tides of the northeast Atlantic Ocean. *Phil. Trans. R. Soc. Lond.* **A298**, 87–139.

Charnock, H. 1955. Wind stress on a water surface. *Quart. J. R. Meteor. Soc.*, **81**, 639–640.

Charnock, H. 1981. Air–sea interaction. In *Evolution of physical oceanography*, ed. B. A. Warren and C. Wunsch, pp. 482–503. The MIT Press, Cambridge, Massachusetts.

Collar, P. G. and Vassie, J. M. 1978. Near surface current measurements from a surface-following data buoy (DB1), Part 2. *Ocean Engng.*, **5**, 291–308.

Csanady, G. T. 1973. *Turbulent diffusion in the environment*, D. Reidel, Dordrecht, Holland.

Csanady, G. T. 1981. Circulation in the coastal ocean. *Advances in Geophysics*, **23**, 101–183.

Csanady, G. T. 1982. *Circulation in the coastal ocean.* D. Reidel, Dordrecht, Holland.

Darbyshire, J. 1963. The one-dimensional wave spectrum in the Atlantic Ocean and in coastal waters. In *Ocean wave spectra*, pp. 27–39, Prentice-Hall, Englewood Cliffs, N. J.

Defant, A. 1961. *Physical oceanography*, vols. I and II. Pergamon Press, Oxford.

Draper, L. 1961. Wave recording instruments for civil engineering use. *Proc. Conf. Wave Recording for Civil Engineers, National Institute of Oceanography, Jan. 1961*, pp. 7–17.

Draper, L. 1963. Derivation of a 'design wave' from instrumental records of sea waves. *Proc. Instn. Civ. Engrs.*, **26**, 291–304.

Draper, L. 1967. Instruments for measurement of wave height and direction in and around harbours. *Proc. Instn. Civ. Engrs.*, **37**, 213–219.

Dronkers, J. J. 1964. *Tidal computations in rivers and coastal waters*, North Holland Publishing Company, Amsterdam.

Duxbury, A. C. 1965. The union of the Columbia River and the Pacific Ocean – general features. In *Ocean science and ocean engineering*, pp. 914–922. Marine Technology Society, Washington, D.C.

Dyer, K. R. 1973. *Estuaries: a physical introduction.* John Wiley, London.

Fearnhead, P. G. 1975. On the formation of fronts by tidal mixing around the British Isles. *Deep-Sea Res.*, **22**, 311–321.

Flather, R. A. 1979. Recent results from a storm surge prediction scheme for the North Sea. In *Marine forecasting*, ed. J. C. J. Nihoul, pp. 385–409, Elsevier, Amsterdam.

Franco, A. S. 1981. *Tides: fundamentals, analysis and prediction.* Instituto de Pesquisas Tecnologicas, Sao Paulo, Brazil.

Garratt, J. R. 1977; Review of drag coefficients over oceans and continents. *Monthly Weather Review,* **105,** 915–929.

Garrett, C. J. R. 1972. Tidal resonance in the Bay of Fundy and Gulf of Maine. *Nature,* **238,** 441–443.

Garrett, J. C. R. 1974. Tides in gulfs. *Deep-Sea Res.,* **22,** 23–35.

Garrett, C. J. R., Keeley, J. R. and Greenberg, D. A. 1978. Tidal mixing versus thermal stratification in the Bay of Fundy and Gulf of Maine. *Atmosphere-Ocean,* **16,** 403–423.

Garvine, R. W. 1971. A simple model of coastal upwelling dynamics. *J. Phys. Oceanogr.,* **1,** 169–179.

Gibbs, R. J. 1970. Circulation in the Amazon River Estuary and adjacent Atlantic Ocean. *J. Mar. Res.,* **28,** 113–123.

Gibbs, R. J. 1982. Currents on the shelf of north-eastern South America. *Estuar. Coastal Shelf Sci.,* **14,** 282–299.

Glen, N. C. 1979. Tidal measurement. In *Estuarine hydrography and sedimentation,* ed. K. R. Dyer, pp. 19–40. Cambridge University Press, Cambridge.

Godin, G. 1972. *The Analysis of tides,* Liverpool University Press, Liverpool.

Gower, J. F. R. (ed.) 1981. *Oceanography from space.* Plenum Press, New York.

Halpern, D. 1976. Structure of an upwelling event observed off Oregon during July 1973. *Deep-Sea Res.,* **23,** 495–508.

Hamilton, P. and Rattray, M. 1978. A numerical model of the depth dependent wind-driven upwelling circulation on a continental shelf. *J. Phys. Oceangr.,* **8,** 437–457.

Hart, T. J. and Currie, R. I. 1960. The Benguela Current. *Discovery Reports,* **31,** 123–298.

Hasselmann, K. *et al.* 1973. Measurements of wind-wave growth and swell decay during the Joint North Sea Wave Project (JONSWAP). *Ergänzungsheft zur Dt. Hydrogr. Z.,* Reihe A, Nr. 12.

Heaps, N. S. 1965. Storm surges on a continental shelf. *Phil. Trans. R. Soc. Lond.,* **A257,** 351–383.

Heaps, N. S. 1967. Storm Surges. *Oceanogr. Mar. Biol. Ann. Rev.,* **5,** 11–47.

Heaps, N. S. 1969. A two-dimensional numerical sea model. *Phil. Trans. R. Soc. Lond.,* **A265,** 93–137.

Heaps, N. S. 1972. Estimation of density currents in the Liverpool Bay area of the Irish Sea. *Geophys. J. R. astr. Soc.,* **30,** 415–432.

Heaps, N. S. 1974. Development of a three-dimensional numerical model of the Irish Sea. *Rapp. Proc. Verb. Cons. Int. Explor. Mer.,* **167,** 147–162.

Heaps, N. S. 1978. Linearized vertically-integrated equations for residual circulation in coastal seas. *Dt. Hydrogr. Z.,* **31,** 147–169.

Heaps, N. S. and Jones, J. E. 1979. Recent storm surges in the Irish Sea. In *Marine forecasting,* ed. J. C. J. Nihoul, pp. 285–319. Elsevier, Amsterdam.

Hendershott, M. C. 1977. Numerical models of ocean tides. In *The sea, vol. 6: Marine modelling,* ed. E. D. Goldberg, *et al.*, pp. 47–95. Wiley–Interscience, New York.

Hendershott, M. C. and Speranza, A. 1971. Co-oscillating tides in long, narrow bays: the Taylor problem revisited. *Deep-Sea Res.,* **18,** 959–980.

Hidaka, K. 1954. A contribution to the theory of upwelling and coastal currents. *Trans. Amer. Geophys. Un.,* **35,** 431–444.

Holligan, P. M. 1981. Biological implications of fronts on the northwest European continental shelf. In *Circulation and fronts in continental shelf seas,* pp. 35–50. The Royal Society, London.

Houghton, R. W. and Mensah, M. A. 1978. Physical aspects and biological consequences of Ghanaian coastal upwelling. In *Upwelling ecosystems,* ed. R. Boje and M. Tomczak, pp. 167–180, Springer-Verlag, Berlin.

Hughes, P. and Barton, E. D. 1974. Stratification and water mass structure in the upwelling area off northwest Africa in April/May 1969. *Deep-Sea Res.,* **21,** 611–628.

Huntley, D. A. 1980. Tides on the north-west European Continental Shelf. In *The North-west European Shelf seas: the sea bed and the sea in motion, II Physical and chemical oceanography and physical resources,* ed. F. T. Banner, M. B. Collins and K. S. Massie. Elsevier, Amsterdam.

Huyer, Adriana, 1976. A comparison of upwelling events in two locations: Oregon and Northwest Africa. *J. Mar. Res.,* **34,** 531–546.

Ishiguro, S. 1972. Electronic analogues in oceanography. *Oceanog. Mar. Biol. Ann. Rev.,* **10,** 27–96.

James, I. D. 1977. A model of the annual cycle of temperature in a frontal region of the Celtic Sea. *Estuar. Coastal Mar. Sci.,* **5,** 339–353.

James, I. D. 1978. A note on the circulation induced by a shallow-sea front. *Estuar. Coastal Mar. Sci.,* **7,** 197–202.

James, I. D. 1981. Fronts and shelf-circulation models. In *Circulation and fronts in continental shelf seas,* pp. 85–92. The Royal Society, London.

Jelesnianski, C. P. 1965. A numerical calculation of storm tides induced by a tropical storm impinging on a continental shelf. *Monthly Weather Review,* **93,** 343–358.

Joseph, J. and Sendner, H. 1958. Uber die horizontale Diffusion im Meere. *Dt. Hydrogr. Z.,* **11,** 49–77.

Kenyon, K. E. 1969. Stokes drift for random surface waves. *J. Geophys. Res.,* **74,** 6991–6994.

Ketchum, B. H. and Keen, D. J. 1955. The accumulation of river water over the continental shelf between Cape Cod and Chesapeake Bay. *Deep-Sea Res.,* **3,** (Suppl.) 346–357.

Kinsman, B. 1965. *Wind waves: their generation and propagation on the ocean surface.* Prentice-Hall, Englewood Cliffs, N.J.

Kraus, E. B. 1972. *Atmosphere–ocean interaction.* Oxford University Press, London.

Lamb, H. 1945. *Hydrodynamics,* 6th ed. Dover Publications, New York.

LeBlond, P. H. and Mysack, L. A. 1977. Trapped coastal waves and their role in shelf dynamics. In *The Sea,* vol. 6, ed. E. D. Goldberg, I. N. McCave, J. J. O'Brien and J. H. Steele, pp.459–495. Wiley Interscience, New York.

LeBlond, P. H. and Mysack, L. A. 1978. *Waves in the ocean.* Elsevier, New York.

Longuet-Higgins, M. S. 1952. On the statistical distribution of the heights of sea waves. *J. Mar. Res.,* **11,** 245–266.

McDowell, D. M. 1977. *Hydraulic behaviour of estuaries,* Macmillan, London.

McLellan, H. J. 1965. *Elements of physical oceanography,* Pergamon Press, Oxford.

Madsen, O. S. 1977. A realistic model of the wind-induced Ekman boundary layer. *J. Phys. Oceanogr.,* **7,** 248–255.

Marmer, H. A. 1951. *Tidal datum planes.* US Coast and Geodetic Survey, Special Publication No. 135.

Miles, J. W. 1957. On the generation of surface waves by shear flows. *J. Fluid Mech.,* **3,** 185–204.

Miles, J. W. 1960. On the generation of surface waves by turbulent shear flows. *J. Fluid Mech.,* **7,** 469–478.

Miller, G. R. 1966. The flux of tidal energy out of the deep ocean. *J. Geophys. Res.,* **71,** 2485–2489.

Mork, M. 1981. Circulation phenomena and frontal dynamics of the Norwegian coastal current. In *Circulation and fronts in continental shelf seas,* pp. 123–135. The Royal Society, London.

Munk, W. H. and Anderson, E. R. 1948. Note on the theory of the thermocline. *J. Mar. Res.,* **7,** 276–295.

Munk, W. H., Miller, G. R., Snodgrass, F. E. and Barber, N. F. 1963. Directional recording of swell from distant storms. *Phil. Trans. R. Soc. Lond.,* **A255,** 505–584.

Mysack, L. A. 1980. Recent advances in shelf wave dynamics. *Rev. Geophysics and Space Physics,* **18,** 211–241.

Neumann, G. 1968. *Ocean currents,* Elsevier, Amsterdam.

Neumann, G. and Pierson, W. J. 1966. *Principles of physical oceanography.* Prentice-Hall, Englewood Cliffs, N. J.

Officer, C. B. 1976. *Physical oceanography of estuaries (and associated coastal waters).* John Wiley, New York.

Okubo, A. 1967. The effect of shear in an oscillatory current on horizontal diffusion from an instantaneous source. *Int. J. Oceanol. Limnol.,* **1,** 194–204.

Okubo, A. 1971. Oceanic diffusion diagrams. *Deep-Sea Res.,* **18,** 789–802.

Okubo, A. 1974. Some speculations on oceanic diffusion diagrams. *Rapp. Proc. Verb., Cons. Int. Explor. Mer.,* **167,** 77–85.

Peffley, M. B. and O'Brien, J. J. 1976. A three-dimensional simulation of coastal upwelling off Oregon. *J. Phys. Oceanogr.,* **6,** 164–180.

Phillips, O. M. 1955. On the generation of waves by turbulent wind. *J. Fluid Mech.,* **2,** 417–445.

Phillips, O. M. 1977. *The dynamics of the upper ocean,* 2nd ed. Cambridge University Press, Cambridge.

Pickard, G. L. 1979. *Descriptive physical oceanography,* 3rd ed. Pergamon Press, Oxford.

Pickard, G. L. and Emery, W. J. 1982. *Descriptive physical oceanography: an introduction,* 4th (enlarged) ed. Pergamon Press, Oxford.

Pierson, W. J. and Moskowitz, L. 1964. A proposed spectral form for fully developed wind seas based on the similarity theory of S. A. Kitaigorodskii. *J. Geophys. Res.,* **69,** 5181–5190.

Pierson, W. J., Neumann, G. and James, R. W. 1955. Practical methods for observing and forecasting ocean waves by means of wave spectra and statistics. *H.O. Publ. 603.* US Navy Hydrogrpahic Office, Washington, D.C.

Pingree, R. D. 1975. The advance and retreat of the thermocline on the continental shelf. *J. Mar. Biol. Assoc. U.K.,* **55,** 965–974.

Pingree, R. D. 1978. Cyclonic eddies and cross-frontal mixing. *J. Mar. Biol. Assoc. U.K.,* **58,** 955–963.

Pingree, R. D. and Griffiths, D. K. 1978. Tidal fronts on the shelf seas around the British Iseles. *J. Geophys. Res.,* **83,** (C9), 4615–4622.

Pingree, R. D. and Pennycuick, Linda. 1975. Transfer of heat, fresh water and nutrients through the seasonal thermocline. *J. Mar. Biol.Assoc. U.K.,* **55,** 261–274.

Pingree, R. D., Pugh, P. R., Holligan, P. M. and Forster, G. R. 1975. Summer phytoplankton blooms and red tides along tidal fronts in the approaches to the English Channel. *Nature, London,* **258,** 672–677.

Pond, S. and Pickard, G. L. 1978. *Introductory dynamic oceanography.* Pergamon Press, Oxford.

Prandle, D. 1975. Storm surges in the southern North Sea and River Thames. *Proc. R. Soc. Lond.,* **A344,** 509–539.

Prandle, D. and Wolf, J. 1978. Surge-tide interaction in the Southern North Sea. In *Hydrodynamics of estuaries and fjords,* ed. J. C. J. Nihoul, pp. 161–185. Elsevier, Amsterdam.

Proudman, J. 1953. *Dynamical oceanography.* Methuen, London.

Ramming, H-G., and Kowalik, Z. 1980. *Numerical modelling of marine hydrodynamics,* Elsevier, Amsterdam.

Redfield, A. C. 1950. The analysis of tidal phenomena in narrow embayments. *Papers in Phys. Oceanogr. Meteorol.,* **11,** (4), 1–36.

Redfield, A. C. 1958. Influence of the continental shelf on tides of the Atlantic coast of the United States. *J. Mar. Res.,* **17,** 432–448.

Redfield, A. C. and Miller, A. R. 1957. Water levels accompanying Atlantic coast hurricanes. *Meteorological Monographs,* **2**, No. 10, 1–23.

Reid, R. O., Vastano, A. C., Whitaker, R. E. and Wanstrath, J. J. 1977. Experiments in storm surge simulation. In *The sea,* vol. 6, ed. E. D. Goldberg *et. al.,* pp. 145–168. John Wiley, New York.

Riley, G. A. 1956. Oceanography of Long Island Sound, 1952–1954, *Bull. Bingham Oceanogr. Coll.,* **15**, 15–46.

Saffman, P. G. 1962. The effect of wind shear on horizontal spread from an instantaneous ground source. *Quart. J. Roy. Meteor. Soc.,* **88**, 382–393.

Schumacher, J. D., Kinder, T. H., Pashinski, D. J. and Charnell, R. L. 1979. A structural front over the continental shelf of the Eastern Bering Sea. *J. Phys. Oceanogr.,* **9**, 79–87.

Simpson, J. H. 1981. The shelf-sea fronts: implications of their existence and behaviour. In *Circulation and fronts in continental shelf seas,* pp. 19–31. The Royal Society, London.

Simpson , J. H. and Hunter, J. R, 1974. Fronts in the Irish Sea. *Nature, London,* **250**, 404–406.

Simpson, J. H., Allen, C. M. and Morris, N. C. G. 1978. Fronts on the continental shelf. *J. Geophys. Res.,* **83**, (C9), 4607–4614.

Simpson, J. H., Edelsten, D. J., Edwards, A., Morris, N. C. G. and Tett, P. B. 1979. The Islay front: physical structure and phytoplankton distribution. *Estuar. Coastal Mar, Sci.,* **713–726**.

Simpson, J. H., Hughes, D. G. and Morris, N. C. G. 1977. The relation of seasonal stratification to tidal mixing on the continental shelf. In *A voyage of Discovery,* ed. M. Angel, pp. 327–340. Pergamon Press, Oxford.

Smith, R. L. 1968. Upwelling. *Oceanogr. Mar. Biol. Ann. Rev.,* **6**, 11–46.

Stommel, H. 1949. Horizontal diffusion due to oceanic turbulence. *J. Mar. Res.,* **8**, 199–225.

Stommel, H. and Leetmaa, A. 1972. The circulation on the continental shelf. *Proc. Nat. Acad. Sci. U.S.,* **69**, 3380–3384.

Suginohara, N. 1977. Upwelling front and two-cell circulation. *J. Oceanogr. Soc. Japan,* **33**, 115–130.

Takano, K. 1954. On the salinity and the velocity distributions off the mouth of a river. *J. Oceanogr. Soc. Japan,* **10**, 93–98.

Takano, K. 1955. A complementary note on the diffusion of the seaward river flow off the mouth. *J. Oceanogr. Soc. Japan,* **11**, 1–3.

Talbot, J. W. and Talbot, G. A. 1974. Diffusion in shallow seas and in English coastal and estuarine waters. *Rapp. Proc. Verb., Cons. Int. Explor. Mer.,* **167**, 93–110.

Tann, H. M. 1976. The estimation of wave properties for the design of offshore structures. Institute of Oceanographic Sciences Report No. 23, N.E.R.C. (unpublished manuscript).

Taylor, G. I. 1920. Tidal oscillations in gulfs and rectangular basins. *Proc. London Math. Soc.,* **20**(2), 144–181.

Thacker, W. C. 1979. Irregular grid finite difference techniques for storm surge calculations for curving coastlines. In *Marine forecasting,* ed. J. C. J. Nihoul, pp. 261–283. Elsevier, Amsterdam.

Tucker, M. J. 1956. A shipborne wave recorder. *Trans. Roy. Inst. Nav. Arch.,* **98**, 236–250.

Ursell, F. 1956. Wave generation by wind. In *Surveys in mechanics,* ed. G. K. Batchelor and R. M. Davies. Cambridge University Press, London.

Welander, P. 1961. Numerical prediction of storm surges. *Advances in Geophysics,* **8**, 316–379.

Wiegel, R. L. 1964. *Oceanographical engineering.* Prentice-Hall, Englewood Cliffs, N.J.

Wood, A. M. Muir and Flemming, C. A. 1981. *Coastal hydraulics.* Macmillan, London.

Wooster, W. S. and Reid, J. L. 1962. Eastern boundary currents. In *The sea,* vol. 1, ed. M. N. Hill, Chap. 11, pp. 253–280. Interscience, London.

Wooster, W. S., Bakun, A. and McLain, D. R. 1976. The seasonal upwelling cycle along the eastern boundary of the North Atlantic. *J. Mar. Res.,* **34**, 131–141.

Wright. L. D. and Coleman, J. M. 1971. Effluent expansion and interfacial mixing in the presence of a salt wedge, Mississippi River delta. *J. Geophys. Res.,* **76**, 8649–8661.

Yoshida, K. 1967. Circulation in the eastern tropical oceans with special reference to upwelling and undercurrents. *Jap. J. Geophys.,* **4**, 1–75.

Zuta, S., Rivera, T. and Bustamente, A. 1978. Hydrologic aspects of the main upwelling areas off Peru. In *Upwelling ecosystems,* ed. R. Boje and M. Tomczak, pp. 235–257. Springer-Verlag, Berlin.

# Index